W9-AZI-983

THE WHITE CASCADE

THE
WHITE
CASCADE

✦ THE GREAT NORTHERN
RAILWAY DISASTER
AND AMERICA'S
DEADLIEST AVALANCHE

GARY KRIST

HENRY HOLT
AND COMPANY
NEW YORK

Henry Holt and Company, LLC
Publishers since 1866
175 Fifth Avenue
New York, New York 10010
www.henryholt.com

Henry Holt® and ⬡® are registered trademarks
of Henry Holt and Company, LLC.

Distributed in Canada by H. B. Fenn and Company Ltd.

Library of Congress Cataloging-in-Publication Data

Krist, Gary.
    The white cascade : the Great Northern Railway disaster
and America's deadliest avalanche / Gary Krist.
      p. cm.
    Includes bibliographical references and index.
    ISBN-13: 978-0-8050-7705-6
    ISBN-10: 0-8050-7705-7
    1. Avalanches. I. Title.

QC929.A8K75 2007
979.7'77041—dc22   2006049047

Henry Holt books are available for special promotions
and premiums. For details contact: Director, Special Markets.

First Edition 2007

Designed by Victoria Hartman
Maps by Bob Pratt

Printed in the United States of America

10 9 8 7 6 5 4 3

For Jon

The difference between civilization and barbarism may be measured by the degree of safety to life, property, and the pursuit of the various callings that men are engaged in.

—*James J. Hill*

CONTENTS

AUTHOR'S NOTE

The White Cascade is a work of nonfiction, adhering strictly to the historical record and incorporating no invented dialogue or other undocumented re-creations. Unless otherwise attributed, anything between quotation marks is either actual dialogue as reported by a witness or else a citation from a diary, memoir, letter, telegram, court transcript, or other primary source. In some quotations I have, for clarity's sake, corrected the original spelling, syntax, or punctuation.

Where there is significant disagreement among sources about the exact time and sequence of certain events, I have chosen what I judge to be the most likely account, giving precedence to documents created during the crisis (such as telegrams and diaries) over those created afterward from memory (such as memoirs and court testimony). Some information comes from newspaper articles of the time, which—in light of the rather permissive journalistic ethics of 1910—can be more than a little unreliable. In these cases, I have done my best to separate true reportage from the inventions of overimaginative deadline writers. Details I believe to be apocryphal are either identified as such in the text or else omitted.

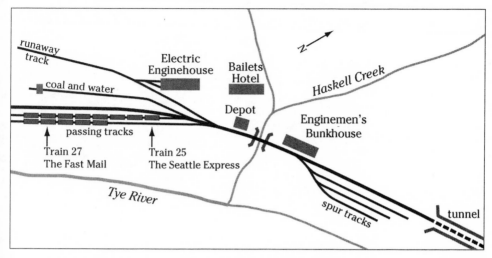

Schematic Plan of Wellington

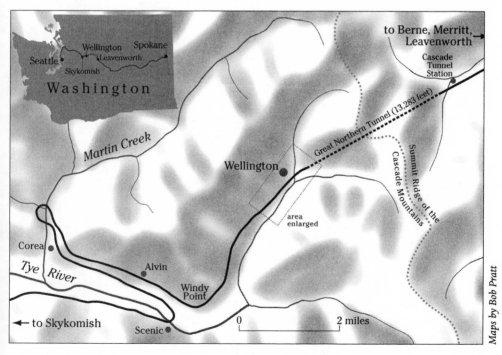

Wellington Orientation Map

Maps by Bob Pratt

THE WHITE CASCADE

PROLOGUE

A Late Thaw

Summer 1910

The last body was found at the end of July, twenty-one weeks after the avalanche. Workmen clearing debris from the secluded site, high in the cool, still snow-flecked Cascades, discovered the deteriorating corpse in a creek at the mountainside's base. Trapped under piles of splintered timber, the dead man had to be Archibald McDonald, a twenty-three-year-old brakeman, the only person on the trains not yet accounted for.

Bill J. Moore was on the wrecker crew that found him. Moore's team was one of many that had been grappling with the hard, ugly work at Wellington over the previous five months. For the first few days following the avalanche—after the storm had finally tapered off and the isolated town could be reached—the men had done little but dig for victims in the snow. Bodies were scattered all over the mountainside, some buried as deep as forty feet. Once located, they had to be piled up—"like cordwood, in 4-by-4 stacks"—and carried to a makeshift morgue in the station's baggage room, where they could be identified. Wrapped in blankets and tied to rugged Alaskan sleds, they'd been evacuated in small groups, each sled maneuvered by four men with ropes, two ahead and two behind, in silent procession down to their mourning families.

After the dead were gone, the crews had turned to opening and fortifying the right-of-way, blasting away acres of compacted snow and timber, laying the groundwork for huge concrete shelters to protect the rail line from future snowslides. Temporary spur tracks had been built along the side of the ravine so that the wreckers could begin their recovery work. Some of the train equipment, like the heavy steam and electric locomotives, had been only lightly damaged, but the wooden mail cars, sleepers, and passenger coaches were completely shattered. Each scrap had to be hoisted back up to the tracks and carted off on a flatcar. The job had taken weeks. All that remained in the ravine afterward, strewn among rocks and ravaged trees, were a few twisted metal pipes, a ruptured firebox door, a woman's torn, high-buttoned shoe.

✧

For nineteen-year-old Bill Moore, the unearthing of the final victim would mean yet another funeral to attend, yet another lost friend to lay to rest. Moore had often worked with Archie "Mac" McDonald, a fellow brakeman. The Great Northern Railway's Cascade Division was full of men like Moore and McDonald. Regarded as something of a hardship post, the division was often avoided by those with the seniority to land positions elsewhere, and it employed more than its share of young rookies. Rootless and unattached, they had to find family wherever they could.

So Moore, like many others, had found it among his fellow railroaders. There was a good reason why railway unions were called "Brotherhoods"; trainmen in the Age of Steam regarded themselves as a breed apart, united by their rough and highly specialized work. In this remote, dangerous territory, where the daily battle against the elements required the highest levels of teamwork, trust, and personal sacrifice, these bonds were especially strong.

For the men of the Cascade Division, the Wellington Disaster thus represented the decimation of an entire close-knit community. Although newspaper reports had given far more ink to the trains' lost passengers (business leaders, women, and children made better copy), nearly two-thirds of the fatalities had come from a relatively small population of trainmen, railway mail clerks, and track laborers. Among them had been several whom Moore considered close friends.

To those who had escaped, one question was unavoidable: Why them and not me? On the night of the avalanche, Moore had been down at Skykomish station, at the foot of the mountains. His train—the last westbound freight to make it over the mountain—had tied up there when the storm reached its critical stage, immobilizing all traffic throughout the range. Had his schedule or the storm's timing been slightly different, it might have been his train trapped for six full days, his body entombed in snow. Such an arbitrary twist of fate was difficult to get over. As Moore would later write: "I will never forget this as long as I live."

Others were less inclined to accept what had happened as fate. Tragedy, they claimed, was not the ending this story had to have. Four days before the terrible events of March 1—shortly after the two trains had become marooned at Wellington station, just below the very summit spine of the Cascades—the passengers and crews had received a stark portent of what was to come. A chef and his assistant, working overnight in a railway beanery at a nearby station, had just put the next day's biscuits into the oven to bake. Outside, the "howling, cantankerous blizzard" that had been raging for days was pummeling the surrounding mountains, rattling the doors of the beanery in their frames. Sometime around 4:00 A.M., in a narrow gully high above the station, the overloaded snowpack began to falter. Within seconds, a torrent of loose snow began slipping down the gully.

As the flow quickly broadened and deepened, it gathered momentum, fanning out into a rolling, churning river of white headed straight for the station below. Surging onto the valley floor, the powerful slide grazed a corner of the depot and twisted the entire building off its foundation. But the beanery stood directly in its path. Hit point-blank by the rushing wall of snow, the rough wooden structure imploded, its timbers rupturing, its roof collapsing to the ground under the intense weight.

For many hours afterward, rescuers digging at the site could find only one of the two dead men inside, though they managed to recover several hot biscuits from the oven.

Over the next few days, as the railroad fought desperately to clear the tracks, slides began falling everywhere. The Pacific Northwest had been inundated with heavy snows for days, and as the weather warmed and the snowfall turned to rain, mountains across the region shrugged off their heavy loads. In the mining country of Idaho, two huge avalanches smashed the sleeping towns of Mace and Burke. A landslide near Seattle annihilated a horse barn, trapping six animals inside and wedging the head of an eighty-year-old rancher under a crosscut saw. Snow shearing off another slope swept a small house into a ravine, the two terrified men inside riding the plummeting cabin like a bobsled for three hundred feet. And in British Columbia, a railroad gang near Rogers Pass was engulfed by an even more massive slide, leaving scores of foreign workers dead, some of them frozen upright in casual postures—"like the dead of Pompeii."

In the midst of this, Great Northern Railway trains Nos. 25 and 27 sat paralyzed at Wellington, slowly being buried under the snow. The men of the Cascade Division made Herculean, round-the-clock efforts to release them, but, as the *Seattle Times* would report, "so fierce is the storm that the attempts of this army of workmen, aided by all the available snow-fighting machinery on the division, are futile." The stress, meanwhile, was taking its toll: "Passengers by Sunday were in a frantic state of mind," one survivor would later report. "It was with difficulty that we could keep the women and children . . . from becoming actually sick in bed from the long strain."

Suffering most acutely was Ida Starrett, a young widowed mother from Spokane. Her husband, a Great Northern freight conductor, had been killed just weeks before at the railroad's main yards in Hillyard, Washington. Having settled his estate, Ida was now traveling with her elderly parents to start anew in Canada. In her care were her three children—nine-year-old Lillian, seven-year-old Raymond, and an infant boy, Francis.

Two other families were in similar straits. The Becks—mother, father, and three children aged twelve, nine, and three—were moving back to the warmth of Pleasanton, California, after two years of hard winters in Marcus, Washington. John and Anna Gray, with their eighteen-month-old boy, Varden, were on their way home after an even more difficult trip. John had broken his leg and was all but immobile in a hip-to-ankle cast. Anna was distraught, in tears every night. "We knew we were in a death trap," she wrote. "We were so much afraid that terrible week and could talk about nothing else."

In desperation, some of the passengers proposed escaping down the mountain on foot, but railroad officials wouldn't hear of it. "To hike out," as one of them put it, "is to take your life in your hands." A worker who made the attempt was soon trying to outrun a rumbling slide racing down the mountain toward him. "He had scarcely gone a step," a companion later reported, "before the walls of snow on each side quivered, then smashed together and he was caught breathless in a mass of snow." Choking on the viscous, powder-dense air, thrashing arms and legs to keep afloat amid the churning debris, he was carried hundreds of feet down the mountain "with the speed of an express train."

Understandably, most passengers elected to remain aboard the trains after that, but the railroad's rescue effort soon veered toward crisis. Food was running low, coal supplies were dwindling, and the temporary workers hired to shovel snow began quitting in droves. On the trains, fear and frustration gave way to blank despair. It seemed inconceivable to many that a snowstorm, no matter how vicious and protracted, could bring the entire northwestern quadrant of the country to a standstill. This was 1910, an era when, as a prominent lecturer of the day opined, "the final victory of man's machinery over nature's is the logical next step in evolution." Modern railroads like the Great Northern—with their tunnels and snowsheds, their fleets of rotary snowplows, their armies of men—were supposed to be unstoppable, the ultimate symbols of twentieth-century America's new mastery over its own geography and climate.

✧

In the end, however, it was nature that had triumphed at Wellington. What was—and still is, a century later—the deadliest avalanche in

American history had given the story a brutal end, killing ninety-six men, women, and children. And the toll had been as arbitrary as it was appalling: Of the three families aboard, one perished, one was entirely spared, and the third was ravaged, seeing half its members die.

Five months later, there remained troubling questions about how and why all of it had happened. Why, for instance, had those two trains been brought up the mountain in the first place, given the severity of the storm? Why, once they were trapped at Wellington, had they been left on the side of a steep slope and not moved to a safer, flatter place? Some critics questioned whether a railroad line even belonged in a steep and slide-prone place like Wellington. Wasn't the practice of running trains up into that mountain wilderness an act of supreme arrogance that made disaster all but inevitable?

These were difficult questions, especially for those who knew the full story of what had happened at Wellington. Punishments and remedies were obvious only to those ignorant of the complex facts. As for Great Northern railroaders like Bill J. Moore—working long hours in a place that even in midsummer could seem eerily hostile and forbidding—they could spare little time for such recriminations. They had trains to move, an outpost in the mountains to rebuild, an economically vital railroad line to secure against the wilderness.

And they had Archie McDonald to take care of—one last dead brother to carry back home.

1

A Railroad Through the Mountains

This winter is hell of a time.

—*Nyke Homonylo,*
trackwalker

Monday, February 21, 1910
Everett, Washington

District weather observer G. N. Salisbury delivered the bad news early
Monday morning: It was going to snow—again. Another late-winter
storm, this one chilled by record-breaking low temperatures, would be
sweeping into the Pacific Northwest, bringing heavy precipitation to
the entire region.

In Everett, some thirty miles north of Seattle, February's relentless
barrage of storms seemed to be making the editor of the *Daily Herald*
giddy: "Cold Wave Is Hieing Hither," trilled the front-page story in
Monday's paper. "It behooves residents to immediately saly [*sic*] forth to
the woodpile and split a goodly supply of fuel, for indications point to
the fact that the mercury is planning to take the toboggan."

For James Henry O'Neill, standing sentinel in his office at Everett's
Delta rail yards, the news was cause for more serious worry. As superintendent of the Great Northern Railway's Cascade Division, he was the
man responsible for keeping vital mail, freight, and passenger trains

moving through the entire western half of Washington State, and he knew that even a minor storm entering his territory could easily balloon into a crisis. Just twenty-four hours earlier—on Sunday, the purported day of rest, when he should have been at home with his wife and baby—O'Neill had been mired in railroad troubles all day. A foot of snow had fallen in the mountains to the east, overwhelming his track-clearing snowplows and delaying two of his most important trains at the station in Skykomish. Today he had another train stranded at Nason Creek with a broken-down locomotive. These all-too-typical headaches could only get worse.

After three years as Cascade Division superintendent, O'Neill had learned a lot about adversity from nature. "Probably no other stretch of railroad in the United States at this time," wrote railway historian James E. Vance, "was so taxing in its operation." The problem was simple geography; virtually all mainline Great Northern trains entering or leaving the Puget Sound region had to surmount one huge and un-avoidable obstacle: the Cascade Mountains. On clear days O'Neill could actually see them from his office windows, suspended over the horizon like a perpetual taunt.

Rising up precipitously from the coastal plain about forty miles east of Seattle, the Cascades formed an enormous geological wall bisecting the Pacific Northwest from north to south, catching moisture from every weather system that crossed them. The unhappy consequence for those on the west side of the range was Puget Sound's notoriously soggy weather. For James H. O'Neill, the result was almost constant railroad chaos for seven months of the year: floods and mudslides in spring and fall, blizzards and avalanches through the long mountain winter. Even in a normal year, the rail lines through the Cascades—Seattle's most direct link with the rest of the country for everything from hat pins to harvesters—were all but impossible to keep open.

This year had been anything but normal. Snow was typically rare in the Pacific-warmed cities on the coast, but in the winter of 1909–10 even Seattle, Tacoma, and Everett were being savaged. With one week left before month's end, Seattle had already surpassed its previous record for snowy days in February. And in the high Cascades—the snowiest region in the contiguous United States and territories—the snow season had lately turned downright brutal. Long before Christmas arrived, mudslides had already started causing accidents and delays throughout O'Neill's territory. By January the mudslides had turned into snowslides, coming down with such frequency that a wrecker train sent up into the mountains to clear up a slide-damaged freight had itself been demolished by a slide.

And now, just when the snow season was supposed to be winding down, this new storm was hieing its way hither, promising to make the superintendent's long winter even longer.

✧

Thirty-seven-year-old James O'Neill—sturdy, austerely handsome, with a chiseled, intelligent face softened by intimations of wry humor around the eyes—had been railroading in and around the northern snow belt for his entire career. Born in Canada in 1872, he'd moved as a child to Buxton, a scrubby Dakota prairie town that owed its existence almost entirely to the fact that the Great Northern Railway (then known as the St. Paul, Minneapolis & Manitoba) ran through it. His father was a section foreman, and before young Jim had memorized his multiplication tables he could recite the makeup of every scheduled freight train that lumbered past the yard where he played. Railroading and Catholicism being the twin family religions, and Jim showing little inclination for the priesthood, there was never much question about what he was going to do with his life. But as one forty-year railroad veteran would later write, "Boys did not go to work on the railroad simply because their fathers did. What fetched them were the sights and sounds of moving trains, and above all the whistle of a locomotive. I've heard of the call of the wild, the call of the law, the call of the church. There is also the call of the railroad."

When he was just thirteen, Jim O'Neill had answered that call, abandoning his formal education and leaving home to start work as a dollar-a-day waterboy for an extra work gang at Devils Lake. By age fifteen he was already operating out of Grand Forks as a freight train brakeman—a notoriously hazardous job and one that, because of his youth, he could keep only by indemnifying the railroad of all liability in case of accident. Two years later, he got a promotion to conductor, running extra freights at three cents a mile. He was dubbed "That Kid Conductor from Buxton" and was soon earning a reputation for keeping his trains on time no matter what the weather.

O'Neill's education in handling the really deep snow began somewhat later, after he was transferred to the Montana Rockies. Vaulting steadily up through the railroad's hierarchy, he became first a trainmaster at Great Falls and then, in quick succession, superintendent of the Montana and then the Kalispell divisions. His swift advancement was no mystery: O'Neill was a prodigy, a precociously shrewd manager with seemingly inexhaustible reserves of drive and will. Never content to oversee operations from a steam-heated office, O'Neill became known for assessing and solving problems right out in the field, almost before they happened. And on the Great Northern Railway, the northernmost transcontinental line in the United States, that typically meant dealing with the consequences of snow.

"I never saw more pluck, energy, and determination bundled up into one man," a colleague would later say of him. "I have known O'Neill to wade snow waist-deep for ten miles to get to a slide. He is first on the scene when there is trouble and last to leave."

The description is doubtless colored by affection—O'Neill was almost universally well liked—but his willingness to work side by side with his men was fabled at the Great Northern. Once promoted to an office job in the cost-accounting department at company headquarters in St. Paul, he lasted less than a year. "I hated it," he would later admit to a reporter. "When winter came, I found myself longing to be out in the weather." Before eight months had passed, he was out on the line again, battling the snow.

But that was over a decade ago. By February of 1910—facing his third winter as head of the Cascade Division—O'Neill had already put in almost a quarter century on the Great Northern. At thirty-seven, he was reaching an age when hiking through acres of deep snow was perhaps better left to younger men. He also had a family to think of now. In October 1908, O'Neill—who had made his own way through life since the age of thirteen—had finally married. Berenice C. McKnight, a tall, doe-eyed, Pre-Raphaelite beauty fourteen years his junior, had followed him from Montana after his promotion to Cascade Division chief. Together they had set up house in a modest, three-story, Prairie-style home at 1713 Hoyt Avenue in Everett. And within ten months of their marriage (O'Neill's gift for efficiency manifesting itself in all areas of endeavor), Berenice had already given birth to a child: Peggy Jane O'Neill, born August 3, 1909.

By the beginning of November—when the first substantial snows hit the high Cascades—O'Neill would have had precious little time for the delights of fatherhood. He was division superintendent, responsible for the smooth running of several hundred miles of railroad, and his duties were legion. "Fully one-half of his time," declared an 1893 *Scribner's* article about the job of railway superintendent, "will be spent out-of-doors looking after the physical condition of his track, masonry, bridges, stations, buildings of all kinds. Concerning the repair or renewal of such he will have to pass judgment." Nor did his job stop there:

> He has to plan and organize the work of every yard, every station. He must know the duties of each employee on his pay-rolls, and instruct all new men, or see that they are properly instructed. He must keep incessant and vigilant watch on the movement of all trains, noting the slightest variation from the schedules which he has prepared, and looking carefully into the causes therefor, so as to avoid its recurrence.

Add to this the complications of a major mountain crossing and an average of fifty feet of snow per year, and the scope of O'Neill's job becomes abundantly, even painfully, clear.

✧

As hard as the superintendent's job was on O'Neill, it can only have been harder on his wife. A woman barely into her twenties caring for a newborn child in a strange town, Berenice must have watched the weather reports as closely as her husband did, knowing that any approaching storm could cause him to disappear for days or even weeks on end. The O'Neills did employ someone to help Berenice with the baby and the housekeeping—Carrie F. Bailey, the only live-in servant on the block—but a forty-five-year-old Irishwoman could hardly substitute for a husband.

These recurring separations must have been especially difficult since, judging from surviving letters and other family memorabilia, the O'Neills' marriage was one of unusually intense affection. "Here is the *most* important thing in my life," Berenice wrote on the back of one of Jim's studio portraits in her scrapbook. On the back of another she scribbled two lines of the Thirty-seventh Psalm: "Mark the perfect and behold the upright, / For the end of that man is peace." Never shy about professing her emotions, Berenice regularly presented her husband with notes of such unreserved tenderness that he must have lived in terror of their ever falling into the hands of his railway colleagues.

The couple had met in Kalispell, the Great Northern's onetime base of operations in the Montana Rockies, probably in early 1907. (In her scrapbook, Berenice kept a photograph of the two of them taken in what appears to be the yard of her family home. Berenice is standing in the shade of a tree, hugging a cat in her arms; Jim, looking rakish in a white, wide-brimmed hat, reclines on the lawn behind her. On the back of the photograph is an inscription in Berenice's elegant hand: "The summer I met 'The Man.'") As a railroad superintendent, "The Man" would have been a figure of some standing in Kalispell, but he was a newcomer to town, barely educated and of no family to speak of. His pursuit of the much younger, much better-connected Berenice— a gifted painter and pianist whose father was a prominent local businessman—would have caused some comment.

Even so, O'Neill approached the task with his usual unflagging energy and efficiency. In the sequence of telegrams he sent to her in the summer of 1907—each one carefully preserved in that same scrapbook—one can trace the swift and steady progress of their intimacy, beginning with a telegram dated June 3, 1907:

—To MISS BERENICE MCKNIGHT
AM ON MY WAY TO CALIFORNIA, IF CONVENIENT WOULD LIKE TO SEE YOU. TELEPHONE ME AT THE BUTLER HOTEL 5 P.M. I LEAVE IN THE A.M. JIM

—Berenice Dear

If you have no engagement this afternoon, come down about 3 p.m. and we'll take a ride. Will look for you. Jim

—Berenice Dear

This is a peachy day for boating. Would you come for a boat ride? You know I love you more than anybody on earth. Lots of love. Always, Jim

That the courtship was telescoped into a few short weeks is unsurprising, considering O'Neill's constant need to be on the road. But by the time he received his next promotion—to Cascade Division superintendent in October of the same year—the couple's bond was solid enough to weather the separation. Within a year they were married and in possession of a lease. To Berenice's delight, Jim even managed to carve a few weeks out of his schedule for their honeymoon, a rail trip to the East aboard his private business car—one of the more enviable perquisites of division superintendency—festooned for the occasion with quantities of roses and carnations.

Since then, two full winters of snow had passed; at this point, nearing the tail end of a third, Berenice had a better understanding of what it meant to be the wife of the Cascade Division superintendent. True, the current of playful affection between them seems to have persisted (a February 1909 telegram reads, "Berenice Dear—Expect to be in Seattle tonight. . . . Have many pretty things to tell you and of course have a few big kisses left"), but Jim's absences must have taken a toll. To be married to James H. O'Neill was, in a very real sense, to share a husband with the Great Northern Railway—and no number of love telegrams, however effusive, could make up for the fact that the other partner in this threesome seemed to be getting most of the attention.

✧

Everett, Washington, meanwhile, was hardly a town likely to provide Berenice with much distraction. Like many new settlements in the rapidly developing Pacific Northwest, it was viewed as a place with a big future, soon to outstrip those hidebound cities of the East, but at the moment Everett was no Little Paris on Puget Sound. Built on a narrow peninsula between the muddy Snohomish River and a ship-cluttered inlet called Port Gardner Bay, it was—according to one visitor, the Reverend Louis Tucker—a place "with none of the social graces." Self-promoted as "The City of Smokestacks," Everett was the quintessential western mill town, a rough and gritty industrial center teeming with

> 12 sawmills, 16 shingle mills, 2 flour mills. A smelter with capacity to reduce 350 tons of ore a day; a precious metal refinery, arsenic plant, immense paper mill, the largest saw and shingle machinery manufacturers on the Pacific coast, iron works, foundries, creosoting works, shipyards, 6 planing mills, sash and door factories, brewery, stove works, tannery, and scores of other industries.

Having been literally hewn from virgin forest less than twenty years earlier, it was now an outpost of heavy industry plunked down on the edge of a timbered wilderness. And although the town often spoke of itself as a rival to Seattle—"as a terrier yaps at a great Dane"—the claim was still mostly swagger.

Everett's inhabitants could be as coarse and unpolished as the town itself. "Sailors and lumbermen reeled through the avenue at all hours," wrote the ever-scornful Reverend Tucker. That these men were likely reeling toward Everett's infamous Market Street bordello, which drew its clientele from mining and lumber camps for miles around, was something the reverend was apparently too delicate to mention. The town did offer less scandalous types of amusement—everything from *The Merry Widow* at the Everett Theater to Norris's Trained Baboons at the Rose—but most townspeople struck the reverend as too overburdened with work to appreciate much of it.

Yet Everett definitely had its appeal. The waterfront areas may have been grim, but the O'Neills' neat, airy neighborhood was more than pleasant. And although the seventeen-year-old town had already endured several of the boom-and-bust cycles for which raw western settlements were notorious, it was certainly prospering in 1910. On mild evenings the couple could stroll with the baby a few blocks west from Hoyt Avenue to admire the rows of smart new mansions on Grand and Rucker, homes owned by the wealthy mining and lumber barons who had built the town up so quickly from nothing. Once there, standing on the high bluffs overlooking the busy gull-streaked waterfront, they could look down on a vast panorama of healthy and humming industry.

By some standards, of course, that sweep of erupting smokestacks and ramshackle sawmills and shingle mills would have been considered irredeemably ugly. For those less sentimental about unspoiled landscape, however, there was doubtless a rough, mesmeric grandeur to the spectacle, with the feverish glow of all-night furnaces pulsing through columns of rising steam, accompanied by the percussion of great industrial machines and the stark glissando whine of mill saws. Armies of men would march to and from their factories for each of the day's three shifts, and over the whole scene (at least when the wind was blowing seaward from the pulp mill) would hang the sweet, sherry-wine perfume of newly cut wood—the scent of great fir and cedar forests being transformed, log by log, into the building blocks of a growing industrial civilization.

For a railroad man like O'Neill and his family, there was good reason for pride in the sight of all that furious productivity. It was the railroad, after all, that had made the transformation of the Northwest possible, serving as the essential catalyst for turning a fallow wilderness into the colossal wealth-producing machine they saw below them. "All of that land," a U.S. congressman had once remarked, alluding to the entire American West, "wasn't worth ten cents until the railroads came." Unlike most places in the world, where railroads were built primarily to connect existing centers of population and industry, in the American West railroads had actually *created* those centers. Lines were run out into the wilderness with the expectation that settlement and development would spring up in their wake.

"Railroads are not a mere convenience," Miles C. Moore, an early governor of the Washington Territory, had once claimed. "They are the true alchemy of the age, which transmutes the otherwise worthless resources of a country into gold."

The results of that alchemy were now plain to see, in Everett and throughout the West. What once had been considered an undifferentiated wasteland—"the Great American Desert," as easterners referred to most of the continent west of the Mississippi River—was now a productive part of the American commonwealth, a rich patchwork of cities and towns and farms, of ranchland and forests that could be harvested for their timber, minerals, and coal. Thanks to the railroad, the task of conquering the West, which had begun with the Lewis and Clark expedition back in 1803, had been brought to triumphant completion in just decades.

In Washington, which had remained unlinked to the American rail system until the mid-1880s, development had necessarily started late even by western standards. But once that connection had been made, growth was explosive. The population of Seattle, which in 1880 stood at less than 10,000, had by 1910 mushroomed to over 237,000—a twenty-four-fold increase in thirty years. Growth rates in some of the smaller cities in the state—Spokane, Wenatchee, and especially Everett—had been even more extreme. "Everything seems to have happened within the last ten years," the journalist Ray Stannard Baker said of the Pacific Northwest in 1903.

The so-called instant civilization of the Northwest, however, was often superficial. Even in that thoroughly modern year of 1910, much of Washington State retained the quality of a raw frontier territory. Cities such as Seattle and Spokane, though vibrant and on the rise economically, were still what journalist Mark Sullivan called "towns with a marble Carnegie Library at 2nd Street and Indian teepees at 10th." And their main link to the rest of civilization was still a few thin lines of iron running through a vast expanse of mountainous forest and empty prairie—a link that in winter was fragile at best.

✧

No one knew all of this better than Superintendent James H. O'Neill. "The true alchemy of the age" couldn't work its economic magic unless the trains were kept running, and in the Cascade Division that was never an easy task. That's why the Great Northern had labored hard over the past two decades to secure its main line through the mountains. Millions of dollars had been spent above and beyond the original cost of construction, principally for the erection of wooden snowsheds, huge rooflike structures built over the track in areas especially susceptible to snowslides.

This work was still ongoing. That very morning, in fact, the GN had announced an ambitious new chapter in its efforts to fortify the line over the Cascades: "Two and a half millions will be spent by the Great Northern Railway company this year in the state of Washington," the *Herald* reported. The focus of the work was to be a radical alteration of the railroad's right-of-way up the west slope of the mountains, where snowslides were typically most troublesome. The company proposed to clean and grade a strip of land five hundred feet wide along a portion of the line, essentially laying down an impregnable thoroughfare through the wilderness, too broad to be burdened by onslaughts of nature like mud- or snowslides.

These promised improvements, however, could do little to help O'Neill as he sat in his office at the Delta yards, contemplating the coming storm. Over the past three winters, he and his men had earned a reputation for their ability to handle massive snowfalls. During O'Neill's tenure as superintendent there had been remarkably few major line closures on the mountain line and—unusual in those days of frequent rail accidents—no passenger fatalities whatever. This was an impressive record—and one he would now have to defend. Slides were already causing problems in the division's usual trouble spots, such as Windy Point and Tumwater Canyon. Another foot or two of new snow could only further destabilize the snowpack. This worrisome weather situation would also be exacerbated by another difficulty O'Neill was facing—an ongoing strike of railway switchmen (the workers who assembled and reshuffled trains in rail yards), which had been disrupting the division's operations ever since the end of November.

With such a bleak outlook before him, O'Neill knew that he could not simply remain in Everett and hope for the best. Telephone and telegraph wires were sure to go down at some point during the storm, severing communications between his office and the field. To stay on top of the situation, he would have to head up into the mountains himself to direct operations on the ground. And he'd have to base himself in the area most likely to experience trouble: Stevens Pass, site of the Cascade Tunnel, the Great Northern's narrow doorway through the Cascades summit ridge.

Unfortunately, this meant that O'Neill would be gone from Everett for at least several days. Berenice would have to endure yet another lonely, anxious week—lonelier and more anxious than usual, given the fact that she had just learned she was pregnant again. Conceived in December, only three and a half months after Peggy Jane was born, the child who was to be James O'Neill Jr. was already well on his way.

But O'Neill had no other choice. Telegrams calling for help were already pouring into the superintendent's office from all over the division. So he began issuing instructions to his young stenographer, Earl Longcoy. O'Neill's business car—the A-16, his portable office and sleeping quarters—was to be prepared for service. Tomorrow it would be tagged onto the end of eastbound GN train No. 4. The superintendent, accompanied by Longcoy and the A-16's steward, Lewis Walker, would hitch a ride on No. 4 as far as Wellington, the small station at the west portal of the Cascade Tunnel. Along the way, he'd coordinate his team of snow-fighting supervisors: trainmaster Arthur Blackburn, a sixteen-year veteran of the GN, and assistant trainmaster William Harrington, that year's designated "Snow King," in charge of rotary snowplows. J. C. Devery, O'Neill's assistant superintendent, would meanwhile supervise traffic from Leavenworth, at the eastern foot of the range. Wherever and whenever the inevitable crisis developed, O'Neill wanted to be prepared—with all of his troops in the field, ready for battle.

The military metaphor would prove to be apt. What O'Neill would be facing in those mountains over the next long and grueling week would be the equivalent of a campaign of war—a battle unprecedented in the history of American railroading. Like any military campaign, it would involve legions of men in action, hard-won victories alternating with even harder defeats, and countless individual acts and decisions that, in retrospect, would seem foolish, cunning, incomprehensible, or surpassingly heroic. It would be a conflict fought with the most advanced technologies of the age, against unrelenting time pressure and under the most extreme physical and psychological hardships, for stakes as high as they could be.

As in any combat situation, moreover, the credit for success or the responsibility for failure would inevitably fall on the shoulders of one man—the man whose position rendered him accountable for every judgment made and every action taken. Fairly or unfairly, this would be James H. O'Neill's war. And now, on this cold but still deceptively calm Monday evening, the battle's first skirmishes were about to begin.

2

The Long Straw

What has become of Spokane's boast that buttercups may always be found in bloom on Cannon Hill by Washington's birthday?

Perhaps the groundhog heard it and wanted to get even with the inconsiderate people who sneer at his power.

"Coldest day of the year," said Weather Observer Stewart this morning.

Everyone knew it, anyway, but an I-told-you-so air became general when it was learned that the thermometer at the Government station registered 4 below zero at 7 o'clock this morning. Until today, January 6 held the cold record for the winter, with a mark of 8 degrees above zero.

And the forecast for Wednesday is "More snow."

—Spokane Inland Herald

Tuesday, February 22, 1910
Spokane, Washington
Early Evening

Time was not going to be a problem. That, at least, was what Lewis C. Jesseph could reasonably assume as he entered the Havermale Island rail station in Spokane on this frigid Washington's Birthday evening. The thirty-two-year-old lawyer, well regarded for his meticulous preparation of court cases, had planned his trip carefully, giving himself a full thirty-six hours to get from Spokane to Seattle to Olympia, a distance of less than four hundred miles. Even if the train he was now heading for—the Great Northern Railway's No. 25, known in Spokane as the Seattle Express—ran into significant delays, he'd still get over the mountains in plenty of time to make his connection. That would put him in the capital early enough to enjoy a leisurely dinner, telegraph his wife, Flora, and still get a good night's rest before his hearing on Thursday morning. Assuming his sleeper wasn't too crowded or noisy, he'd even have an opportunity to rehearse his presentation once or twice more.

This was to be an important case for Jesseph. Several months earlier he had lost a suit in the Superior Court of Stevens County in Colville, the small city north of Spokane where he lived and practiced. He was now appealing the case to the Washington State Supreme Court, and though he could have filed his brief on paper, he'd decided to argue the case orally before the panel of judges. As a former city attorney for Colville, Jesseph was practiced in the art of legal persuasion, and he was determined to use his argumentative skills to get the lower court's judgment reversed.

Wintry weather hadn't figured into his calculations. By late February the Spokane region was typically well on its way to spring thaw. But as Jesseph made his way down the steam-wreathed platform of the GN's handsome mottled-brick station, sparse, wind-blown snow flurries began to spiral from the dark sky overhead, swirling through the halos of the station's sputtering arc lights.

It was just after 7:00 P.M. when Jesseph climbed aboard the sleek, burgundy-colored cars of train No. 25. After the chill outside, the warmth of the train's interior must have come as an enormous relief. Jesseph's berth was in one of the two steam-heated sleepers—the Winnipeg and the Similkameen—located well behind the chuffing and cinder-spewing locomotive. Built by the renowned Pullman Company and recently remodeled, these sleepers represented the height of early-twentieth-century railroad luxury, with elegantly arched, leaded-glass clerestory windows, ornate gas lighting fixtures, and interiors finished in polished mahogany and plush vermilion. There was even a snug little gentlemen's lounge at one end of each car and an equally compact ladies' sitting room at the other.

Train No. 25 offered yet another distinctly modern amenity. Its powerful H-class Pacific engine was also pulling (in addition to two day coaches, a mail car, and a baggage car) a suave and stylish observation car, where the male passengers could gather to play cards, discuss business, smoke, drink, and swap stories without fear of offending feminine sensibilities. Overall, while not the most opulent train on the Great Northern line (that distinction belonged to the famous Oriental Limited, which ran between Seattle and the railway's corporate home of St. Paul, Minnesota), the Seattle Express did provide a distinctly civilized environment in which to cross the bleak emptiness of central Washington State.

Jesseph had barely settled himself into his seat when a familiar figure appeared in the aisle beside him: John Merritt, an old friend who was also, by chance, the opposing lawyer in Thursday morning's supreme court case. Despite a more than twenty-year difference in their ages— Merritt was in his late fifties, looking somewhat stooped and overweight these days—the two had become cronies in Spokane years ago, when Jesseph was in law school. Upon hearing that Jesseph was planning to argue the supreme court case in person, Merritt had decided to do likewise, and had by coincidence booked the same train.

At exactly 7:30 P.M., after the conductor's requisite cry of "All aboard" and two long blasts from the engine's whistle, the Great Northern Railway's Seattle Express pulled away from the Spokane station, right on schedule.

Passing under the station's tall, Italianate clock tower, the train veered slightly to the north and almost immediately crossed a bridge over the Spokane River. Below, barely visible in the evening gloom, was the rushing, partially frozen torrent of the city's celebrated falls, around which, just a scant few decades earlier, Spokane Indians had pitched their tepees. But here, as in Everett across the state, the railroad had performed its quick transforming act, and the bunchgrass prairie around the falls had long since given way to broad avenues and multistory office buildings. Far from the old frontier town of some eighty ranchers, fur traders, and prospectors it had been in 1879, Spokane was in 1910 a busy modern metropolis of 104,000 souls, with half a dozen daily newspapers, numerous theaters, electric streetcars, and even its own fifteen-story skyscraper—the headquarters of the Old National Bank, not quite finished but already magnificent on its prominent corner of West Riverside Avenue. As No. 25 began picking up speed, clattering through the outlying districts west of the city center, Jesseph, Merritt, and the other passengers could look out on what had rapidly become the largest metropolis between the Twin Cities and Seattle.

Even a large western city, however, had little in the way of an electrified urban area in 1910, and it was not long before the lights of downtown Spokane were left behind. The exterior darkness soon turned the train windows reflective, redirecting the passengers' attention toward the gaslit interior of the cars, toward one another. There would be, by the time the train's complement was full, about fifty-five passengers aboard—a mix of men and women, children and adults, leisure travelers and those on personal or professional business. Lawyers were the largest contingent; in addition to Jesseph and Merritt, there were three other attorneys aboard. The passenger list also included two real estate men, an electrician, a civil engineer, a clergyman, and the inevitable three or four "drummers" (the ubiquitous traveling salesmen of many a Rotarian's joke and many a mother's cautionary tale to her daughter).

Ida Starrett, the recent widow from Spokane, was already on the train, with her three young children seated around her and her elderly parents sitting nearby. The other families were also aboard—the Grays, the Becks, and a young streetcar motorman with his three-year-old daughter. There were also several women traveling alone: a white-haired grandmother named Sarah Jane Covington, who was coming home from a visit to Spokane; Libby Latsch, the head of her own hair-accessories company; and Nellie Sharp, a young, newly divorced freelance writer working on a travel article.

Mrs. Covington, a petite sixty-nine-year-old of a somewhat intellectual bent, was well known in her home city of Olympia for her charity and reform work. Some weeks earlier she had traveled to Spokane to care for an ailing son. Melmoth A. Covington's illness had started innocuously enough: one day he'd received a minor scratch on the wrist from a pet cat. But the wound had quickly become infected, and within three days he was in the hospital, his arm grotesquely swollen. Mrs.

Covington had arrived in town just in time to witness her son's harrowing treatment: "Two or three Drs. worked over him," she later wrote to her daughter. "They injected serum in his breast and that made him extremely weak; then they cut three gashes in his arm, which was swollen very much. . . . When I first saw him, they were spraying it with stuff that burned and smarted so as to make him holler out."

Yet Melmoth had recovered steadily. His mother, feeling comfortable enough to leave him, was now heading back home, after nearly a month away from Olympia. And although she was not a confident traveler, she could reassure herself with the thought that she would soon be reunited with her husband, in plenty of time to celebrate their fifty-first wedding anniversary on March 3.

Not far from Mrs. Covington on the sleeper Winnipeg sat Edward W. "Ned" Topping, a curly-haired, powerfully built twenty-nine-year-old salesman from Ashland, Ohio. Employed by his father's family business— the Safety Door Company, a manufacturer of hardware for barn doors— Ned was ostensibly traveling cross-country in search of new markets. But he actually had another, sadder motive for being on the road. The previous August, his wife, Florence, had died in childbirth. After watching their son grieve for months, Topping's parents had decided that he needed something to distract himself from the loss of both a wife and an unborn daughter. So they had sent him on this trip west, taking his twenty-two-month-old son, Bill, into their own care until his return. And although the idea behind Ned's trip was to get his mind off matters back in Ashland, his letters indicate that he was thinking about little but home and family.

"Mother," he wrote while on the train, "I am so glad that your trip to Akron was so successful & that the doctor found nothing wrong with little Bill. I'd like to have seen him acting up on the train. I suppose the Durrs"—the child's maternal grandparents—"thoroughly enjoyed your visit, for I know how they like to see him and I'll be anxious to hear from your own lips the story of the trip."

Since his departure from Ohio, he'd apparently had news of his younger sister's engagement: "I can hardly believe that Ruth is wearing a ring," he continued, perhaps thinking of his own wife's ring, the stone of which he himself now wore in a setting made after her death. "I know she must be very happy. I'm glad, exceedingly so, and further believe she has made a wise choice. She will have a new life now entirely."

The subtext in all of this was clear: Despite being surrounded by novelty—the sights and sounds of a strange, new territory very different from the place he had left behind—Ned Topping was yearning for nothing so much as further reminders of home: "I hope father and the rest will get busy pretty soon and write me, for letters do come so good way out here."

The person with perhaps the oddest reason for being aboard the Seattle Express that night was Mrs. Nellie McGirl—or, as she now preferred to be called, Miss Nellie Sharp. Recently separated from a husband in Oakland, Nellie had been staying in a Spokane hotel with a friend—Mrs. Herbert Tweedie, whose husband also seemed to be out of the picture—planning the next step in their lives. The two women had decided to spend a few weeks researching a travel article about the lingering traces of the old Wild West in Washington and Montana, with an eye to selling the piece to the popular magazine *McClure's*. From Spokane, one of them would head east to cover the cowboys and homesteaders of the great Montana plains; the other would go west to interview the loggers and fishermen of the more temperate Washington coast. In the interest of fairness, they had drawn straws to determine who would take which territory.

Nellie, a decidedly stout twenty-six-year-old of ebullient good humor, had drawn the long straw. As winner of the contest, she had chosen what seemed the more desirable option: heading west to the coast. So Mrs. Tweedie had packed her friend onto the Seattle Express that evening. Their plan was to meet again in Spokane after a few weeks in the field—their notebooks brimming with fabulous tales about their escapades—and begin assembling the article. Whether or not they'd be able to get the story published in a prestigious magazine like *McClure's*, the project would be a new beginning for them, the start of a bright new chapter in their lives.

This, at least, was what Nellie Sharp had planned for herself. And as the porters on train No. 25 began preparing the Pullman cars for the night, pulling down the cunningly stowed sleeping berths, it was unlikely that Nellie—or any of the others aboard—was anticipating any greater adventure than that. Traveling hundreds of miles over a mountain range was far from the weeks-long ordeal it had been just decades earlier. America at the beginning of the twentieth century was a population on the move, alive with what William Dean Howells once called "the American poetry of vivid purpose." This kind of journey was a routine affair in 1910, something undertaken for the most commonplace reasons: to visit a son or daughter, to consult on a local engineering project, to sell a few loads of "patented safety door hangers."

At Wenatchee, one of the last stations before the foothills of the Cascades, Henry H. White boarded the train. A salesman for the American Paper Company, White had been away on business and was now returning home to the Fenimore Hotel in Seattle, where he lived with his wife. A plainspoken, sometimes pugnacious man, he was, by his own admission, "not of a disposition to anticipate trouble," but rumors of a severe snowstorm ahead were worrisome to him. Though White had been crossing the Cascades monthly for the past six years, this was only his fourth trip on the Great Northern's line through Stevens Pass, and he had never made the trip during such a bad storm.

Even so, as White climbed aboard the sleeper Winnipeg and found his berth, there was no palpable sense of alarm on the train. News of the storm, while perhaps disturbing for some, didn't trouble those familiar with the railroad's operations in the Cascades. As Lewis Jesseph was later to write: "We knew that the Great Northern Railway had constructed many snowsheds to protect the right-of-way from the slides and that the rotary snowplows could clear the exposed track." The splendid cocoon of a Pullman sleeper would in any case have seemed all but impermeable to those carried within its portable environment of safety and comfort.

"About eleven o'clock we retired," Jesseph wrote, evincing a sense of trust that was probably shared by most of those aboard. By morning, they knew, the train would already be approaching the coast, with the storm-tossed mountains far behind it.

✧

9:00 P.M.

Berne, clear and calm, no new snow

Cas. Tunnel, snowing light, east wind, 10° above

Wellington, strong wind, snowing, 20° above

Scenic, snowing medium hard, blowing hard, 18° above

Handled freight and passenger traffic with rotary protection and without any unusual delay.

—*J. C. Devery,*
assistant superintendent
Cascade Division Operations Diary

Wellington, Washington
Toward Midnight

The situation was under control. Twelve hours after his arrival on the mountain, James H. O'Neill could safely say that much. Yes, there had been some small problems—and at least one situation on the west slope that had resulted in significant delays—but his men were taking the storm in stride. From his temporary command post in the tiny station at Wellington, high in the mountains, O'Neill could look out on a railway line that, if not quite running smoothly, was at the very least running— a victory in itself.

Unfortunately, however, victories never lasted very long in the Cascade Division. No sooner was one train dragged over the mountains than another was on the way to take its place—a procession that never ended, day or night. Though there were still some reactionaries in the country who opposed nighttime and Sunday operation of trains, railroading in 1910 was emphatically a twenty-four-hours-a-day, seven-days-a-week proposition. To a modern railroader, the idea of any kind of downtime for a mainline rail system would have seemed almost unbelievably quaint.

So the superintendent knew that it was far too early to celebrate.

The snow had begun in earnest a few hours earlier and was now coming down as thick as he'd ever seen it. Although storms in the Cascades rarely lasted more than twenty-four or thirty-six hours, O'Neill understood that there was still plenty of time for trouble to erupt.

Surprisingly, the only real problem so far had been caused not by snow but by the extreme cold. That morning, after bidding his wife and daughter good-bye and boarding his business car for the trip to the mountains, O'Neill had felt the temperature plummet. By the time he reached the station at Scenic Hot Springs, a small resort on the west slope, it had fallen to ten degrees above zero—cold enough for ice on the tracks to start playing havoc with stopped trains. And this was exactly what had happened. Overnight, an extra-long westbound freight train had become immobilized by ice and hard snow while standing halfway onto the passing track at Scenic. An attempt to pull the freight free had succeeded only in dislocating the drawbar of one of the freight cars. The train had broken in two with its back end sticking out onto the main line, blocking traffic in both directions and delaying no fewer than three first-class trains.

Arriving on the scene and conferring with his trainmaster, Arthur Blackburn, the ever-efficient O'Neill had quickly organized a team of seventy-five to one hundred shovelers to keep the train's undercarriage free of the drifting snow. Then he'd ordered up a spare engine to extricate the damaged freight car, reconnect the two halves of the train, and pull it completely off the main track. The maneuver had required some complex railroading, but within a couple of hours the job was done. Traffic had begun moving again. Leaving Blackburn in charge at Scenic, O'Neill had reboarded his business car and continued up the hill.

It was already midday by the time he'd arrived at Wellington. Ordering his business car left on a sidetrack, O'Neill had made his way to the depot and established himself in the station's small telegraph office. And ever since then, he'd been hovering over the operator's shoulder, receiving reports and issuing instructions by telegraph and telephone up and down the line. As trains passed through the station on their way east or west, he would take time to consult with the engineers and conductor of each, asking them about conditions, weighing their impressions against his own encyclopedic knowledge of the division and its weak points. O'Neill understood from long experience that if he was to have any hope of keeping his trains on time, he'd need every bit of intelligence he could get.

O'Neill's principal focus was on the deployment of his fleet of Cooke rotary snowplows. These state-of-the-art snow-fighting machines were heavy, reinforced railcars, each with a huge bladed wheel attached to the front. Propelled by one or two trailing locomotives, a rotary would lumber along the tracks at a top speed of ten miles per hour or so, the rotating blades of its fanlike wheel slicing into drifts as high as thirteen feet, throwing the snow in high, parabolic arcs to the edge of the right-of-way. Rotaries were difficult to maintain, awkward to operate, and gluttonous of coal and water—and they certainly weren't pretty—but they *were* effective: A fleet of half a dozen could normally keep a division's worth of track free of snow and open for traffic.

O'Neill currently had four of the division's five rotaries operating, and he needed every one of them. Earlier in the evening he'd issued an order that all first-class trains (i.e., high-priority, time-sensitive trains such as those carrying passengers and mail) should be directly preceded over the hill by a rotary. With the wind blowing so hard on the west slope, a newly plowed track could be clogged by drifts within an hour or two; a train without a snowplow escort could easily bog down—and the last thing O'Neill needed was a train full of passengers marooned on an exposed mountainside, slowly being buried under windblown drifts of snow.

So far, at least, this plan was working well. Eastbound trains No. 2 and No. 26, under the protection of snowplow X800, were at that very moment climbing in procession up the west slope toward Wellington. Another plow, the X801, was waiting at the western edge of the mountains, ready to accompany No. 44, which had just left Everett. Westbound train No. 1—the Oriental Limited—had passed through Wellington about an hour earlier and was being preceded down the mountain by rotary X807. And O'Neill's fourth rotary, the X802, was heading off to meet westbound No. 25, the Seattle Express (the train carrying Jesseph, Topping, and the others), which was now approaching

Leavenworth, at the eastern edge of O'Neill's territory. Overall, traffic in the Cascade Division was in remarkably good shape.

But there was one more train approaching the Cascades that O'Neill was worried about more than all the rest: No. 27, the Fast Mail from St. Paul. This was the highest-priority train on the line, rushing mail cross-country from St. Paul to Seattle in a mere 47.25 hours. Inaugurated the previous September, the Fast Mail had quickly become a key (and extremely profitable) element in the GN network, part of a nationally crucial relay system designed to move mail from New York to the West Coast in just three days. In order to maintain this schedule, however, the Fast Mail had to travel significant stretches of its route at speeds in excess of sixty miles per hour. The penalty for late arrivals in Seattle was heavy, and if they occurred too frequently were likely to cause the U.S. Post Office Department to take the lucrative contract to one of the GN's all-too-willing competitors.

In the first month of its existence, the Fast Mail had turned in a brilliant performance: From its first run on September 27, 1909, until October 30, it had racked up a perfect record of thirty-four consecutive on-time arrivals, often making up significant delays inherited from the Chicago, Milwaukee and St. Paul Railway, the line relaying mail to the GN from Chicago. One St. Paul–to–Seattle run had even been made in 44 hours and 35 minutes—a blistering pace by all standards of the day. "The Fastest Long-Distance Train in the World" was how one journalist from the *Brooklyn Standard Union* had described it. "It runs like a scared cat."

Then November arrived and the Fast Mail's record took a sudden and decisive turn for the worse. It ran hours late on November 2, 14, and 22. On December 5, the Great Northern's "hottest train" gave its worst performance yet, arriving a full 12 hours and 45 minutes behind schedule. The main trouble, of course, had been heavy weather in the Cascades.

Now, on the night of February 22, the Fast Mail was threatening to fall short of even that dismal December record. Thanks to delays coming through the Montana Rockies, the train was roughly six hours late already. Getting over the Cascades under current conditions would probably put it even further behind schedule.

So O'Neill faced a conundrum. There were currently two important first-class trains heading west into his territory, but only one rotary—the X802—available to serve them. Should he hold the Seattle Express at Leavenworth until the Fast Mail caught up with it? If he did so, he could send the rotary ahead of both trains, giving both a newly cleared track as they made their way up the east slope of the mountains. Doing so, however, would also mean putting the Seattle Express, a train nearly as time-sensitive as the Fast Mail, several hours behind schedule.

Alternatively, O'Neill could release the Seattle Express promptly upon its arrival at Leavenworth and, without waiting for the Fast Mail, send it up the hill with the X802 ahead of it. Assuming that the mail train wasn't too far behind—and that the snow wasn't drifting too quickly—the Fast Mail would still have a relatively clean track ahead of it; but those were two significant assumptions. The fierce winds on the west side of the summit might soon work their way over to the east. Did O'Neill really want to take that kind of chance with his highest-priority train?

There was also a third option, one that O'Neill dreaded even to consider. If conditions on the hill turned critical—if a heavy snowslide came down or another train got iced up on the main line—the superintendent could always request permission to send trains over the line of one of the other GN-affiliated railroads connecting Spokane with the coast—namely, the Northern Pacific or the Spokane, Portland & Seattle. These lines also ran through the Cascades, but their crossings were located far south of the Great Northern's always dicey route through Stevens Pass. The SP&S line, for instance—also known as the North Bank road—followed a route much less vulnerable to the depredations of mountain snowstorms, tracing the north bank of the Columbia River across the range. If any route remained open during the storm, that would probably be the one.

The inevitable drawback of detouring trains over either line was that it would put them many more hours behind schedule, and there was no reason—yet—for such a drastic measure. If nothing else, it was a matter of pride. To reroute the trains now, because of something as normal as a late-winter snowstorm, would be to admit defeat even before the battle was truly under way.

O'Neill, however, was a careful man, and this storm was beginning to look like a bad one, even by Cascade standards. Just an hour earlier, when the Oriental Limited had come through, O'Neill had asked its engineer, J. C. Wright, what he thought of conditions. Wright, a fourteen-year veteran of the Cascade Division, had given O'Neill something to think about: The storm, he'd said—at least right at the top of the mountain around Wellington—was quite simply the worst he'd ever seen.

✧

It was snowing heavily, very heavily . . . [as if] somebody was plucking a chicken; it was falling out there so fast that you could not see very far, like looking across the canyon you could not see, on account it was just a dense fall of snow.

—*Alfred B. Hensel,*
mail clerk

Wednesday, February 23, 1910
Leavenworth, Washington
1:30 A.M.

Most of the passengers had already been asleep for hours when the Seattle Express pulled into the Leavenworth station. A small, picturesque mountain town sitting at the foot of a virtual wall of craggy, snow-covered peaks, Leavenworth was a Great Northern division point, where crews were changed and locomotives could top up their supplies of coal and water. It was also the point at which the really difficult terrain began for westbound traffic. Helper engines were added to the front or back of Seattle-bound trains here; the extra horsepower would assist them on the steep grades and sharp curves ahead. After Leavenworth, the line would enter a slotlike opening in the Cascades massif, following the Wenatchee River up a twisty canyon between brooding, steep-sided peaks of six to eight thousand feet. The effect was like entering a gargantuan maze, and on a slick, ice-covered path heading straight up. Even a relatively light passenger train would need the added help to get through.

It was snowing but calm at Leavenworth as the helper engine was attached to the front of the Express and a few more passengers boarded. Conductor Joseph L. Pettit, coming on duty for the night, took charge of the train. In an era when train conductors were fabled for their arrogance and imperiousness, Joe Pettit was a notable exception, by general consensus a kindly, avuncular man. Tonight, though, even he could be excused for being less than cheerful. Pettit knew what the weather was doing in those mountains up ahead. It was going to be a rough trip, and it was he, as conductor, who would have to deal with disgruntled passengers if they ran into heavy delays.

The train idled, steaming in the cold night while its crew awaited orders. They weren't long in coming: superintendent O'Neill had decided he could not afford to wait until conditions improved. Time was simply too valuable to waste. So he chose to release the passenger train and let the Fast Mail catch up as it might. According to the latest reports, the mail train was making good time from Spokane, and since the wind had not yet picked up on the east slope, the line up to Stevens Pass was clear. There was no reason, then, to delay the passenger train.

At about 1:30 A.M., O'Neill conveyed his instructions to the dispatcher: Pettit and the crew of the Seattle Express were given the go-ahead to proceed.

Before the Express could leave, however, one of its passengers—a Mrs. Blanche Painter—stepped down from the train to the station platform. A milliner from Everett, she had been on her way home on a through ticket when she decided quite suddenly to stop over in Leavenworth to see some friends. Though she would later claim that the impulse was spontaneous, it was certainly a strange hour for an unannounced visit, and even finding a hotel room at 2:00 A.M. would have been difficult in a small town like Leavenworth. Nevertheless, Mrs. Painter did detrain, intending to complete her journey the next night. Luggage in hand, she left the Express and headed toward the depot—with no idea of how monumental a decision she had just made.

Meanwhile, final preparations were under way for the train's departure. At 2:15 A.M. rotary X802 pulled out of Leavenworth, its fan blades spinning, making easy work of the light snow cover on the tracks. The express followed a short time later, carrying its cargo of sleeping passengers. The time was 2:30 A.M. For better or worse, they were heading up into the mountains.

3

Last Mountains

No sun can penetrate these forests. The very life that is there
seems a hushed, awed life. . . . In the presence of such savage
loneliness, one feels how like an acorn's fall and rotting man's
death would be.

> —*Hamlin Garland*
> *"Western Landscapes"*

To pioneers of the Oregon Trail in the mid-nineteenth century, they
were known as the "Last Mountains." Rough, precipitous, and densely
timbered, they erupted from the western plateau like a final geological
insult, one last obstacle between exhausted emigrants and the fertile,
temperate river valleys of the coast. After the arduous two-thousand-
mile journey from their starting point in Missouri, westering travelers
might have thought that they'd endured just about every hardship the
continent could possibly serve up. Then came the Cascades.

"The crossing of the Rocky Mountains . . . was insignificant in comparison to the Cascades," wrote an early western journalist of a trip
over the Oregon Trail. Few passes penetrated the range, and those that
did were swathed in dense, junglelike forests that made any progress agonizing. With little grass to graze on, hungry livestock would eat the
poison laurel leaves and die. The danger from rockslides, floods, and avalanches, moreover, was relentless. For would-be settlers transporting
their worldly possessions on wagons and oxcarts, these obstacles were

all but insurmountable. Many early pioneering groups chose instead to stop at a place on the Columbia River called The Dalles, disassemble their wagons, load them onto rafts, and then brave the perilous rapids of the Columbia gorge in order to get through the range.

Not that the Cascades are particularly lofty. Compared to the giants of the Rockies, most Cascade peaks are of relatively modest height, at least on paper. As a very young and complex mountain system, though, the Cascades are steeper and more rugged than the Rockies, riddled with blind canyons that end at sheer, towering cliffs. Worse still, the Cascades are, as one writer has put it, "restless with the restlessness of youth. They break off in hunks and slide down canyons; they toss off their mantles of trees and sling them down roaring rivers. . . . It is as though the hundreds of peaks in the Cascade chain remembered the exciting period only a few million years ago when they first boiled up out of the retching earth and threw themselves against the north-west skies."

Even this forbidding terrain, however, couldn't hold back the tide of Manifest Destiny for long. Good land lay beyond those mountains, and by midcentury it had been declared free for the taking. Thanks to the massive territorial gains of the 1840s—the annexing of Texas, the winning of California, the Southwest, and the Colorado plateau in the Mexican War, and the signing of an 1846 treaty giving the United States control of the Oregon Country—the nation had increased in size by roughly 50 percent in a single decade. Vast new territories had to be settled, requiring that obstacles to travel be neutralized as quickly as possible.

This need was especially urgent in the Pacific Northwest. By the early 1850s new towns were sprouting up all over the Oregon and Washington coast. If these settlements were to grow into the New Yorks and Bostons of the West, the Cascades would have to be overcome. So travelers began to search for alternative routes to bypass the Columbia River bottleneck. Primitive trails and wagon roads were hacked out of the mountain wilderness, cutting across the mountains wherever a usable pass could be found. But these flimsy connections—slow, hazardous, and virtually useless in winter—could provide only a limited solution. It soon became clear that what was needed to tame this area was the technology of the iron horse.

The dream of a railway connection to the Northwest was as old as the railroad itself. As early as 1835—five years after the first few miles of track had been laid in the East—an Oregon pioneer named Samuel Bancroft Barlow was already mentally projecting those tracks northwestward, writing treatises in support of a railroad line to the Columbia River. Asa Whitney, a prosperous New York entrepreneur, took up the cause ten years later, petitioning state and federal governments for permission to build a railroad from Michigan to the Pacific. By the 1850s, even Congress was convinced, realizing that the sooner the West was linked to the rest of the country by rail, the sooner America's dreams of an ocean-to-ocean civilization could be achieved.

The sum of $150,000 was therefore appropriated to fund surveys of four possible railway routes to the Pacific. They included the northern route originally proposed by Asa Whitney plus three others, spaced at rough intervals like horizontal stripes across the western half of the country. Also, since the Pacific surveys fell under the jurisdiction of the War Department, led by a regionally loyal young southerner named Jefferson Davis, a fifth, deeply southern route was belatedly added to the list.

In charge of "The Northern Pacific Railroad Exploration and Survey" (the Whitney route) was one Isaac Ingalls Stevens, a young army major who had served honorably in the Mexican War. Having campaigned actively for his friend Franklin Pierce in the latter's successful presidential bid in 1852, Stevens was due for a political plum. He was granted two of them. Not only was he given command of the northern railway survey, he was also made the first governor of the newly organized Washington Territory.

By the summer of 1853, Stevens had already assembled his reconnaissance party and divided it into three. One group, under his own leadership, was to focus on surveying the northern plains westward from the Mississippi River. Another team would head toward the Rockies and the Bitterroot Mountains of Montana and Idaho. To the third group—led by another army major, a moody and irritable young

Philadelphian named George B. McClellan—would fall the hardest part, the Cascades. "The amount of work in the Cascade Range and eastward . . . will be immense," Stevens warned the future commander of the Union armies in the Civil War. "We must not be frightened [by] long tunnels or enormous snows, but set ourselves to work to overcome them."

It was not the kind of task to which McClellan was well suited by temperament. Showing the same distaste for action and effort that would later cause Abraham Lincoln such consternation, the prickly young major conducted the shoddiest of surveys in the Cascades, often relying on questionable testimony from local Indians to substitute for the hard work of actual exploration. Unsurprisingly, every pass he considered turned out to be too steep, too rocky, and/or too snowbound for train tracks. Pronouncing himself "thoroughly disgusted with the whole concern," he quarreled repeatedly with Stevens and with his own subordinates, though he did finally admit, grudgingly, that one particular pass, the Snoqualmie, might just be railworthy. Even so, he remained unconvinced that any truly practicable route existed through the northern Cascades—a doubt he had no qualms about expressing directly to Secretary Davis.

As matters played out, the results of the northern survey would prove to be largely academic. The always partisan Davis eventually selected the route he had probably chosen even before the surveyors took their first steps west: the southern route from New Orleans through Texas and Arizona to California. Not that it mattered. By the end of the 1850s, with the slavery issue turning critical and North-South tensions rising, the idea of a transcontinental line was soon eclipsed by the more pressing matter of civil war.

Paradoxically, the start of the War Between the States proved less of a hindrance to railroad advocates than might be imagined. With southern opponents suddenly and decisively engaged elsewhere, plans for a line to the Pacific could go forward without much regional stonewalling. The first Pacific Railroad bill, approved by Congress in July 1862, did authorize a centrally located line from Omaha to Sacramento, but the second nod went to the Pacific Northwest. On July 2,

1864, the Northern Pacific Railroad bill was signed into law by that former railroad lawyer himself, Abraham Lincoln, mandating that the nation's second transcontinental line extend from Lake Superior to Puget Sound. And although one arm of it would follow the well-trodden Columbia River Gorge through the Cascades to Portland, the main line to the coast would run through the relative terra incognita to the north of the river, right through the high Cascades.

The Last Mountains, though, had not in the meantime become any less problematic to cross. The Northern Pacific quickly sent several groups of surveyors out to the northern Cascades, but none turned up anything close to an easy pass. After reviewing their reports, the chief engineer of the project reluctantly found himself in agreement with the now nationally prominent George McClellan: "There is no place to cross the mountains north of Snoqualmie Pass where a great deal of money would not be necessary both in first cost of construction and in subsequent operation."

It ultimately took over two decades (not to mention a bankruptcy or two), but the Northern Pacific did finally put its line through the mountains—at Stampede Pass, a close neighbor of the Snoqualmie. It was hardly an ideal route (in the very beginning the line was forced to include a stretch of track at the ridiculously steep grade of 5.4 percent), but it did get the job done. Upon completion of the NP's Cascade line in 1887, trains could finally reach Puget Sound on a fairly direct route from the East, giving the Washington Territory what it had been seeking for decades—"the entering wedge," as one newspaper had put it, to "open our great oyster, the world of enterprise and prosperity."

But while the Northern Pacific connection did put parts of Washington on the grid of the American railway network, it still left vast portions of the territory underserved—including Seattle, which was stranded at the end of an inconvenient branch line from Tacoma. The city that would eventually become the region's giant was therefore still without direct connection to the East, almost forty years after its founding.

Fortunately, the person who would finally give the city its own transcontinental was even then hatching plans to take train tracks where none had ever gone before—straight through those same northern

Cascades that had given the early pioneers such trouble. Soon to be dubbed the Empire Builder of the Northwest, he was a man who would change the fate not only of Seattle but of the entire northwestern quarter of the United States—and one who would eventually play a critical role in the events unfolding at Stevens Pass in the late winter of 1910.

✦

Give me enough Swedes and whiskey and I'll build a railroad to Hell.

—*James J. Hill*

He was, according to one of his own biographers, "the shaggy-bearded, barb-wired, one-eyed son-of-a-bitch of western railroading." It was a description that even his staunchest admirers would have been hard-pressed to contradict. James J. Hill—conceiver, builder, and eventual éminence grise of the Great Northern Railway—was by all accounts intimidating and irascible. Physically, he was a great wolverine of a man: thick-necked, burly-chested, with stocky arms and legs that over-clever journalists were wont to compare to railroad ties. His blunt-featured face was framed by a thick, domed forehead and a matted snarl of steel-gray beard. But his most arresting feature was his piercing left eye—his one good eye, the right having been blinded in a childhood archery accident. The angry flash of that eye was to be—over the course of a long and stupendously productive life—a much-feared phenomenon in the highest business and political circles in the land, the bane of countless railroad underlings, business rivals, and more than a few presidents (of banks, of railroads, of the United States). In an age that saw the likes of J. Pierpont Morgan, Jay Gould, and Andrew Carnegie, James J. Hill more than held his own.

Born poor in the Ontario backwoods in 1838, Hill had come to the United States as a young man with little except a few dollars in savings and an almost diabolical capacity for toil. Once established in St. Paul, Minnesota (a.k.a. "Pig's Eye" in those early days), he had worked his way up the frontier economic ladder from steamship clerk to prominent local capitalist, mainly by investing his extraordinary energies in any and every business that seemed to have a profit in it. Combining a healthy opportunism with an intimate knowledge of the western frontier's infrastructure needs, Hill soon made a small fortune in such stubbornly unglamorous businesses as warehousing, freight forwarding, and the wholesaling of everything from coal to apple cider.

As the economic potential of the railroad became glaringly obvious, however, Hill quickly turned his attention to that most capital-intensive of industries. Partnering with four other men, he managed to assume control of a small, St. Paul–based railroad that had fallen into bankruptcy after the Panic of 1873. Before long, Hill was hatching big plans for his new acquisition. Like Asa Whitney before him, he saw both wisdom and profit in opening up the great northwestern wilderness with a railway line from the upper Midwest to the Pacific—a modern-day Northwest Passage that could also provide a link to the markets of China, Japan, and the rest of Asia.

Principal among Hill's many challenges was the fact that the Northern Pacific had already realized a version of his dream with its own line from Minnesota to the coast. This meant tough competition for every potential traveler and carload of wheat or lumber the territory could produce. Unlike the NP, moreover, Hill's Pacific Extension would have to be built without the generous land grants and subsidies that the U.S. government had provided to the earliest transcontinentals. Running as it did north of the NP line and south of the Canadian border, it would also have even harsher and more barren territory to traverse, including the worst of the high, dry plains of western Dakota and eastern Montana. So tremendous were the risks that early critics began referring to the entire plan as "Hill's Folly"—a railroad that would likely end up carrying nothing but buffalo bones.

But while Hill harbored no illusions about the difficulties of implementing his line, he had a clearer sense than anyone of how those difficulties could be surmounted—thanks mainly to his close study of the particulars of the Northwest's climate, soil, and natural resources. To overcome the route's geographical disadvantages, he would focus (obsessively, some would say) on keeping costs low and maximizing efficiency in every aspect of construction and operation. By taking advantage of the very latest innovations in railroad technology and traction power, and harnessing them with the organizational principles of what would soon be called "scientific management," Hill would make the Great Northern the first truly twentieth-century western railroad—the first one worthy of the adjective "modern."

It remained only to build the thing. "What we want," Hill famously told his engineers, "is the best possible line, shortest distance, lowest grades, and least curvature that we can build." This was a tall order, but early surveys through the Rockies were encouraging. The GN's newly hired locating engineer, John F. Stevens (better known to posterity as the chief engineer of the Panama Canal), quickly located an excellent pass over the continental divide in Montana—the so-called Lost Marias Pass, which turned out to be the lowest and most practicable Rockies crossing of any transcontinental yet built.

Hill had known from the beginning, however, that the greater challenge would be getting the line across those ever-troublesome northern Cascades. The only known viable passes—the Snoqualmie and the NP's Stampede, as well as the water-level Columbia River route—were all too far south; using any of them would have involved taking the tracks on a long detour, something that the parsimonious Hill could simply not tolerate. So when, in 1890, the time came to plot the route over the Cascades, Stevens was again dispatched, in hopes that the young engineer could repeat the magic of his Marias Pass accomplishment.

But, like numerous locating engineers before him, Stevens soon found himself stymied by the region's pitiless terrain. "The process of reconnaissance for a railway line," he would later write, "is largely one of elimination—to find out where *not* to go." And for the first few weeks of his reconnaissance, Stevens was finding no end of places not to go. Realizing that his cantankerous employer would accept no failure, Stevens was nonetheless determined to remain in those mountains until he had a feasible pass to recommend. So he persisted.

Finally, following a lead developed by an earlier GN surveyor, A. B. Rogers, Stevens located what seemed the best pass in the region and essentially declared it feasible for a railway line. Stevens Pass was arguably a very poor place for a railroad. The plotting of a workable rail line through the pass eventually proved to be an engineering challenge of mind-boggling complexity, requiring sharp curves, brutal grades, elaborate switchbacks, and even a baroque horseshoe-shaped tunnel—all of which violated Hill's most cherished principles of efficient railway design.

By this point, though, Hill was a man in a hurry. While he clearly understood the high operational cost of every degree of curvature and every percentage point of grade on Stevens's proposed line, he also recognized that his Pacific Extension had to start producing revenues immediately for the railroad to survive. So Stevens's route—no matter how imperfect—was accepted. Over the next two years, three thousand men worked twelve hours a day, seven days a week, to build it. And on the evening of January 6, 1893—at a point near what would later become Scenic Hot Springs—the last spike of the Great Northern Railway's Pacific Extension was driven.

Rejoicing was general up and down the Washington coast. In Seattle, some local boosters even started claiming that the city would soon outstrip San Francisco in both size and importance. Such boasts may have been excessive, but they were not entirely without foundation. Within a decade of its completion, "Hill's Folly" would utterly transform the entire region. Describing the entrepreneur's accomplishment some years later, Seattle luminary Thomas Burke hailed the new railroad as "the most judiciously planned, the most economically constructed, and the most wisely managed line that has ever served a new country. . . . [Hill] has, in less than fifteen years, given four new states to the Union with an aggregate population of more than 1,500,000 people!"

True to the old rhetoric, then, the iron horse had worked its alchemy on the Pacific Northwest. The wilds of Washington State were, by the beginning of the new century, tamed and civilized at last. "The twin ribbons of iron or steel," as historian Carlos Schwantes has put it, "converted inhospitable terrain into friendly space."

◆

But in the early morning hours of February 23, 1910—as Great Northern train No. 25 began its climb into the high Cascades from

Leavenworth—the friendliness of that terrain was starting to look a little doubtful. Even if they'd been awake, the passengers on the Seattle Express could not have seen their surroundings in the snow-seared darkness, but what they were heading toward was a mountain wilderness still as intimidating as any in the country. And they would be crossing it via a stretch of track that even the officials of the Great Northern itself regarded as "the weakest link in our transportation chain."

In one of his original reports on the discovery of the pass in 1890, John Stevens had noted that "there was no evidence whatever that the pass in question was known to anyone. . . . There were no signs of any trails leading to or from it, within ten miles in either direction." Given the massive snows, precipitous alpine terrain, inhospitable remoteness, and always unpredictable weather, there were some very good reasons why this pass had been shunned even by Indians on foot before the coming of the Great Northern Railway—reasons that the passengers aboard the Seattle Express were soon to discover for themselves. For no matter what the railway propagandists might say to the contrary, there were indeed places in the country too wild to be tamed by the technology of the railroad—and Stevens Pass might be one of them.

4

A Temporary Delay

Dear Mother & all of you,

I wrote you last night that I expected to reach Seattle this a.m. Here I am at the summit of the Cascades, snowed in since 6:30 this morning. Such a snow you never saw. It's banked up to the top of the window here and we can't go or come. Can't get any information as to when we'll get out.

—*Ned Topping*

Wednesday, February 23, 1910
Cascade Tunnel Station
7:00 A.M.

When Lewis Jesseph awoke on Wednesday morning, it was immediately apparent to him that something was wrong. The train he was on, which should have been rocking along the flat coastal plain toward Puget Sound, was instead standing at a dead halt. The comforting sounds of a steam train on the move—the deep, resonant churning of the engine, the clatter of metal wheels on metal rails, the far, always wistful cry of the locomotive whistle—were notably absent. Instead, the train seemed to be swaddled in an ominous silence. When he lifted the shade on the window beside his berth, all he could see outside was white.

Jesseph sat up in the tight space of the sleeping berth, pulled on some clothes, and climbed out into the stuffy corridor of the Pullman.

He made his way to the men's lounge at the end of the car, where he shaved and finished dressing. As he cleaned up, the porter assigned to the Winnipeg—a dapper young black man from Mississippi named Lucius Anderson—entered the tiny lounge.

"Good morning, Porter," Jesseph said to him. "Where are we?"

"We're at Cascade," Anderson replied, meaning Cascade Tunnel Station, at the east portal of the two-and-a-half-mile tunnel under the summit of Stevens Pass.

"Have we been here long?" Jesseph asked.

"Several hours, but we hope to be on our way any time now." Then the porter added an observation that cannot have been welcome to a man intent on making a court date in a still-distant city: "The storm is very bad."

Jesseph finished dressing and returned to his berth to find John Merritt. The two attorneys discussed the delay, then decided to go outside to assess the situation for themselves. What they saw when they stepped down from the Pullman's vestibule was not encouraging. "I was born and had lived all my life in a northern climate," Jesseph would later write, "but never before had I seen a snowstorm like this one. There was no wind . . . [but] it fell so thick and fast that at a distance of twenty-five feet an object was almost indistinguishable."

What Jesseph would have seen, had the visibility allowed it, was a tiny alpine village sitting in a small basin surrounded by high serrated peaks. Cascade Tunnel Station, at an altitude of 3,382 feet, was an intensely isolated place with only one reason to exist: to service the railroad tunnel from which it took its name. Built from nothing barely twenty years earlier, the town consisted primarily of a depot, an engine roundhouse and turntable (for turning locomotives and snowplows), an electric substation and motor shed, a few cottages, a bunkhouse for train crews, and a number of makeshift shacks created by removing the wheel trucks from the bottoms of old boxcars. The bulk of its wintertime population consisted of crews of transient snow shovelers, typically down-on-their-luck types recruited from places like Skid Road in Seattle. Cascade Tunnel Station was, in short, a rough, workaday, and sometimes unsavory place, even under a forgiving blanket of snow.

Henry White, the traveling salesman for the American Paper Company, was also up and about by now, and hungry for breakfast. Stopping Joseph Pettit in the aisle of the Winnipeg, he asked the conductor where the dining car was. Pettit told him that there was none on the train (one was usually added farther down the line), but that arrangements had been made to feed the passengers at the station "beanery," a rudimentary cook shack above the depot where the engine crews ate.

Gathering White and the others into small groups, the conductor and the Pullman porters led them out into the blinding storm, guiding them up a narrow path to the plain, half-buried shack. Essentially a single large room hammered together out of raw lumber, the beanery was hardly a pleasant place. A huge potbellied heating stove radiated at one end of the room, opposite an equally massive flat-topped cookstove. Between them stretched a dozen or so rough-hewn, grime-streaked wooden tables set with white enamelware and dented tin cups.

However primitive the setting, the beanery's chef, Harry Elerker, and his waiter, John Bjerenson, did know how to produce food in bulk. Finding themselves with so many extra mouths to feed, they rose to the occasion. Before long the passengers and crew of the Express were digging into an ample breakfast of flapjacks, eggs, cooked cereal, and tinned fruit. "It was a dirty hole," Ned Topping later wrote to his mother of the beanery, "but the stuff tasted good."

Naturally, the passengers were eager to know what was keeping them stalled there. Gathering information from Pettit and the other railroaders, a few managed to piece the story together: One of the rotary plows, having bogged down during the night in the snow west of the tunnel, was now blocking the main line. Once it was shoveled out, the Seattle Express would be on its way—perhaps by afternoon, but probably not until nightfall. This was hardly comforting news, especially to Jesseph and Merritt, who would now quite possibly miss their Thursday morning court appearance. Since the two lawyers represented both sides of the case, though, they could at least hope that the supreme court would make no decision without them. They returned to their berths in the Winnipeg after breakfast, determined to make the best of their unanticipated leisure.

Back on the train, Sarah Jane Covington was getting up after a long sleep-in. Told of the delay, the old woman was alarmed but tried to be philosophical about her situation. Though she knew no one aboard, the crew and the other passengers were being kind to her; several even offered to bring her breakfast from the cook shack. To help pass the time, she pulled a few sheets of paper from her handbag and started to jot down some notes: "Feb 23," she wrote. "We are snowed in at the mouth of the Tunnel, 20 minutes of eleven A.M. I just got up from my bed. The mts. are beautiful and we are all resting easy. They say we may be here all day. The cars are warm and very nice."

Standing behind the Seattle Express by now was the Fast Mail train, which had reached Cascade Tunnel Station a few hours after the passenger train. Alfred B. Hensel, one of the mail train's crew of eight clerks, was also gazing out at the storm in some dismay. He had been working the Spokane-to-Seattle run for the past six weeks—enough time to know what kind of snowfalls a Cascade storm could unleash—but this one looked particularly ominous. Here at Stevens Pass, in fact, it was coming down more copiously than he'd ever seen it. A careful and conscientious worker (his daughter would later recall watching him practice his mail-sorting skills for hours on end in his bedroom), he took pride in the speed and efficiency of the Fast Mail system. The fact that the current delay had nothing to do with his own performance didn't ease his frustration much.

Not that his luck had been perfect before this. Hensel, twenty-nine years old and rather stylish with his sleek mustache and neatly parted slicked-down hair, had been a railway mail clerk for almost six years now, and like anyone who'd worked on steam trains for any length of time, he'd experienced his share of misadventures. Once while he was on the Northern Pacific's mail run to Lewiston, Idaho, his train had been charged by a large, aggressive, and apparently very confused bull. Incredibly, the animal had succeeded in derailing the train's locomotive. The consequences were not particularly dire—except for the bull, which did not survive the encounter—but the following year the mail clerk was involved in a far more serious accident. His train was being pushed up the Lewiston grade by an extra-large locomotive that, because it was too big for the normal station turntable, had been attached backward at the end of the train. Somehow the weight of the water in the engine's forward tender shifted on a curve, flipping over the locomotive and the mail car. Hensel was thrown through the skylight of the mail car as it toppled, injuring his feet.

Since then the mishaps had been less dramatic—mostly snow delays like the current one. But for a member of the Railway Mail Service, which operated under the motto "Certainty, Security, Celerity," anything that interfered with the timely delivery of the mail was a serious matter. A division of the U.S. Post Office Department, the RMS contracted directly with the railroads to carry the mail, and it kept close tabs on the performance statistics for each line. To keep the mail moving efficiently, clockwork precision was required of every service employee, with mail bags being picked up and dropped off at every station—often without the train even slowing down—and then sorted en route.

In February 1910—as Hensel surely would have known—the consequences of any major snow delay were likely to be especially damaging for the GN. Mail contracts were coming up for renewal that spring. Great Northern officials were hoping not only to renew the contract for the company's lucrative existing run but to secure some contracts now held by its rival Union Pacific. (James J. Hill, who at seventy-one was still chairman of the GN board, had even threatened to discontinue Fast Mail service unless the company was granted a larger slice of the mail business.) Late February was also the time when the quadrennial weighing of the mail was taking place—a sampling process that would help determine the railroad's entire annual payment from the Post Office Department for the next four years. Given that the GN's share of mail money in 1909 had been over $44 million, it was clear that a significant amount of the railroad's revenue was at stake.

Even so, there was little that Hensel or his colleagues could do to help matters. Their part of the delivery job was finished. All of the mail on the train was already sorted, packed away in neatly labeled canvas sacks that now hung on hooks around the mail car like sides of beef in a slaughterhouse. Hensel and his colleagues could only bide their time as the ever more expensive hours ticked by, knowing that it was now up to superintendent O'Neill and his snow-fighting crews to clear the line and get those trains moving again.

✧

> Wellington, Feby 23, 1910
> Situation 7:30 A.M. . . . . Conditions on west slope very bad. Snowing and blowing so hard cannot see over 100 feet. . . . . Nos. 25 and 27 tied up at Cas. Tunnel until we can get rotary out of snow west of Wellington. . . . . Do not consider it safe to start even passenger trains present weather conditions.
>
> —J. H. O'Neill,
> telegram to E. L. Brown,
> general superintendent,
> Great Northern Railway, St. Paul

Wellington
Midmorning Wednesday

It was one of those ironies that railroaders on the Cascade Division just had to learn to live with: One of O'Neill's rotary plows, those magnificent specimens of twentieth-century snow-removal technology, had gotten stuck in the very snowdrifts it was supposed to be clearing.

The plow—the X807, under the direction of conductor Homer Purcell—had left Wellington at about 3:30 A.M., heading west to clear the track and meet up with an eastbound train in Skykomish. About a mile and a quarter out of Wellington, the plow had encountered a moderate snowslide on the track measuring about two hundred feet long and twenty feet deep. Purcell and his crew had attempted to buck right through the snow, but it turned out to be of the wet, heavy, late-winter sort that the men called "Cascade cement." The compacted mass soon clogged the rotary's cutting wheel, stalling it. Worse, since the plow had been jammed with such great force into the slide, the rotary's pusher engine couldn't pull it back out again. Purcell had been forced to send to Wellington for some extra snow shovelers to free it. The whole process had eaten up no fewer than four full hours.

Unfortunately, during that time both the Seattle Express and the Fast Mail had reached the Stevens Pass vicinity. With the line ahead blocked, O'Neill had had no choice but to sidetrack both trains. He'd decided to stop them at Cascade Tunnel Station, on the east side of the summit ridge, where the weather was slightly less extreme. With any luck, it would just be a temporary delay. Within a few hours the trains could be brought through the tunnel to Wellington and then taken right down the west slope of the mountains.

But the storm hadn't made anything easy that night. No sooner had rotary conductor Purcell and his men gotten through the first slide than they'd encountered a second—a bigger one this time—another mile down the line at Snowshed 3.3, near a place on the mountain called Windy Point. Considering the size of this new slide, they'd figured at least half a day would be needed to work through it. Frustrated, Purcell had relayed the bad news back to Wellington: The delay was going to be significantly longer than expected.

Now, at midmorning—as O'Neill racked up his twenty-fourth sleepless hour on the mountain—the situation was starting to look even grimmer. Other problems were cropping up all over the division, with drifts and small slides blocking the track in several places. The biggest mess was down at Scenic Hot Springs. Because of the extremely low visibility, eastbound passenger train No. 44, following its rotary out of Scenic station, had slammed right into the back of the rotary's pusher engine. The plow was not damaged—because of the racket of the spinning fan and the howl of the wind, its crew didn't even realize it had been hit—but No. 44's locomotive had broken its pilot, as well as a coupler and a drawbar farther back in the train.

O'Neill, a man given to chain-smoking even when not under stress, was finding little reason to cut back now. Since daybreak the storm had only gotten worse. With the wind blowing hard, snow was piling up rapidly against anything that wasn't moving, including trains. Even at Cascade Tunnel Station, where the wind was less fierce, the snow was drifting at an astonishing rate. Despite the fact that O'Neill had many of his force of three hundred temporary snow shovelers working to keep the two stalled trains free of drifts, the men were barely keeping pace.

It was a type of situation with which O'Neill was all too familiar: Whenever storms got bad enough on the mountain, problems would begin to compound. Trouble at one place on the line would cause a delay at another place, which, by drawing resources off other tasks, would in turn precipitate more trouble somewhere else. Unless the individual crises were resolved quickly, the whole system would eventually start to break down, stranding trains all over the division.

What O'Neill and his men needed to avoid such a predicament was for the storm to abate at least temporarily, giving the rotaries time to work through the buried sections of track and the shoveling crews a chance to make headway against the windblown drifts. Certainly the storm had to pass soon. The snow had started at Wellington at about 4:00 A.M. on Tuesday. It was now after 9:00 A.M. on Wednesday. Judging by his experience with past Cascade storms, the superintendent could reasonably expect this one to end sometime within the next twelve hours.

Until that time came, O'Neill needed to focus on handling the trains already on the mountain. He had explored the possibility of rerouting some of his approaching traffic via the Northern Pacific, but that company's officials had demurred, having their hands full with slide troubles of their own. So, after consulting by telegraph with his superiors in Spokane and St. Paul, he had made a difficult decision. Trains scheduled to depart for Stevens Pass were to be held at their stations of origin. Those already en route would, if possible, be stopped and turned around, perhaps to await later rerouting. The trains already on the mountain—including No. 25, the Seattle Express, and No. 27, the all-important Fast Mail—would simply have to tie up where they were until the line was clear.

At 9:30 A.M. O'Neill handed a scrawled telegram form to the operator on duty. Addressed to O'Neill's lieutenants up and down the line and copied to his superiors in the East, it contained a message no railway superintendent ever liked to send: "Will not run any trains until conditions change for the better." This was news dire enough to reach the ears of everyone in the company, including James J. Hill himself. But

O'Neill didn't see any alternative. As drastic—and expensive—as the action was likely to be, he was shutting down the entire division.

✧

SIX TRAINS STALLED ON GREAT NORTHERN

Everett, Wednesday, Feb. 23—The worst storm of years is heaping snow on the right of way of the Great Northern Railway in the Cascade Mountains as fast as the rotary plows clear away the drifts. . . . Last night from four to five feet of snow fell and the situation continues bad, as the storm shows no sign of abating.

—Seattle Times

Cascade Tunnel Station
Early Wednesday Afternoon

"Well, it's 1:00 P.M. now and snow getting deeper all the time."

Ned Topping, back on the Seattle Express after his excursion to the beanery, had picked up his pen again to continue the letter to his mother. The young widower from Ohio had spent most of the morning reading and writing and smoking, occasionally glancing out the window to marvel at the sheer density of the snowfall. Every time the train jolted or a rotary plow passed by, his hopes of getting under way would rise, only to be dashed again when nothing else happened. Alone with his thoughts now, he found himself again dwelling on his family at home:

"This is the 23rd," he continued, "six months ago that Florence died, and little Billy 22 months old yesterday—I have been thinking lots about it. There's a little fellow two seats in front of me suffering with his teeth, and an old man in the back of the car battling with a carbuncle on his neck. All this with other troubles and stalled out in the snow. . . . I wish you could see the surroundings. You never saw such piles and piles of snow in your life."

The teething child (who clearly reminded Topping of his own young son) was probably eight-month-old Francis Starrett, squirming in the arms of his mother, Ida. Mrs. Starrett was doubtless having trouble keeping her three young children happy during the delay, and the uncertainty of the weather could not have been helping. Still reeling from the death of her husband, she was in a kind of limbo, not even sure yet whether she would continue living in Spokane or move back to Canada with her parents. Mr. and Mrs. May had persuaded their daughter to come home with them at least temporarily—the $500 she had received from the Great Northern for the death of her husband, they knew, would not go far—but Ida still felt too unsettled to make a choice.

One of the more trying moments of the morning—for Ida and for everyone else aboard—had come after breakfast, when the Seattle Express had been taken into the mouth of the tunnel. This was done to allow the Fast Mail to pull forward to the water tank, but although the train was inside for only half an hour, the experience was decidedly unpleasant, offering passengers a glimpse of a place that would figure more prominently in their future than any of them could then realize. Many had complained to conductor Pettit. "It was draughty and dirty," passenger George Loveberry would later explain. "And of course there is always a smell of gas, and cold." Even the Great Northern railroaders found the tunnel difficult to bear. According to engineer J. C. Wright, it was "the dirtiest, blackest hole that a man ever went into."

Nasty as the tunnel was, it was a distinct improvement over what had been there when the Great Northern first ran trains over these mountains in the mid-1890s. Although a tunnel under Stevens Pass had been planned from the beginning, the time and huge expense of digging through three miles of granite was more than James J. Hill felt he could afford at the time. So for the first seven years of the Cascade Division's existence, trains were pulled over the pass via an elaborate system of switchbacks.

Depending on the perspective of the observer, the GN's Cascade switchbacks were either "a miracle of engineering" or "every railroad man's nightmare." Consisting of eight long and often sharply curved segments, the switchbacks zigzagged up the face of the steep summit ridge, carrying even heavy freight trains up a slope seemingly impossi-

ble for an adhesion railroad to surmount. With powerful 110-ton con-
solidation locomotives added to both the front and the back, a train
would be hauled up one segment of track onto an end spur, where it
would stop, reverse, and then start up the next leg in the opposite direction. Three such reverses were required to lift the train to the east summit of the pass, with five more required for the descent on the west
side—all at a punishing grade of 3.5 to 4 percent. The maneuver, which
had to be handled by specially trained crews, required so much tractive
effort that each locomotive consumed over three thousand pounds of
coal in the process. And even though the twelve-mile route could sometimes be completed in seventy-five minutes or even less, under adverse
circumstances the trip could take up to thirty-six hours—a pace that
works out to a blistering average speed of three hours per mile.

This switchback system, though eccentric, did prove to be remarkably safe. Although the route had earned the nickname "Death Mountain" during construction, the switchbacks had operated for seven years
without a single fatality—even during the legendary winter of 1897–98,
when a reported 140 feet of snow fell at Stevens Pass. Even so, they
were always considered a temporary expedient, and so once the American economy began to recover from the 1890s depression, Hill ordered
construction to start on the long-delayed summit tunnel.

Begun in 1897, the Cascade Tunnel proved to be a massive three-
year, round-the-clock effort employing a huge force of laborers (with, at
any given time, "800 working, 800 sleeping, and 800 standing at the
bar," as one account had it). The engineering challenges of drilling
through a heavy, water-saturated conglomerate of granite, slate, and
rockslide debris proved daunting enough, but the real struggle was re-
taining the men to do it. Given the remoteness of the construction site,
the GN was forced to hire "birds of passage"—transient laborers with
no local ties or responsibilities to keep them on the job if the work became too unpleasant. Turnover rates were staggering, often reaching
50 percent per month. Those workers who did stay were not always
model citizens. In fact, the construction camp at what would later be
called Cascade Tunnel Station became so notorious for drunkenness, violence, and prostitution that at least one eastern journalist gave it that

coveted moniker of all Wild West settlements: "the wickedest town on earth."

Between bouts of debauchery, there was apparently still enough time for the men to get their work done, and by December 1900 the 2.6-mile Cascade Tunnel was complete. Hailed as an unprecedented feat of engineering (despite the fact that in 1882 the Swiss had dug a tunnel in the Alps that was over three times as long), the tunnel certainly did improve the profile of the GN's Cascade line. But it also created a few new problems of its own. Steam locomotives laboring eastward up the tunnel's 1.9 percent grade would produce voluminous amounts of smoke, gas, and heat, creating serious ventilation problems. Temperatures in engine cabs often reached two hundred degrees Fahrenheit, leading some crew members to bury themselves in the coal pile to escape the heat. Smoke accumulations sometimes became so intense that even the tunnel's emergency telephones would cease to operate.

"You couldn't see for the smoke boiling out of the ends of the tunnel when steam engines entered," telegrapher Warren Tanguy would later remember. "On a hard pull, if a train got stuck and a brakeman or fireman got down to see what was wrong, he might be put to sleep. The heat reflecting from the roof would burn you up and the gas would asphyxiate you." In a typical incident in March 1901, a freight engineer, overcome by heat and fumes, either jumped or fell off a locomotive stalled in the tunnel. Trying to find cooler, fresher air, he crawled over to the drainage ditch that carried spring water out of the tunnel. Even here the gases were overpowering: The engineer was found dead in the ditch a short time later.

What could have been a far worse tragedy was narrowly averted two years later, when a train carrying over a hundred passengers broke down in the tunnel. While attempting to fix the problem, the engineer, fireman, and conductor all succumbed to the fumes and collapsed. As the passenger cars slowly began to fill with gas, an off-duty fireman named Abbott, riding as a passenger, fought his way forward to the locomotive and released the brakes. The train proceeded to roll downgrade, gathering momentum until it shot backward out of the tunnel at Wellington, at which time Abbott was still sentient enough to trigger the emergency brakes. The train screeched to a stop in the Wellington yard, its crew and most of its passengers unconscious but still very much alive. In recognition of his valiant action, the quick-thinking fireman received a citation and (perhaps more welcome) a $1,000 personal check from James J. Hill himself.

No one knows how many people actually died in such incidents in the first years of the tunnel's operation; as one Wellington telegrapher later recalled, "Many a hobo stole his last ride going through the . . . tunnel." The death toll was evidently sufficient to earn the Great Northern the wrath of the local press. "If Mr. Hill still [refuses] to remedy this worse than evil," fumed the *Seattle Mail and Herald,* "then the people have their recourse. They should send him through his own tunnel on his freight train."

Even Hill, famously impervious to such rhetorical broadsides, couldn't ignore the problem forever. The obvious solution was to electrify the line from Wellington to Cascade Tunnel Station, allowing trains to be pulled through the bore by smokeless electric locomotives, also called "motors." This tunnel electrification, completed in July 1909, did effectively solve the suffocation problem, but many of the kinks in its unusual three-phase system were still to be worked out. The electric locomotives failed often, leaving it up to the polluting steam engines to carry trains through. The interior of the tunnel was thus still caked with a soft, slimy layer of soot three or four inches thick. ("You can put your hand on the walls," O'Neill once remarked, "and your hand would sink into the refuse.") Little wonder that the passengers had found their half hour in the tunnel so unsavory.

Out on the passing track east of the tunnel, though, they could at least breathe freely and see something beyond their windows besides soot and smoke. And as evening approached on what was to be their first full day in the mountains, there was even a bit of entertainment to watch out there. Two of the rotaries (the X800 and the X802) were being connected end to end in the rail yard, forming a two-headed "double rotary" that could clear snow in either direction without being turned around. The sight of this powerful snow-fighting machine—a plow on either end and no fewer than three steam engines in a row between them—must have given the passengers at least some hope that the tracks could be cleared by morning, even with the storm still raging.

The show didn't last very long, and once the double rotary had left the yard, traveling west through the tunnel to help clear the still-blockaded line, there was little more for the passengers to see. Most of them retired early, salesman Ned Topping among them. "It's now nine P.M.," he wrote in his letter home, "and we are still here so I'm going to turn in." Then he closed the day's entry with an observation he'd be repeating in one form or another for more days than he could ever have imagined then: "Outlook now," he wrote, "is stuck all night."

5

***

Over the Hump

Q: How long did it take you to get coal and water on your
rotaries?
A: Oh, I should judge we were there three or four hours.
Q: How long would it ordinarily take, in good weather conditions?
A: Well, two engines and the two rotaries, coal and water, would
probably take fifteen or twenty minutes.

—M. O. White, *rotary conductor*

Thursday, February 24, 1910
Wellington
After Midnight

It would be, O'Neill knew, another sleepless night. Wednesday evening
had already bled seamlessly into Thursday morning, and still no trains
were moving on the Cascade line. In the small office of the Wellington
station, O'Neill had been keeping each of his three telegraphers furiously busy through a long eight-hour "trick," or shift. One by one they
had succeeded each other at the key—William Flannery, a transplanted
Ohioan, was on duty from 8:00 A.M. to 4:00 in the afternoon; Basil
Sherlock, the small, officious second-trick man, worked from 4:00 P.M.
to midnight; and the third operator, an unassuming young man named
W. V. Avery, was now manning the graveyard shift. Known to his

colleagues as "Mississippi," Avery was a southerner by birth, with no previous experience in wintertime mountain railroading, and he was ill-prepared for the operational chaos triggered by a northern Cascades snowstorm. Like many railroad telegraphers of the day, he was a highly itinerant character, never spending very long at any one job, and he was utterly new to the Cascade Division. As luck would have it, he had started at Wellington just three days earlier—at midnight on February 21, four hours before the current storm had begun.

Through the shifts of all three of these telegraphers, O'Neill himself had doggedly remained on duty, stopping only occasionally for an hour's nap or a quick meal prepared by his steward in the A-16. Short breaks were all that O'Neill felt he could allow himself. Conditions had become so bad that tasks normally requiring a few minutes to accomplish were now taking several hours. The crew of the double rotary, for instance—the one that Ned Topping had watched being assembled in the Cascade Tunnel yard—had spent well over three hours just getting the plows and their engines filled up at the Wellington water tank. Homer Purcell's single rotary had also taken far longer than expected to work through the slide at Snowshed 3.3. Many of the extra gang workers, citing fatigue, had simply refused to work, leaving the task of shoveling the snow down to a depth of thirteen feet—the maximum depth the rotaries could handle—to the train crews themselves. As a result, night had already fallen by the time Purcell had broken through the slide and could continue plowing west.

The fact that the coal supply was dwindling only compounded these difficulties. Wellington was not a regular coaling station for through trains, which typically took on their fuel at Leavenworth at the eastern edge of the mountains and at Skykomish in the west. O'Neill tried to have an ample emergency reserve on the mountain to keep his rotaries well supplied during heavy snowstorms, but something had gone wrong this week. Perhaps as a result of the ongoing switchmen's strike, a scheduled delivery of four extra cars of coal had somehow been bungled at Leavenworth. So although O'Neill had started the storm with 140 tons at Wellington—ample under normal winter conditions—this was now proving to be inadequate. With the rotaries consuming enormous quantities of fuel in their round-the-clock labors, stores were rapidly running out. On Wednesday afternoon, O'Neill had fired off an angry telegram to G. W. Turner, the chief dispatcher at Everett: "WILL BE OUT OF COAL HERE TOMORROW. WHEN WILL YOU HAVE SUPPLY DELIVERED?" But with no regular trains moving, there was little Turner could do. Without a replenished coal supply at Wellington, the rotaries would soon have to start recoaling all the way down at Skykomish, adding yet another kink to the smooth operation of the superintendent's mountain line.

At least O'Neill knew that the GN was not alone in this sea of troubles; the entire northwestern tier of the country was now reeling under the onslaught of this storm. Certainly every railroad with a line through the Cascades was having enormous difficulties. The Milwaukee Road (a.k.a. the Chicago, Milwaukee, and Puget Sound) had shut down its Cascade operations entirely, and the Northern Pacific had several passenger trains stalled at its own tunnel at Stampede Pass. A theater company on one blockaded NP train had even taken the long delay as an opportunity to put on a show, commandeering an empty baggage car for a performance of *The Merchant of Venice*.

O'Neill, however, had only tobacco to distract him, and he was almost certainly partaking copiously of his trademark small cigars. In February 1910—thanks to the tide of fastidious progressivism that was then sweeping the country—cigarettes were prohibited in the state of Washington; it was illegal not only to manufacture or sell them but even to possess them. Cigars, on the other hand, were still perfectly legal, due in large part to the fact that one of the anti-cigarette bill's original sponsors—State Senator Orville Tucker of Seattle—was an avid cigar smoker. (The story goes that Tucker even set fire to his Olympia hotel room while discussing the legislation with colleagues. "Senator Tucker," the *Seattle Post-Intelligencer* blithely reported, "had been too enthusiastic wrestling with a refractory match.")

But even cigars in heavy doses could provide O'Neill with only limited consolation. He had, all told, six trains in distress on his Cascade line, not to mention numerous others delayed elsewhere in the division—and all of them were losing time and money with every idle hour.

Finally, at about 2:00 A.M. on Thursday, some good news arrived: Homer Purcell's rotary, incommunicado for most of the night, finally chugged into the Wellington yard. Rimed with ice and windblown snow, the battered-looking plow bore mute testimony to Purcell's own rough night. After finally bucking westward through the slide at Snowshed 3.3 late on Wednesday, he had met trainmaster Arthur Blackburn's rotary—the X801—which had been working eastward up the line from Scenic. The two plows had proceeded to a small station on the mountain called Alvin, where they had combined into a double rotary and started back toward Wellington. Even that trip of less than four miles had turned into a slog, but they had finally reached Wellington after five hard hours, clearing the tracks as they went.

To O'Neill, the meaning of this breakthrough was clear: The line west was open again. Unless another slide had come down sometime in the past few hours, those two trains stuck at Cascade Tunnel Station now had their escape route off the mountain.

The superintendent did not hesitate. Although Purcell, Blackburn, and the rest of the crew of the double had not slept in well over a day, he ordered the disheveled trainmen to turn right back again and make another plowing run down to Scenic to keep the line clear. Then he contacted the operator at Cascade Tunnel Station, instructing him to prepare the Fast Mail and the Seattle Express for action.

Shortly thereafter, the snow that had been falling relentlessly for the past forty-eight hours started to let up. It seemed possible to O'Neill that the storm might be lifting at last. That would have made it a relatively long storm by Cascades standards, but not an unprecedented one. So now, with two double rotaries at his disposal and another single rotary—the X808—almost ready to head toward the mountains from the repair shop in Everett, O'Neill even allowed himself a bit of optimism. In a message relayed by telegram up and down the line, he predicted that the Cascade Division would be open for operation again by 6:00 A.M. Thursday. With no new snow to complicate plowing efforts, the opening of the line should proceed easily now. And if the storm was truly past, he might even be able to get back to Everett to spend the weekend with Berenice and the baby.

It was to be a premature declaration of victory. Though word of

O'Neill's prediction would percolate down to the Seattle papers ("O'Neill has won the fight of his life," the *Post-Intelligencer* would proclaim on Thursday's front page), the battle was still far from over. At about 4:30 A.M.—even before Blackburn and Purcell had recoaled their double rotary—the storm roared back with all of its previous intensity. Tangled in snowdrifts at the water tank, the plow did not start heading west again until well after 6:00, and even then the going was not easy.

"If anything, it is snowing harder than it was last P.M.," O'Neill reported, with obvious chagrin, in an 8 A.M. telegram to headquarters. "Strong northwest wind and drifting very badly. . . . All of our extra gang men are tired out and we are unable to get them to work. . . . It is drifting so bad that track drifts in immediately after rotary passes over."

As difficult as conditions might be, however, the line was still open as far as anyone knew, and O'Neill was determined to seize the opportunity to get those two trains off the mountain. To make sure that nothing else went awry, he decided to oversee the job of digging them out himself. This would at least give him a reason to get away from that smoke-filled telegraph office and out into the weather. Leaving the grateful telegrapher to his own devices, O'Neill joined assistant trainmaster William Harrington—his "Snow King"—on the other double rotary. Together they made ready to head east to Cascade Tunnel Station, where they would begin the process of extracting those trains from the Cascade cement.

✧

Thursday 10:40 A.M.—This makes 30 hours here in this spot. It's still snowing hard. . . . Conductor this morning says snow over there [at Wellington] is 20 ft deep and slides back as fast as taken away. I'd give $10.00 to have the Kodak so's to bring back to you all my present surroundings.

—Ned Topping

Cascade Tunnel Station
Midmorning Thursday

The passengers awoke on Thursday morning to a scene dishearteningly similar to the one that had presented itself twenty-four hours earlier. Still the snow was coming down; still the two trains sat idle at Cascade Tunnel Station. The character of the snowfall itself, however, had changed overnight. "The flakes became larger and heavier," Lewis Jesseph would later report, "but did not fall so thick and fast." The result was better visibility. As the passengers trudged up to the beanery for another breakfast, they could finally see far enough to glimpse the mountain peaks all around them. Faced with those steep walls of white punctuated only by the skeletal remains of burned-off firs and pines, they realized—many for the first time—how isolated and remote they really were.

There probably wasn't much overt contact at the beanery between the well-dressed passengers and the unkempt and overtired railroaders— one imagines them sitting uncomfortably at opposite ends of the room, sneaking glances at each other through the rising steam of their coffee cups—but word was soon spreading through the dining hall that the food supply was running low. With the storm preventing delivery of any new provisions, chef Elerker's limited stores were proving inadequate to the task of feeding so many extra mouths. Some said that if the trains were to remain at Cascade Tunnel much longer, food would have to be rationed.

When Mrs. Covington heard this rumor back on the Winnipeg, she confided her growing concern to her diary. "Thursday 24th, 10 A.M.," she wrote. "They say it has snowed 13 ft in 11 hours. . . . The mts. loom up a thousand feet or thousands. . . . They keep saying the provisions are getting low and they can't get water for the train."

Right beside the tracks, visible through Mrs. Covington's frost-rimed window, some workers were trying to clear snow from the roof of the station roundhouse. The old woman drew a small picture of the scene in her diary. The men were digging from the top of the roof down to the eaves, creating trenches whose walls towered several feet above their heads. Under different circumstances, the sight of those dwarfed figures battling feebly against the snow might have been amusing to her. But Mrs. Covington was in no state of mind to be amused. Though her diary indicates that she was well cared for, she confessed to feeling anxious and alone, particularly after news spread through the train that a snowslide somewhere on the eastern slope had taken out the telegraph line. The day before, she'd been able to send a wire to her son Melmoth telling him she was safe. Now, however, she felt adrift, without direct connection to the husband, seven children, and twenty-two grandchildren who were her life.

"The tel. wires are down," she wrote in her diary—adding, with perhaps a touch of melodrama: "No communication with the world."

Most of Mrs. Covington's fellow passengers were taking the situation with somewhat more equanimity. Along about midmorning, lawyers Jesseph and Merritt, retreating to the observation car, blandly took note of the fact that their supreme court case was being called in Olympia even as they sat here, 170 miles away. (Contrary to Jesseph's expectations, the court ultimately did go forward with the hearing; the justices ended up deciding the case based solely on the written record— in Merritt's favor.) Two boys—probably the eighteen-year-olds Milton Horn and Frank Ritter—entertained themselves by stepping out to the station platform to play their horns in the snow. Ned Topping was even trying to use the unexpected spare hours to get some work done, hatching new strategies for the family's barn-door business: "Say father," he wrote in his letter home, "Don't you think it would be a good scheme to have the Steel Co. cut us up some steel—that is, shear it to lengths & widths ready for the machine in case we get the new machines before the shear? This would save some time and in order to have it sheared correctly, one of the boys or myself could go direct to the mill and superintend the shearing."

Meanwhile, three-year-old Thelma Davis was busy charming everyone aboard. Her father, George, a small, half-Iroquois man who worked as a streetcar motorman, was taking her to see her mother in Seattle, and the child had quickly become the pet of the train. With her thick, dark, shoulder-length hair and plump, pretty features, she was apparently finding no shortage of surrogate mothers on the train—to the relief of her father, who doubtless had long ago run out of ideas to entertain her.

Others on the Express were also making a social event of the delay. John Rogers, a Seattle real estate man, had been inspecting mining properties in central Washington with his lawyer, former judge James McNeny. Now the two were taking it upon themselves to spread a little goodwill through the train. "We visited from coach to coach," Rogers would later recall. "[We] joked with the sick, and did our best to keep everybody reassured. Conductor Pettit," he added, "was foremost in everything of that sort."

Joe Pettit, though not out laboring in the wind-whipped snow like most of the other railroaders, was certainly performing a job just as difficult—dealing with fifty-five impatient and underoccupied passengers. Being the father of five young children, he was undoubtedly well schooled in patience and diplomacy. Even so, he can't have had an easy time of it keeping everyone satisfied.

And there were some among the passengers whose situation made Pettit's job especially delicate. John Gray, for instance, with his broken leg in a heavy cast, could not even be moved from his berth. Ada Lemman, a slender, thirty-nine-year-old woman suffering from an unspecified nervous condition, was an even more ticklish problem; accompanied by her attorney husband, Edgar, she was now on her way to a hospital in Port Townsend for treatment, and by popular report she was more than a handful to deal with, always on the edge of hysteria.

Perhaps worst off was sixty-year-old J. R. Vail, a sheepherder from Trinidad, Washington, afflicted with a swollen carbuncle on his neck. Little information survives about his illness, but the fact that he was being transported by a professional caregiver—Catherine O'Reilly, a young nurse from the Sacred Heart Hospital in Spokane—hints that the infection was already a serious condition, and one that, in this age before antibiotics, could very easily become much worse.

For the majority of Pettit's other charges, the primary ailment to be endured at this point was cabin fever. "It's awful being held up like this,"

Ned Topping wrote. "Can't get off the train for exercise on account of snow and storm." Letting ill temper get the better of him, he even began complaining about the beanery again: "Have had 4 meals now at the camp. A dirty grease hole—oilcloth on tables and half-wiped dishes. Eat alongside of the scum of the earth."

Toward late afternoon on Thursday, the spirits of Topping and everyone else aboard got a lift when they began to see signs of renewed activity in the Cascade Tunnel yard. The men he'd called "the scum of the earth" were now out in the storm beside the trains, digging away the snow and ice that had accumulated around each car. The double rotary from yesterday was also back, cleaning up the tracks between the trains and the tunnel.

"It's now about 5:00 P.M.," Topping wrote as the afternoon light began to falter. "Snow is nearly stopped and clearing up some. Engines are steaming up & this gives a faint hope."

That faint hope was soon fulfilled. Before long, the good news was spreading like a warm breeze through both the Seattle Express and the Fast Mail. The trains, after the better part of two days, were finally going to proceed west.

✧

Look for Nos 25 + 27 to leave Tunnel about 5 P.M. Rotaries digging them out now.

—J. H. O'Neill,
telegram to E. L. Brown,
Great Northern Railway, St. Paul

Cascade Tunnel Station
Late Thursday Afternoon

Anyone looking for an explanation of James H. O'Neill's popularity among his men need only consider his actions on the stormy Thursday afternoon of February 24. As superintendent, O'Neill was the highest-ranking official on the entire Cascade Division—the rough equivalent of, say, a major general in the army of the Great Northern

Railway. Yet here he was, sleepless and badly shaven after two full days on duty, digging snowdrifts from the wheel trucks of a train coach. Having come over to Cascade on the rotary with Harrington and a gang of laborers, O'Neill had quickly checked in with the station operator, issued his instructions, and then grabbed a shovel to help the gangmen dig.

This wasn't merely a gesture calculated for show. According to more than one report, when O'Neill cleared a frozen switch or crawled under a disabled rotary to lend a hand on the bridge jack, he really did the job. As someone who had worked his way up from the very lowest positions in railway service, he was familiar with nearly every dirty task there was to do on a steam railroad, and he knew how to get cooperation from even the lowest-paid extra gangmen, typically foreigners with whom he didn't even share a language. "In two minutes," a colleague once said of him, "he can have a . . . gang of foreigners doing team work and moving together like oiled machinery."

It was a scene reminiscent of one involving O'Neill's illustrious boss, James J. Hill. According to a famous story, the Empire Builder once grew impatient when his train became immobilized in a Dakota blizzard. Seeing the snow shovelers outside his window start to flag, he decided to take matters in hand. As his biographer Stuart Holbrook tells the story: "President Hill of the railroad came out to snatch the shovel from one man and send that bemused working stiff into the president's private car for hot coffee, while he himself shoveled snow as though driven by steam. One after the other, the gandy-dancers were spelled off and drank fine java in unaccustomed elegance while the Great Northern's creator and boss wielded a shovel. *That* was Jim Hill for you."

That was also Jim O'Neill for you, and it was probably this prodigious work ethic that had first attracted the Empire Builder's attention. Later profiles of O'Neill depict him as a favorite of Hill's as far back as his Montana days, when the latter allegedly chose the young conductor to oversee his train whenever business took him to the western divisions. Hill may have been attracted by O'Neill's similar background (both men were transplanted Canadians with humble beginnings and little formal education), but it was more likely O'Neill's hardworking competence that truly endeared him to the old man. "He does not sit in his private car writing and directing the work," a Great Northern colleague once said of the superintendent. "He is 'on the job' all the time. He sets the pace for his men, works with them, and accomplishes results."

Despite O'Neill's energetic shoveling efforts with the gangmen, however, the task of moving the two trains at Cascade Tunnel Station ended up being anything but simple. Twice during the process the lead rotary of the double was thrown off center, a problem requiring precious time to correct. Even after the trains had been freed of snow, the electric locomotives were still unable to budge them from the passing track. O'Neill and his men were eventually forced to uncouple the individual cars of each train and dislodge them one by one, reassembling them on the track in front of the tunnel portal.

It was a slow, almost unfathomably cumbersome chore. And before it was finished, a snowslide somewhere between the tunnel and its hydroelectric plant in Tumwater Canyon took out the power and communication lines to the east. The job of pulling out the trains therefore had to be finished by the steam locomotives, which would then have to carry them through the unventilated tunnel. The only bright spot in the situation was that the trains would be moving downgrade as they traveled to Wellington. With gravity providing most of the tractive effort, the steam locomotives could "drift" through the tunnel, throttles barely open, making any danger of asphyxiation remote.

Toward evening—with the job of moving the trains now under control—O'Neill finished up at Cascade Tunnel Station and hopped a ride on the rotary west through the tunnel. It was growing late, and he needed to get back to a working telegraph key to report to his superiors in St. Paul.

But there was yet another snag awaiting him at Wellington. The second double rotary—the one that was supposed to have plowed the tracks down to Scenic by now—was instead back at Wellington, sitting idle in the snow. Hard as it was to believe, conductor Purcell and his crew had encountered another snowslide on the line west—near

Snowshed 3.3 again, at precisely the same point where the first major slide had come down twenty-four hours earlier. Worse, while attempting to buck through it, the lead plow of the double, the X807, had swallowed a fallen tree stump embedded in the snow. The stump had ravaged the bowels of the plow and broken its hoist mechanism, causing the plow to list hard to one side. Although Purcell and his men had effected a makeshift repair of the machine, it was all but useless for heavy-duty work.

Even a man as stoic as James O'Neill must now have been beyond frustration. With the westward line blocked yet again, those two trains would not be able to continue down the mountain for at least several more hours. Nor could they be held back at Cascade; the dwindling food supply at the beanery had to be conserved for the use of the workers there. So O'Neill decided to put the trains at Wellington, at least for the moment. West of the Wellington station were several passing tracks where both trains could wait until the line was clear again. The passengers could then eat their supper at Bailets Hotel, a small railroaders' hostelry not far away. The proprietor, W. R. Bailets, reportedly had plenty of food on hand, and would welcome the extra business.

Fortunately, there was at least one encouraging development concerning rotary snowplow X808, the fifth of the division's rotaries. Under the direction of the division's master mechanic, J. J. Dowling, it had now reached Scenic, clearing the line from the coast and allowing several eastbound trains stranded since early Wednesday at Skykomish and Scenic to return to Seattle. Dowling's rotary had also picked up two cars of coal at Skykomish and was pulling them up the west slope. If O'Neill's rotary crews could somehow limit their consumption of coal, supplementing the supply in the coal chute with coal from various locomotives not in current use, they might just be able to scrape by until Dowling's two carfuls arrived. Until that time, O'Neill would put disabled rotary X807 on the coal-chute track alongside his own business car, where the rotary's coal supply could be plundered if necessary.

That still left the matter of clearing up this new slide at Snowshed 3.3, and the rotary crews, many of which had been on duty for two days straight, desperately needed a break. Rather than leave the plows idle while their operators slept, O'Neill decided to supplement their crews with the relatively well-rested men from the electric motors. He and Blackburn would take the double rotary west with these extra men to attack the slide at Snowshed 3.3 overnight. Harrington would meanwhile take the remaining single rotary—the X801—back through the tunnel to deal with the slide that had taken down the power lines on the east slope.

With the process of moving the trains to Wellington well under way, the superintendent and trainmaster Blackburn boarded the double rotary and began to head west toward Windy Point. Weary as he was, Jim O'Neill seemed determined not to rest until his division was back in working order.

✧

24th of Feb. at night. They are moving us through the Tunnel to a little hamlet called Wellington.

—*Sarah Jane Covington*

Wellington
Thursday Evening

At approximately 7:45 P.M. Great Northern Railway train No. 25 emerged from the western portal of the Cascade Tunnel into the muffled silence of the Wellington yard. Night had already set in, and with the electricity out, the few lights visible in the tiny, snowbound settlement were dim and irregular, the buildings lit only by gas lamps and flickering lanterns. As the train glided past the embattled-looking station, the passengers could see, standing on the slope behind it, a large wooden building with the words HOTEL BAILETS painted in block letters across its facade. It was here, according to conductor Pettit, that they would go to get their supper—a welcome piece of news. After the beanery, Bailets's dining room was bound to seem like Delmonico's.

Still moving, No. 25 was shunted off the main line onto one of the sidings that paralleled it for some distance beyond the station. Here the train shuddered to a stop. Happy to have made even this small advance—at the very least they were now "over the hump," on the westward side of the summit ridge—the passengers peered through the train windows at their new surroundings. To the right of the cars, standing on the various side tracks of the Wellington lower yard, were some of the casualties of the railroad's ongoing fight against the storm: the disabled rotary X807, an extra steam engine, and three of the four powerful GE electric motors, now paralyzed by the downing of the power lines. At the very end of the spur track, opposite a small sand house and a tall wooden coal chute, sat an elegant-looking business car: the A-16, the private car of superintendent O'Neill, nearly invisible under mounds of snow.

The exact nature of their new position would not be evident to most of the passengers until daybreak, but the passing track on which they had been placed was located on a fifty-foot-wide ledge that had been gouged out of the mountainside during construction of the line. Above the ledge was a steep, sparsely timbered slope running two thousand feet straight up to the top of Windy Mountain. Below, just beyond a second, still-unoccupied passing track to their left, was the continuation of the slope—a sharp drop down to frozen Tye Creek. The train, in other words, was perched on a narrow shelf, with a steep ravine below it and acres of heavy wet snow on a mountainside above it.

After wrapping themselves in coats and hats against the cold, the passengers disembarked and headed toward the hotel. Henry White, Ned Topping, and the others walked back along the newly cleared tracks, filing between the high snowbanks as if through stark white corridors. The snow was falling copiously but gently now; the fierce winds had died down to a gentle breeze. As they passed the Wellington depot, Topping took note of the snow gauge affixed to the back of the building. It registered seventeen feet of snow on the level, with more still accumulating.

Once seated at their tables in the pleasant, high-ceilinged dining room at Bailets—amid the lace curtains, potted plants, and hanging chromolithographs of various specimens of fish and game—the passengers tried to learn whatever they could about the progress of the snowplows. No one at Bailets, though, could say with any certainty how long the trains would be delayed at Wellington. Conductor Pettit, ever optimistic, assured them that the wait would be brief, especially now that the storm seemed to be tapering off, but it's doubtful that anyone really believed him. The drifts of snow at Wellington were even more imposing than those they'd all been staring at for two days at Cascade Tunnel Station. With the snow still falling, the passengers had to be wondering if it would be yet another day—or even two—before they got out of that icy wilderness and down to the safety of the coast.

After dinner, several of the passengers decided to bundle up and have a look around the storm-battered town. To their surprise, it proved to be even smaller than its counterpart at the other end of the tunnel. Surrounded by roadless mountains, Wellington had no proper streets—just walkways, some of them wooden, connecting the various buildings. Instead, the town's main street seemed to be the railroad line itself. Virtually every major structure was arranged on or near it, tracing the inside arc of the broadly curving tracks as they ran along the edge of Windy Mountain.

The entire settlement, in fact, turned out to be little more than what the passengers had seen from the windows of their moving train. Just outside the tunnel portal was the upper rail yard—essentially three spur tracks built on an artificial flat created from tunnel debris. A large enginemen's bunkhouse stood here, and on the banks of a small creek beyond were a few sorry-looking shanties and small houses. West of the creek was the depot, the section house, and the roadmaster's office. And on the slope behind were two privately operated businesses, the Bailets Hotel (where they had eaten supper) and a seedy-looking tavern called Fogg Brothers Restaurant.

This, in short, was "downtown" Wellington. A few other structures lay west of the depot—the coal chute, sand house, and water tank; a new shed for the four GE electric locomotives; the parallel sidings where the Seattle Express stood—but aside from these and a few other assorted structures, there was nothing else. From the western switch of the passing tracks, the main line simply ran under a short wooden snowshed and continued on down the mountain toward Windy Point. The next settlement of any size was Scenic Hot Springs, a long ten miles down the twisted right-of-way.

"8:00 P.M. Thursday," Ned Topping wrote, continuing his letter back on the train. "Well, we've pulled through the 3-mile tunnel and are on the west side of the Cascades. Don't know whether we will go on or not. Just talked to Porter—poor fellow has a sick baby & is anxious to get home. Other babies I have mentioned have been good, but it's tough to see them held up this way. Am going to turn in soon."

Many others on the train were also retiring early, apparently hoping that sleep would make the hours of waiting pass more quickly. Those who stayed up a little longer would have seen the Fast Mail arriving from Cascade Tunnel at about 10:15. This much shorter train—carrying A. B. Hensel and the other mail clerks—was held at the station for a short time. Then it proceeded west to the second passing track, alongside the Seattle Express, right on the edge of the drop to Tye Creek below.

It was to be the last tranquil evening for the seventy-odd people aboard the two trains. By morning, news would arrive that would change the complexion of their collective predicament, turning what until then had been an inconvenient delay into something far more ominous and frightening. For now, though, they could all bed down with relative peace of mind. Progress seemed imminent: The storm appeared to be passing; the rotaries would be working through the night to clear the line. Only a few people aboard would still have been awake when, toward 3:00 A.M., the wind started picking up again, rocking the Pullmans gently, sweeping up the snow and depositing it in ever deeper drifts on that brooding, sparsely timbered slope above the trains.

6

A Town at the End of the World

Too high for forest trees, too rocky for even the mountain shrubs to thrive, what was there to tempt men to such an unrewarded climb?

—Seattle Times
on Wellington, Washington

To call it a "town" is to exaggerate its size and population. To call it a "village" would be to romanticize its soot-smeared industrial squalor. To call it just a "station" would be to ignore its roadless isolation and the rough magnificence of its setting. Instead, the men of the Cascade Division had a different name for the place where the Seattle Express and the Fast Mail now stood. To them, it was simply "the end of the world."

Wellington, Washington, with a year-round population of about one hundred, was a settlement cobbled together in the wilderness of Stevens Pass during the initial laying of the transcontinental line to Seattle—in the early 1890s, when the Great Northern first established a construction camp here. Like Cascade Tunnel Station on the other side of the summit ridge, it was at first a rude and makeshift place, deriving its rough character from the nature of the men who built the early western railroads. "As wild a town as any described in western truth or fiction" was how one journalist described it. "Girls from Leavenworth rode the work trains up the mountain. No conductor collected any tickets, and the workmen were always glad of the diversion of being with them. They gravitated to the bar and dance hall as bees do to honey."

In the twenty years since, the town had become considerably less infamous. Nowadays the women of Wellington were more likely to be railroad workers' wives than imported bar girls, and the loose, Wild West anarchy had given way to a quieter Progressive Era–style respectability. But Wellington in 1910 was still as remote as ever, and it was still populated largely by young unmarried men with nothing much to do in their off-hours but drink, play cards, and carouse. And despite catering to trappers and the occasional group of recreational hunters or fishermen, the place was still, above all else, a railroad town. Run almost exclusively for, by, and in the interest of the Great Northern Railway, it was a society unto itself, bound by the rigid hierarchies of a world that is now all but lost—the world of the railroad in the Golden Age of Steam.

It's almost impossible from the perspective of the early twenty-first century to appreciate either the intricate sociology of the great American steam railroads or their centrality to American life in the late nineteenth and early twentieth centuries. Freight trains may still be a vital part of the economy, but long-distance passenger rail service is now considered something of an anachronism—too slow, too expensive, and too inconvenient to be a viable option for most travelers. In 1910, though, railroads were at the very center of American consciousness. As businesses, they still dominated the national economy, even with the rise of large trusts like Standard Oil and U.S. Steel. (When the prototype of what would eventually become the Dow Jones Industrial Average was first published in the 1880s, nine of its eleven stocks were railroad or railroad-related issues.) With the national rail network just six years away from its all-time peak of 254,037 miles of track, the railroad industry was actively employing an estimated one-twelfth of the adult male population in America. And for what the astute British observer James Bryce once called "an eminently locomotive people," the railroad was simply an essential and inextricable part of the American cultural identity.

Granted, attitudes toward the major railway companies in 1910 may not have been as positive as in the past, but the sheer magnetism of the railroad itself was still strongly felt. In cities, towns, and rural areas across the country, the local train station was the symbolic heart of everything considered modern and important. Whereas children given to dreams of future greatness might once have fantasized about becoming Pony Express riders or cattle rustlers, in 1910 they imagined themselves locomotive engineers, footloose brakemen, or (for those with a little more financial savvy) president and chairman of the board of one of the great eastern trunk lines.

Much of this appeal had to do with simple aesthetics. There is nothing in the world quite like the charismatic majesty of a huge steam locomotive on the move. The sight of 140 tons of oiled and intricately orchestrated iron barreling along at breathtaking speeds, pistons and connecting rods pumping, whistles bawling, great clouds of white and black smoke erupting with gorgeous profusion from the stack—it all stood as a vivid symbol, a perfect visual metaphor for the bold animal authority of a nation growing into a new sense of power and command in the world. A steam engine of the early 1900s was a statement—it was potency and prestige incarnate. No wonder children stared at them in awe.

Naturally, once those locomotive-dazzled youngsters actually entered the world of steam railroading, the romance was bound to dim significantly. As any genuine railroader could have attested, it was hardly an easy life, given the long hours and hard physical labor. Still, the cachet of being "on the railroad" was felt by even the lowliest trackwalker or engine wiper; to work for one of the great rail systems was to be a member of a distinct fraternity governed by a highly specialized system of rules and rituals. And as with members of that remarkably similar fraternity—the military—no amount of griping about the unfairness, ineptitude, or maliciousness of those in command could mask the railroaders' underlying sense of pride.

That the culture of the railroad so closely resembled that of the military should not be surprising, considering that the one was quite consciously modeled after the other. When long-distance rail systems first began to emerge in the mid-nineteenth century, they faced problems of organization, administration, and discipline that had never been encountered before by any private enterprise. That's why, as historian Harold Livesay has pointed out, they turned for a solution to the only model available at the time: "Only one organization, the military, was experienced in moving large quantities of men and material across long distances. The railroads adapted the military's line and staff organization, often using military nomenclature."

This helps explain why so many early railroad leaders, such as Grenville Dodge of the Union Pacific and the ubiquitous George McClellan (who eventually became president of the Ohio and Mississippi), were former army generals. "These men and others like them," Livesay says, "perfected the first modern bureaucracies for management, capable of controlling complex, round-the-clock operations at places distant from headquarters and coordinated with telegraphic speed."

Crucial to the running of such a complex organization was an attention to procedure expressly designed to minimize any potential for mishap or miscommunication (often as fatal in the world of the railroad as in the world of the army). Hierarchies of authority were rigid, and the chain of command strict and unambiguous. Thus James H. O'Neill, as superintendent of the Cascade Division, was the supreme local authority, the field general in command, responsible for all aspects of the railroad's day-to-day operations in his division. He stood at the head of a group of senior staff officers that included the division's roadmaster (in charge of the physical roadway—tracks, bridges, tunnels, and the like—and the men who maintained it), the master mechanic (responsible for the rolling stock of the division and those who kept it in good repair), and the various station agents and yardmasters (overseeing the workings of individual stations and rail yards). And the most visible area of a division's operations—the movement of the trains themselves—fell under the jurisdiction of the chief dispatcher, who supervised train dispatchers and telegraph operators, and the trainmaster, who oversaw the work of the engineers, firemen, conductors, and brakemen.

It was these train crews—the junior officers and infantrymen of the railroad army—that lay at the very heart of railroad culture in the Age of Steam. They were the most recognizable railway figures to the general public, and the ones whose functions and duties most directly affected the average passenger. The conductor, for instance, was known as the administrative supervisor of a given train. It was his responsibility to keep the record of the train (the paperwork involved in safely running a railroad was—and still is—mind-boggling). He was also charged with overseeing the work of the brakemen, making sure the schedule was adhered to, and, on passenger trains, collecting tickets and looking after the safety and comfort of the passengers. Consistent with these weighty responsibilities, the steam-era conductor (sometimes known in railroad argot as the "con" or "skipper") had a reputation for arrogance and imperiousness—though, as we've seen, Joseph Pettit, the skipper of the Seattle Express, was a notable exception.

While the conductor may have been officially in charge, it was the engineer who actually made the train go, an arrangement that often led to intense rivalry between the two men. According to one former railroader, the unwritten law of railroading was that the conductor's authority ceased at the back end of the tender—that is, at the rear end of the engine and the permanently coupled car that carried its coal and water. In the cab of the locomotive it was the swaggering hotshot known as the engineer who was boss. This "engine runner" (also called a "hoghead" or "hogger" or even "throttle jockey") was the object of the most intense popular fascination—it's been said that even Sigmund Freud dreamed of becoming a railroad engineer.

Assisting the engineer—and stationed on the left side of the locomotive cab, as opposed to the engine runner's right-side post—was the train's fireman. Also known as the "tallow pot" (since it was his responsibility to grease the engine's valves), he was the man charged with keeping the locomotive well stoked with coal—a job that tended to leave its performer "so black that his best friends would not know him when washed up." On a particularly fast or difficult run, at least on engines without mechanical stokers, the fireman could spend virtually his entire long shift "shoveling real estate," or loading coal from the tender into the firebox. It was overall a thankless, exhausting, and poorly paid job, its only compensation being that it served as an apprenticeship for the far more desirable position of engineer.

The real yeomen of the train service were the brakemen, of which there were usually two or more per train, and the switchmen, essentially brakemen who worked in the confines of a single rail yard. Until the widespread adoption of safety appliances such as air brakes and automatic couplers in the 1880s and '90s, the brakeman's job was notoriously dangerous. Early "brakies" had to crawl onto the roofs of moving trains, in all kinds of weather and in any kind of terrain, to apply and release each car's individual hand brake; when assembling trains in a rail yard, they had to stand between converging cars and deftly slip a metal pin into the primitive link-and-pin couplers. Mistakes were frequent, and their consequences often dire. "What're brakemen for anyway," a mangled veteran once complained to an early railroad chronicler. "Nothin' but fodder for cars 'n' engines to eat up." This was not an exaggeration; it was a rare brakeman who still had all ten of his fingers.

Even with the introduction of ever-safer equipment and practices, steam railroading remained an occupation with on-the-job casualty rates that would be unthinkable today—not just for brakemen but for nearly everyone on the payroll. Some of the busier rail yards in the American system, at least in the 1870s, were virtual slaughterhouses, seeing three to five men killed per week. (According to one yard switchman, his sister kept a clean bedsheet reserved at all times, "for the express purpose of wrapping up my mangled remains.") Even as late as 1907, one out of every eight trainmen suffered serious injury every year. In a difficult mountain area like the Cascade Division, the odds of avoiding casualty were even slimmer. Railroading was, in sum, "a miserable living gained by the hardest kind of work, with almost a certainty of being crippled, or meeting death by some horrible means." The fact that there was usually no shortage of applicants for most railroad jobs is, under the circumstances, remarkable—a tribute to the industry's lingering prestige.

✧

The only amusement we had was manufactured right there in Wellington.

—*Basil Sherlock*

Given the harsh and hazardous nature of the steam-railroading life, it's unsurprising that those who led it developed a military-style esprit de corps that manifested itself both on and off the field of battle. In a crisis situation like the one now prevailing at Stevens Pass, they could be counted on to close ranks and make Herculean efforts to meet and overcome the common enemy, whether it be a snowstorm, a mudslide, or even an army of hoboes trying to catch a free ride on a freight train.

On the other hand, in easier times—when the pressure was off and the battle was far in the distance—the fraternity of railroaders could take on a different character entirely. As railroad writer Herbert Hamblen once observed, "It becomes absolutely necessary sometimes for men whose daily lives are passed under the strictest discipline, and in a calling where their nerves are ever at concert pitch, to unbend, relax the rigid tension, and do things which would appear silly under other circumstances, or even vicious." This need for release was especially pronounced in a lonely, female-deprived place like Wellington, where the community of railroaders often resembled the kind of fraternity more commonly found on college campuses: "There was plenty of kidding, shenanigans, and horseplay at Wellington," telegrapher Basil Sherlock would later write of this phenomenon. "They seemed to like a joke, [and] the hotter or the more angry the victim of the joke became, the better the joke."

As one would expect, the victims of these jokes often came from outside the ranks of the railroad family. One favorite target in Wellington, according to Sherlock, was W. R. Bailets, the proprietor of the hotel, who was apparently given to moneymaking schemes of all types. One of his scams involved buying a twenty-seven-pound Thanksgiving turkey to raffle off at his saloon. With the preponderance of young, unmarried men at Wellington, there was probably little serious interest in such a big bird, but Bailets reportedly hounded each man until he bought a ticket. Upon reaching $15 worth of sales, the hotelkeeper would hold a drawing, the lucky winner of which would then be offered a deal: Bailets would buy the turkey back from him for the sum of $7.50. The winner rarely refused, and so Bailets, back in possession of the bird, would turn around and raffle it off again. "Many thought that [the] turkey had paid for itself time and time again," Sherlock wrote of the 1909 raffle, "and that something had to be done about it."

Something was. Seeking revenge for this blatant extortion, several of the railroaders got together at the Wellington station and hatched a plan. It began with two of them faking a fight in the Bailets Hotel saloon. When the scuffle started getting out of hand, "showing signs of possibly damaging the furniture," Bailets came out from behind the bar with a club in his hands to stop it. In the commotion that followed, an accomplice nabbed the caged turkey and whisked it out of the saloon and down to the station. "The turkey was handed to a train that was leaving town and [was] never recovered."

Nor was the joke left at that. The next day a counterfeit sign appeared on a tree in front of the saloon: "Reward of 100 dollars will be paid for information regarding a turkey stolen from me November 23rd 1909. (Signed) W. R. Bailets." The hotelkeeper was furious when he saw it. He tore down the sign and threatened to have the perpetrator arrested for forgery. Then other signs began appearing all over Wellington, reading, "Who oh who stole Bailets' turkey?" One of these signs, posted at the depot, was still there when the Seattle Express pulled into Wellington on the night of February 24.

There seems to have been a distinctly cruel edge to many of the practical jokes played at Wellington. Once—to tease section foreman Bob Harley, a man apparently prone to violating the railroad's ever-unpopular Rule G (forbidding alcohol use)—telegrapher William Flannery faked a report of a landslide two miles down the line that had to be cleared immediately. A quickly sobered-up Harley sprang into action. But Flannery and the rest of the Wellington crew proceeded to frustrate every attempt by the foreman to assemble a work gang and get them down to the alleged trouble area. At the same time, Flannery kept handing Harley fake telegrams from his bosses, chewing him out for the delay. The poor man became increasingly frantic—until, in sheer exasperation, he ran off and drank himself into a stupor.

One recurring prank involved "arresting" strangers in town (usually hoboes or passing hunters) and dragging them before a kangaroo court on trumped-up charges. The ruse was amazingly well orchestrated, commonly involving a cast of dozens, with various local railroaders posing as sheriff (with an old Seattle police badge), prosecuting attorney, witnesses, a jury, and His Honor Judge Grogan, this last played by John Robert Meath, a locomotive engineer who often worked the rotary plows. One such trial—of an itinerant cougar hunter who was hauled in on fake sabotage charges—went on for hours, with the poor defendant never once doubting the legitimacy of the proceedings.

But the denizens of Stevens Pass didn't always base their entertainment on the mortification of others. Sledding was a popular activity on winter days, and many evenings would find the men gathered in the telegraph office, playing cards, telling stories (one famous tale involved a creature named Wah-too-tie, who supposedly lived in the tunnel), or just bantering among themselves. In less remote railroad stations, the telegraph office was supposed to be a private place, off-limits to anyone who didn't have business there. Not so at Wellington. "Many times Superintendent J. H. O'Neill had to elbow his way into the office," Sherlock later recalled, "but [he] never made any objection. I often thought that Mr. O'Neill would rather find the men there than at the saloon."

Even in this boys' club atmosphere, however, there were calmer, more serious moments: "One evening, when things seemed rather dull or tame, everyone waiting for something to happen, two of the men begged another to sing a song. He declined, saying it would disturb the telegrapher. . . . I assured him it would not. [And] with the best Irish tenor voice I ever heard before or since, without a musical accompaniment, he sang 'The Wearing of the Green.' "

There's a distinct poignancy to the image of this cluster of workingmen, gathered together in the dim glow of a tiny wilderness station, rapt as one of their number sings a sentimental ballad a cappella in the night. These were rough, hard-laboring types, predominantly of Irish or Scots-Irish background. They were daily facing high danger, extreme isolation, and unbending, often unfair performance expectations. Under such circumstances, the loyalty of these men to one another—their solidarity and almost tribal feeling of brotherhood—makes perfect sense. The job they were doing was hard and largely thankless, but they were railroad men—and mountain railroad men at that. They found in the very rigors of the life they all led together a source of uncommon pride.

With the arrival of those two trains from the other side of the mountain, however, a distinctly foreign element would be introduced into this closed world of Wellington. Normally, railroaders would have little to do with the travelers who passed through their territory. (Many shared James J. Hill's famous low opinion of passenger service as an annoyance: "like a male teat—neither useful nor ornamental.") But henceforth these particular passengers, who until now had been passive observers of the railroaders' battle against the storm, would become active participants in the Wellington drama as it unfolded over the next few difficult days, creating tensions for which the tiny, insular community was ill prepared. And the immediate catalyst for this change was to come before dawn on Friday morning back at Cascade Tunnel Station, where a deadly avalanche was about to darken the character of the entire situation at Stevens Pass.

7

First Loss

TWO MEN PERISH IN SNOW SLIDES

Two lives have been snuffed out as the result of the heavy snows in the Cascade Mountains, a storm proving more effectual as a traffic blockader than any previously experienced by the Great Northern railway in its countless battles with the warring elements in the rugged mountain range.

—Everett Daily Herald

Friday, February 25, 1910
Wellington
Toward Noon

It was already late morning when the news reached the passenger cars of the Seattle Express.

Up until that time, it had been a relatively uneventful day. Sarah Jane Covington and most of the other passengers had slept late, lazing in their berths until after 10:00 A.M. The winds had started up again, pummeling the two trains with fifty-mile-per-hour gusts, spraying them with bursts of sleet that sizzled against the windows. "Snowing hard," Mrs. Covington wrote in her diary. "Everybody trying to be patient." Henry White, who walked up to breakfast at the hotel through the windblown snow, found the look of the mountainside above the trains a little intimidating. "It was some mountain all right," he would later say. "You had to throw your head back to see the top of it." Returning to the train, he buttonholed Pettit and asked the conductor when they'd be moving on. Pettit was optimistic: Soon, probably sometime today, as soon as the slide ahead was cleared.

Toward noon, though, a shocking rumor began circulating through the train cars. Mrs. Covington overheard it while writing in her diary. Someone told Lewis Jesseph and John Merritt as they were smoking in the observation car. Precise details were scant at first, but gradually the passengers learned the full story: Very early that morning, a scant few hours after the trains had been pulled through the tunnel to Wellington, a powerful avalanche had come roaring down the mountainside above Cascade Tunnel Station. It had smashed full-force into the beanery there, crumpling the thin wooden walls, exploding sacks of beans and flour, and sending the tables and chairs flying. The cook and his waiter—Harry Elerker and John Bjerenson—had been working inside at the time. Both had been crushed and killed instantly.

This news horrified everyone aboard. The beanery, after all, was where they'd eaten lunch the day before. The two victims had been the friendly pair of men who'd served them. Perhaps most disturbing was the fact that the slide had occurred at precisely the spot at which their train had been standing for the better part of thirty-six hours. "Glad we moved from where we were," Ned Topping wrote breezily in his letter home, but his light tone was masking a frightening thought: Had the trains still been there at 4:00 A.M., the entire Fast Mail train and the last two cars of the Seattle Express would have been engulfed by the slide.

For the passengers, everything about their situation on the mountain suddenly seemed different. Until the beanery slide, most had regarded the delay as an annoyance, disquieting but not actually life-threatening. Now, trapped by slides both ahead and behind, they began to appreciate the real danger they were in. Lewis Jesseph, trying to maintain order in the observation car, was startled by the dramatic change in mood. "Some of the women became hysterical," he reported. "Some of the men were abstracted in thought, silent and morose."

Newly sensitized to the menace around them, the passengers began examining their position more closely. Ned Topping noted that the shelf of land on which the trains were sidetracked was really quite precarious. "Perched on the side of a mountain now," he wrote to his mother after lunch. "A wooded hill to my right and a deep valley on [the] other side." And the forest cover on that "wooded hill" was hardly dense enough to provide much of an anchor for the snowpack. Wildfires in the area had been allowed to rage unchecked for years, leaving the woodlands around Wellington little more than a forest of charred stumps tangled in huckleberry brush and cedar seedlings. Was this really the safest place for the trains to wait?

The women aboard certainly didn't think so. Reports of their fearfulness are undoubtedly magnified by 1910 attitudes of male condescension, but some of the women—Ida Starrett, Anna Gray, and the already unstable Ada Lemman—seem to have been utterly terrified by the beanery slide: "On the 25th I overheard a conversation of two ladies and one gentleman on my way back to the depot," telegrapher W. V. Avery was later to testify. "The ladies were worrying as to their safety and the man was jollying them and remarked . . . that they were in no danger."

Porter Lucius Anderson told a similar story in his inquest testimony:

Q: Did you hear any of them talking to Conductor Pettit, any of the passengers?

A: There was a couple of ladies on [the Winnipeg] that was of a very nervous disposition; they continued to bother him about when they would get out and the safest place to put the train.

Q: Did those two ladies attempt to suggest to the conductor that any other position was safer than the position which they were in?

A: They asked him if it would be safe to put the train in the tunnel; he told them that he thought the [position] where they were would be better, because in going to and from their meals they would have to wade through water in the tunnel to get out, and the smoke in the tunnel would be very bad, and it would be very unsanitary in the tunnel, and as far as his knowledge [went], it was the safest position where they were standing.

Q: Did the ladies acquiesce in his decision, or did they insist on
   being moved?

A: No sir, they quieted down for a while—you know how they
   usually are.

Male or female, even the most stouthearted passengers now had to
be wondering whether O'Neill and his men really had the situation under control. True, the Cascade Division was well armed to fight the fury
of a typical Cascades snowstorm, but was this storm at all typical? Just
the night before, hotelkeeper W. R. Bailets had announced to several
passengers that he'd been checking his seventeen years of records, and
as far as he could tell there had never been as much snow accumulated
at Wellington as there was right now.

That had been about twelve hours ago. The snow had been falling—
copiously, continuously—ever since.

✧

> We tried digging food out of the dining hall [at Cascade Tunnel
> Station], but didn't find much. . . . I found a new pair of slicker
> pants and tied the ends and used them for sacks, filling them from
> a box of raisins and a sack of beans we uncovered. We figured
> that might be all we'd have to eat for some time.
>
> —*Warren S. Tanguy,*
> *telegrapher*

Wellington
Friday Afternoon

Superintendent O'Neill had been working with the double rotary, at-
tacking the hard-snow slide at Snowshed 3.3, when word of the beanery
slide reached him sometime before dawn. Others may have been
shocked by the news, but this was unfortunately just the kind of mishap
O'Neill had been fearing. Between noon and midnight on Thursday, he
had watched in dismay as temperatures on the mountain had risen a full
ten degrees, climbing into the low thirties even as the sun set and night

moved in. One thing his long experience had taught him was that rising temperatures and heavy snow cover were a dangerous combination. Add to them the extra stress of the gale-force winds that started picking up after midnight (wind can deposit snow up to ten times faster than it can fall from the sky) and you have a perfect recipe for sliding. That one of the resulting avalanches had hit Cascade Tunnel Station—at a place where there were likely to be people in its path—was merely the grimmest part of his bad luck.

Leaving trainmaster Blackburn in charge of the snow-clearing effort, O'Neill hiked back to Wellington to telegraph the Chelan County coroner about the two deaths. It was not a pleasant duty, but O'Neill found that he also had other unpleasant tasks awaiting him at Wellington. Crises were looming throughout the entire Cascade Division, and the outlook seemed only to be worsening. Rain- and snow-swollen rivers were rising all over the western Cascade watershed, threatening to take out bridges and embankments on the division's coastal line. (Within hours, O'Neill would have two wrecks to deal with on the line between Seattle and Bellingham, both caused by track washouts.) Other snowslides had fallen overnight on the east slope, and though they hadn't caused any fatalities, they were potentially even more dangerous to operations than was the beanery slide. A large avalanche somewhere on that east slope had taken out the telegraph wires again, leaving O'Neill with no direct communication with anyone in the entire eastern half of his division.

This sudden intensification of sliding activity gave O'Neill's problems new urgency. Working out on the rotaries, he and his men were in more peril than anyone on the mountain—a fact that Berenice down in Everett would not have been able to forget—but the two trains at Wellington were not exactly exempt from danger. He was convinced that where they stood now, just west of the Wellington depot, was one of the few places on the mountain immune to avalanches. The trains, however, wouldn't be there forever. Once they were liberated, their journey down to Scenic and Skykomish could become extremely hazardous if the warming trend continued.

O'Neill had faced an eerily similar situation on the west slope shortly after his appointment as Cascade Division superintendent. On a stormy day in December 1907, GN's train No. 4 had been heading upgrade to Wellington in warming conditions much like those currently developing. About a mile past Windy Point, as the train emerged from a snowshed, the lead engineer saw a massive avalanche rumble down the mountain to cover the entrance of the next snowshed on the line. Something about this slide must have spooked the engineer, because instead of merely stopping, he began signaling frantically for a full reverse. Passengers and crew were hurled to the floor as the train suddenly switched directions and began to accelerate back toward the shed they'd just left behind. About fifty feet from the entrance the engineer hit the brakes again. The train shuddered to a stop, its momentum placing it neatly centered under the roof of the shed, which was barely longer than the train itself.

This turned out to be an inspired maneuver. As the train stopped moving, another avalanche came thundering down the mountain, plugging the front end of the shed. Within thirty seconds, a third slide (or an extension of the same one) buried the rear end, trapping the train inside. The crew and forty passengers on train No. 4 remained stranded in the open-sided shed for days, living on the dining car's supplies and rationing coal to keep the train warm. On the tenth day, they all finally abandoned the train and struggled into Wellington on foot.

This vivid precedent was impossible to ignore in the current circumstances. Granted, the chances of a moving train being hit by an avalanche were remote, even under the worst slide conditions. But as O'Neill well knew, every avalanche brought down by a thaw, even if it occurred far from any train, would complicate the operations picture of the entire Cascades crossing, making all trains on the mountain more vulnerable. New slides would also mean more messes to clean up once the storm had finally passed and the rotaries could start catching up.

The storm, however, was not passing, and with the wind roaring back to its previous strength, the plows were floundering again. Harrington's X801 was having trouble even within the confines of the Wellington yard. The superintendent needed it to clear up the slide at Cascade Tunnel Station, but just getting the plow from the depot to the tunnel was proving to be an ordeal. Already it had bogged down once. Caught in the windblown drifts, the plow had sat idle until it could be dug out by the double rotary on one of its fuel runs back to the coal shed. How could O'Neill get his two first-class trains off the mountain when even his rotaries were wallowing helplessly in the tempest?

These were desperate straits, to be sure, but O'Neill had two important factors working in his favor. The first was that outside help was on its way. Dowling and the X808 were still battling up from Scenic on the west slope, getting closer every hour. Another rotary was now en route from the GN's Kalispell Division in the Rocky Mountains to the east; this extra plow was farther away than Dowling's—at this point, it hadn't even reached Leavenworth—but it was making faster progress. There were also two emergency relief trains with extra men and equipment heading toward the pass; one was traveling from Everett in the west and the other was coming with the Kalispell plow from the east.

O'Neill was probably pinning greater hopes on the second major factor working in his favor—namely, simple meteorological probability. It was now official: Never before in O'Neill's three-year tenure in the Cascades (or even in the far longer tenure of Wellington veterans like Bailets and conductor Ed Lindsay) had a winter storm lasted as long as this one had. In a typical Cascades snow season there might be seventy-five days on which snow fell, but almost never would there be more than three in a row without a day's hiatus. Considering this history, O'Neill had every right to expect that the storm would break soon. And once it did break, his three working rotaries might even be able to clear the slides without any outside help at all.

Until then there was the ever-present problem of the coal supply to contend with. O'Neill was doing everything possible to conserve the limited stores he had left, but already the coal chute at Wellington was all but tapped out. On its next fuel run, the double rotary would be forced to pilfer coal from the disabled X807 and a spare locomotive on the coal-chute track. G. W. Turner, down in Everett, was furiously buying coal wherever he could find it. The chief dispatcher's attempts to procure some from the Northern Pacific had failed, so he was finding it necessary to buy on the open market, and for a price that would not please the frugal Great Northern managers. Even if Turner could secure a good supply, however, getting it up to Wellington would be another challenge. O'Neill's need was immediate, and even the coal cars coming up with Dowling's rotary were still hours away.

So O'Neill was weighing his other options. He knew that there was a stash of several coal cars at Merritt on the east slope. Once Harrington and his crew had cleared the beanery slide at Cascade Tunnel Station, they would continue east. If they were able to work through the slides as far as Merritt before running out of coal themselves, they could conceivably refuel there, retrieve those coal cars, and bring them back to Wellington.

But that was still just a remote possibility. The frustrating reality was that it would require coal to get more coal, whether it came from Harrington in the east or Dowling in the west. With no other sources at his disposal, O'Neill simply wasn't sure there would be enough to go around.

❖

The first I heard of the dissatisfaction, or noticed it, was after the slide at the east end that destroyed the eating house and killed the two men there. That seemed to get the women very nervous. They heard of that and they were afraid.

—*Henry White*

Wellington
Early Friday Evening

By the time evening fell, turning the surrounding slopes from white to blue and then dark gray, it was becoming clear to everyone that the trains were going to remain on the passing tracks at least until next morning. Many of the anxious passengers had been able to cable their families—the telegraph wires west from Wellington were sporadically operational—but that was little comfort against the prospect of another long night on the mountain. One woman on the Winnipeg—probably Libby Latsch, a well-turned-out thirty-year-old entrepreneur whose firm, the Northwestern Sales Company, sold something called Always in

Place hair supporters—apparently decided she couldn't stand it anymore without a cigarette and set upon porter Lucius Anderson. "Our nicely dressed woman just came back in the observation [car] & complained of a lack of accommodations for ladies," Ned Topping wrote in his letter. "Said she wanted to smoke, so porter fixed her up in a compartment & I guess she is happy." (This, remember, was a time when cigarettes were illegal in Washington State.)

Sarah Jane Covington doubtless disapproved. "A good many of the passengers on this train are the smart set," the old woman wrote to her husband. "Quite a number play cards and drink, talk slang and any old thing." She herself was finding more productive ways of dealing with the tension—by immersing herself in improving literature. "Am reading the story of a Cooperative Experiment that failed because of the class hatred of its Beneficiaries," she wrote, referring to an article about the Dutch socialist Frederik van Eeden, founder of a short-lived utopian community called Walden. Mrs. Covington, a true product of the reform-minded Progressive Era, was fascinated by such social experiments, and with anything else concerning ways to perfect the human condition. "Van Eeden," she wrote, "became awake to the fact that at least 90% of the misery of mankind was not necessary. It is only the result of bad order, bad organization, inertia, laxity, indifference."

Meanwhile, Henry White and a few others were growing increasingly dissatisfied with Pettit's hollow reassurances that the line would soon be clear. Deciding that it was time to make their concerns known to someone truly in charge, they called a meeting in the plush observation car at the end of the train, inviting Jesseph, Merritt, and several other prominent men among the passengers.

The main instigator of the meeting was Charles S. Eltinge, a fifty-year-old banker recently retired as vice president of Traders National Bank in Spokane. Smooth-shaven, with dark black hair and stern, pinched features, Eltinge was of a mind to complain directly to superintendent O'Neill. According to Merritt, "[He] wanted to know if Mr. Jesseph and I would not take up the question with the company and register a kick about their not getting us out."

This was not something Merritt was prepared to do. He and Jesseph had already talked about the situation and had decided that the train was in no immediate danger. "We would come out and stand on the track and look up the mountain," he later said, "and it seemed to us that where the train stood was probably the safest place . . . unless it was in the tunnel." Being acquainted with O'Neill, Merritt also felt certain that the superintendent was doing everything in his power to free the trains. So he told Eltinge that he wouldn't join in the complaint. "I did not see that there was anything that the company could do that they were not at that time [already] trying to do, and it would not do any good to kick."

Others disagreed. Henry White—who traveled enough to have strong ideas about his rights as a passenger—was determined at least to speak to the superintendent. "[We] decided that we would ask Mr. O'Neill to come in that night and have a talk with us and give us some sort of assurance," White would later report. "And so we told Mr. Longcoy, the private secretary. We saw him and asked him if he would not tell Mr. O'Neill to come over that night, and he said that he would."

At this point in their ordeal, the passengers seem to have been split over the question of whether the trains were in any real peril where they were. Most of the men—at least judging from their own testimony— were still concerned mainly about what the delay was doing to their schedules. ("There was not any question of slides at that time," Merritt would later claim.) The women, on the other hand, were terrified about the possibility of an avalanche. Unswayed by Pettit's warnings about the unpleasantness of the tunnel, they continued to hound him on the topic. So the harried conductor tried another tack, noting that never in the seventeen-year history of the GN line through Stevens Pass had there been a snowslide at the place where the trains now stood. This re-assurance did nothing to quiet the women. "They made the argument," Henry White observed, "that neither had there ever been a slide at [the beanery at Cascade Tunnel Station] . . . and if it could happen there it would be just as likely to happen where we were."

Whether or not Pettit and the other men were swayed by this logic, they didn't act upon it. And, in truth, no one on the trains really had the relevant expertise to judge the level of danger they were in. "There did not seem to be any of us who had any previous experience in snowslides," White explained. "Most of our information came by what you would call the 'grapevine telegraph.' It would come through different parties—so-and-so said this or so-and-so said that—and we concluded it was about time to get something from someone in authority."

The superintendent had therefore been summoned. But as the evening wore on without any sign of O'Neill, the passengers' frustration grew. And they were to get no satisfaction that night. "We waited for Mr. O'Neill until about 10 o'clock," White recalled, "and he did not show up."

The passengers were beginning to wonder if they were being consciously ignored, or at least forgotten about. The fact that rotaries were throwing snow on top of the passenger train each time they passed on refueling runs just added injury to insult. Wouldn't every extra bit of snow piled around the train require time and effort to shovel out once the line opened? Then why was the railroad worsening their entombment?

The answers would apparently have to wait until morning. "Nothing doing," Ned Topping wrote finally, closing out his letter for the night. "Still imprisoned. Conductor thinks we can get out tomorrow." The young Ohioan seemed resigned to the fact that there was little he or anyone else could do to change their situation. But there were some aboard—Henry White, in particular—who were now determined not to let another day pass without making their displeasure known.

✧

> I think the railroad men believed we would [get through]; and we would have, if we could have stopped the snow from falling. But as they would gain one victory . . . here would come another heavy fall of snow and slides.
>
> —*John Rogers*

Berne
Late Friday Evening

There was coal to be had at Merritt. William Harrington knew that much for sure. Whether or not he and the crew of rotary X801 would be able to reach that coal was another question entirely. Between their rotary and the loaded cars at Merritt stood an unfathomable amount of snow, and their path through it would be as perilous and uncertain as that of a ship on a storm-rocked sea.

Harrington, a bluff, work-hardened man in his late thirties, was a figure of considerable substance. "Featured like a Roman gladiator, thewed like an ox, with a chest like a cider barrel," as the sometimes oratorical *Seattle Times* would later describe him, he had been railroading for over twenty years, and he approached every aspect of his job with a stolid assurance born of long experience. Having grown up on a farm in Wisconsin, he was also no novice when it came to working in extreme weather. Still, the effort required to perform even the simplest task in this storm was astounding. It took hours to water an engine, hours to move a few railcars, hours to work through a small slide that should have taken minutes to dispatch. The most absurd struggle had been simply getting the rotary up to the tunnel portal at Wellington. Even after borrowing the helper engine from train No. 25 for extra pushing power (a six-hour maneuver), making any headway at all had been ridiculously arduous. For a rotary plow with two pusher engines to have such trouble moving a few thousand feet was unheard-of.

Once they were through the tunnel and on the far less windy eastern side of the summit ridge, the going had been much easier. After a few hours spent clearing up the beanery slide at Cascade Tunnel Station, Harrington and the rotary crew had changed engines and, at about 6:00 P.M., proceeded east to continue plowing the line. The official version of their mission was that they were headed all the way to Leavenworth at the foot of the mountains, clearing slides as they went. In light of the weather conditions, though, Harrington must have known that taking a single rotary such a long way was hardly possible. More likely, with coal so short on the mountain, he was on an errand to fetch those coal cars at Merritt and bring them back to Wellington—a far more plausible assignment. In any case, they'd clear what they could of the eastern line, making it that much less difficult for the relief train that would be heading west from Leavenworth to bring supplies and reinforcements.

At least Harrington was well staffed on this run. The plow train under his command carried a good score of men, including two entire rotary crews, one of which could plow while the other slept. He also had an ample contingent of shovelers and several of the best snow-fighting railroaders on the mountain—among them J. J. Mackey, one of the division's traveling engineers, and conductor Ira Clary, a diminutive but scrappy Irishman known for his waspish wit. Sporting the black bowlers and felt homburgs worn by many trainmen in the Cascade Division of this era, they would have made an incongruously stylish tableau as they swarmed around the bellowing rotary. But these were rugged and determined men, close-knit, loyal to O'Neill, and expert in the technical aspects of mountain railroading. If there was any chance at all of getting a single rotary through that storm, this was the crew to do it.

Was there a chance of getting through? Harrington was likely beginning to doubt it. Though they had left Cascade Tunnel with a full supply of coal, they'd been encountering small slides and deeply drifted snow all evening. The plow and its pushers had been forced to work consistently hard, burning coal at an alarming rate. There was still plenty of fuel left in the engines' tenders, but the look of the road ahead was enough to have the Snow King worried. Having worked those mountains for several years, he knew that even small slides could be harbingers of much worse to come. Like cockroaches, avalanches didn't typically run in isolation—once you saw two or three of them, you could be certain that many more were lurking, waiting to make an appearance. Given the right conditions, it would only be a matter of time before they began to swarm.

And as superintendent O'Neill also recognized, the right conditions had been falling into place for days. Common sense might suggest that the likelihood of avalanches depends mainly on two factors—the steepness of a slope and the amount of snow that has accumulated on it—but the physics of sliding are actually far more complicated. "Snow," as one modern expert has put it, "is one of the most complex materials found in nature, and it is highly variable, going through significant changes even before it has accumulated as a continuous cover on the landscape." Thus the likelihood of further snowslides in the area would depend not just on what would happen over the next few days, but also on what had already happened in the previous days or even months.

Certainly the enormous amounts of snow falling in the current storm would not be a negligible factor. Precipitation of any type has weight, and lots of new weight will add lots of new stress to the existing snowpack. But whether that new stress can be absorbed safely depends on a number of variables, all determined by the specific conditions under which the snow was deposited. Rapidly changing weather is particularly dangerous, with fluctuating temperatures altering the nature of the snowpack and creating layers of various tensile strength within it.

As everyone at Wellington knew, just such a temperature fluctuation had occurred in the Cascades over the past week. On Tuesday, the current storm had arrived on a blast of arctic air, shattering low-temperature records and forcing the mercury (as the *Everett Daily Herald* had pointed out) to "take the toboggan" to near zero degrees. Since then, temperatures had risen quickly. High winds, moreover, had come and gone all week, loading certain slopes with much greater depths of hard, compacted snow.

The result was that the snowpack clinging to the slopes around Stevens Pass was already a dangerous mixture of strong and weak layers. Depending on what the weather did next, the snowpack could either maintain its current precarious balance, slipping only in especially vulnerable places, or fail more generally, bringing down slides all over the mountain. In the latter case, Harrington and his crew would find themselves with far greater problems than simply running out of coal before reaching the cache at Merritt.

For the X801, then, there was no alternative but to keep plowing. Returning to the tunnel would have been futile if there was no coal there with which to refuel. Besides, if Harrington or any of the others were ever to see home again, they'd have to get this rail line open. Unlike many of the younger men he worked with, Harrington had a family relying on him. His wife, Lillian, and their three young children were all at home in Everett awaiting his return. During the two-thirds of the year that he worked as a regular conductor, the children would actually get to see something of their father; he'd go over the mountain to Leavenworth one day and come back over the hump to Everett by the next. From mid-November to late March, however—when he served as assistant trainmaster in charge of snow removal—Harrington could go days or even weeks without managing to find his way home.

Fortunately, the end of February was already in sight. Within a few weeks, the Cascades snow season would be over. Even if slides began to swarm over the next day or two, they would likely be the last major headache of the winter. The Snow King would get to retire and return to his regular duties until the following November. If nothing else, this was something for Harrington to look forward to.

8

Closing Doors

Q: Had you had a chance to get a meal more than the two or
   three meals you have mentioned in that period?
A: No sir, we did not have any chance to get any meals.
Q: Where did you get your sleep?
A: I got no sleep.

—*John Robert Meath,*
rotary engineer

Saturday, February 26, 1910
Near Windy Point
Early Morning

Shortly before 4:00 A.M. on Saturday morning, after another protracted
night of grinding, unremitting plow work, the westbound double
rotary finally broke through the deep slide at Snowshed 3.3. For superintendent O'Neill, this was a heartening development. The two consecutive slides at this spot had been the principal obstacles preventing the
escape of those two trains at Wellington.

Plowing away this second blockage, however, had taken nearly
thirty-six hours—plenty of time for drifting snow and further slides to
have created problems elsewhere on the mountain. Although the line
was now clear from Wellington to Windy Point, there were still some
seven or eight miles of track between Windy Point and Scenic about
which O'Neill knew little. Master mechanic J. J. Dowling and the X808

had been hacking away at this stretch of track since 3:00 P.M. on Friday, working up from Scenic, but they were as yet nowhere to be seen on the line below. And as much as O'Neill wanted to continue plowing downgrade to meet them, the double needed to be coaled and watered again, and the overworked rotary crews needed some refueling of their own. Reluctantly, therefore, he ordered the double rotary back to Wellington.

While his men were eating breakfast at the station shortly after 5:00 A.M., O'Neill gathered whatever news he could about the other rotaries. With all communication down east of the tunnel, nothing had been heard from Harrington on the east slope, but word from the west was hardly more definitive. At last report, Dowling and the X808 were still far closer to Scenic than to Windy Point, delayed by a small slide and a burst flue on the rotary that had taken some hours to repair. There was, in short, still no verifiable path off the mountain in either direction.

O'Neill also had another new predicament to deal with. Over the course of the past few days, his battalions of temporary snow shovelers had been growing steadily less cooperative, grumbling about pay and the harsh and increasingly dangerous conditions. Many had been putting in only halfhearted efforts, working more slowly and resting more frequently with each passing hour. Even the passengers had noticed their tendency to goldbrick. "Hello there, Bill," one of the male passengers had shouted from the train to a group of idling laborers, "if you aren't careful you will hurt your shovel!" This taunt had done little to increase the shovelers' motivation. Then, on Friday, a fistfight had broken out between two drunken section crews at the saloon. O'Neill knew that it would only be a matter of time before the men stopped doing any work at all.

Now even the passengers were starting to turn troublesome. It was sometime on Friday night, probably during one of the double rotary's quick trips back to Wellington for water, that the superintendent had first heard from Longcoy about the passengers' request to see him. O'Neill was not at all eager to oblige; after all, he had more than enough to occupy him without having to field unanswerable questions from nervous passengers. And so—understandably if not quite admirably—he had told Longcoy to make excuses for him. O'Neill instructed the stenographer to say that he was "too sleepy" for a meeting that night.

It was no mystery to O'Neill why these men wished to see him; they obviously wanted the Seattle Express moved off the flank of Windy Mountain. Given appearances, their concerns were not unreasonable. O'Neill wasn't blind to the deepening snowfield on the mountainside above the trains, and he realized that the increasing instability of the snowpack was justifiably worrying to people ignorant of the behavior of slides. But he was convinced that the passing tracks at Wellington were actually one of the least slide-prone places on the mountain. Years of experience had shown that snowslides in the area almost invariably came down on slopes pleated with ravines or draws. There had been a small gully, for instance, creasing the mountainside above the beanery at Cascade Tunnel Station. Here, on the slope above the passing tracks at Wellington, there was no such interruption in the smooth face of the mountainside. That's why there was no snowshed protecting the tracks there. No protection was considered necessary.

And the simple fact of the matter was that there was no other suitable place at Wellington to put those trains. The tunnel, whatever the passengers might think, was an utterly impractical alternative. The only other sheltered place would have been under one of the snowsheds. Snowshed 2, not far west of Wellington, might have been long enough to cover at least one of the trains, but there was only one track—the main line—going through that shed; leaving a train there would have blocked the double rotary's access to the coal chute and the water tank. Nor were snowsheds entirely indestructible; it was not unheard-of for a big slide to collapse a wooden snowshed, crushing whatever stood beneath it. Since these sheds were naturally located in places known to be susceptible to avalanches, moving the Seattle Express under Snowshed 2 would also have been taking it from a place with no slide history to a demonstrably slide-prone area.

The last possibility—moving the trains to the spur tracks on the flat area near the tunnel portal—posed its own insurmountable difficulties. Given the amount of snow that had fallen, clearing those tracks would have taken O'Neill's entire force of men at least two days of hard labor to accomplish. Putting a passenger train on a spur track would also have run counter to the rules of standard operating procedure. Besides, O'Neill wasn't convinced that the spur tracks were any safer than the passing tracks. Yes, the steep mountainsides were somewhat more distant from the tracks there, but that area—where the switchbacks had been located years earlier—had been the site of frequent slides in the past. A large avalanche coming down that gully-creased mountainside could easily travel far enough to bury any trains standing on the spurs.

Moving the trains was therefore simply out of the question; O'Neill felt he had no better alternative than to keep them exactly where they were. Instead of redeploying all of his manpower and steam power to the futile task of clearing the line between the trains and the tunnel, he would continue to devote all of his efforts to getting the trains off the mountain and out of danger entirely.

To do that, of course, he had to finish clearing the line down to Scenic, which meant working his already exhausted men even longer, not to mention finding more fuel to run the rotaries. After breakfast, O'Neill was relieved to learn that the plow crews had managed to solve at least the latter problem. By raiding supplies in the motor shed, the unused engines, and elsewhere, they'd collected enough coal to fill the rotary train's tenders to full capacity. Depending on conditions, then, they would have a good ten to twenty more hours of work time— enough, O'Neill hoped, to at least secure access to one of his two potential replenishment sources of coal: either the carloads traveling up the mountain from the west with Dowling or the two or three cars being freed by Harrington to the east.

Shortly after sunrise, refueled but woefully unrested, O'Neill and his force of thirty-five trainmen and snow shovelers reboarded the double rotary and headed back west. The snow was still coming down hard, but the wind had now fallen off to a breeze, promising to make the work of plowing considerably easier. With any luck, they would plow their way to a rendezvous with Dowling sometime that day, opening the line and allowing the trains to head down the mountain at least as far as Scenic.

Luck, however, was in horribly short supply in the Cascades that week: Just a few miles from Wellington, as the rotary was making its way west over the already plowed line, a new slide appeared out of the swirling snow ahead of them. It had fallen sometime in the few hours they'd been gone, and it had come down—incredibly—at Snowshed 3.3, precisely the same point at which the earlier two slides had come down.

What O'Neill may have muttered under his breath at this moment is not recorded. He was known as a man who always kept his temper. Probably he waited for the rotary train to stop, then jumped across to the high bank of snow beside the tracks and, without comment, waded forward through the drifts to examine the slide. From what was visible through the falling snow, he could see it was a large one—almost fifteen hundred feet long, according to his subsequent report. Though the slide was relatively clear of timber, its depth varied from ten feet in some places to over thirty feet in others. It would be at least another full day's work to clear it up.

Enraging as this situation may have been, there was only one thing O'Neill could do. Returning to the rotary, he called out the shovelers and set them to work breaking down the face of the slide.

✧

> Saturday—noon—still here—snowing hard—report this AM that there is six miles of uncleared track—some places 30 ft deep. They are working from Seattle toward us and we may get [out] tonight—tho I'm not believing anyone.
>
> —*Ned Topping*

Wellington
Saturday Afternoon

By Saturday even the children had grown testy and quarrelsome. There were a total of four boys and four girls on the Seattle Express, and keeping them all peacefully occupied was proving to be a chore. Seven-year-old Raymond Starrett and the three-year-old Beck boy seemed to be getting along well enough; the younger child had a toy train that Ray was simply fascinated by, and the two of them would spend hours pushing it along the floor of the crowded car. But the boys wanted no part of Thelma Davis, the three-year-old girl from Seattle, whom Ray regarded as hopelessly spoiled. Whenever Thelma didn't get her way, she would dissolve into tears, requiring continual comforting by one of the older Beck girls. Although it was explained to Ray that little Thelma was missing her mother, who was back at the family's Seattle apartment, he was not very sympathetic. Since he himself had recently lost a father, he felt he could have limited sympathy for a girl who was just missing a temporarily absent parent.

The adults did what they could to keep the children amused. Whenever there was a lull in the storm, some of the younger passengers would take them outside to build snowmen and have raucous snowball fights among the drifts. Sometimes the girls were gathered into sewing circles to patch together makeshift dresses from scraps. When things got really bad, Lucius Anderson, the "jolly" porter on the Winnipeg, would tell stories. Once—to Ray Starrett's delight—he even did a tap dance.

Back on the observation car, salesman Henry White was still fuming about O'Neill's failure to appear the night before. Spotting Longcoy, White and a few other malcontents hailed the young man and asked whether the superintendent had received their message. He had, Longcoy replied, but Mr. O'Neill had been too busy and then too sleepy to come over and see them last night. Now he was gone again—down to Scenic on unspecified business. This last bit of information was actually an expedient fabrication—O'Neill was still with the rotary at Snowshed 3.3—but even this answer did not yet satisfy White. "We insisted that [Longcoy] send a message—either a wire or a telephone [call], or send somebody to Scenic and tell Mr. O'Neill we wanted to see him right away." In reply, Longcoy spun out yet another fib: "He told us that Mr. O'Neill was sick abed and could not get away."

Whether Longcoy—a devout Baptist who was also an active member of the Everett YMCA—was improvising on his own here or merely passing along excuses concocted by O'Neill is impossible to say. The sickness story was in any case a risky lie to tell, and one that was eventually exposed. (Two days after this exchange, White would ask conductor Pettit about O'Neill's ill health: "I asked him how Mr. O'Neill was and he said, 'He is all right.' . . . I said, 'Isn't he sick?' He said, 'No, he has not been sick.' ") The pretense of O'Neill's incapacitation, though, was enough to keep White quiet, at least for the moment. And the salesman was further mollified when he encountered Pettit a short time later and asked the inevitable question about progress. "It looks now as though we will get away this afternoon," the conductor offered (perhaps because he had not yet heard about the third slide at Snowshed 3.3).

Other passengers found reassurances elsewhere. Lewis Jesseph, approaching the situation with his usual lawyerly thoroughness, busied himself questioning local experts on the issue of moving the trains. He consulted with some old mountain men in Wellington, who assured him that the trains were "perfectly safe" where they were. He also had a conversation with hotelkeeper W. R. Bailets, resident at Wellington since 1892, who confirmed that he had never seen any slides on the slope over the passing tracks.

Some of the women, though, still refused to be comforted. Ida Starrett and Anna Gray, both mothers of infant children, were naturally more fearful than others, but the real problem was Ada Lemman, the woman suffering from nervous prostration. Although the Lemmans' child—a sixteen-year-old daughter—was safe with relatives in Ritzville, Ada had become increasingly unstable since the beanery slide. A graduate of Whitman College in Walla Walla, she was unusually well educated for a woman of her day, and was apparently unwilling to take the word of alleged experts over the evidence of her own senses. So she and some of the others used one of the few tactics of persuasion available to women at this time, but to little avail: "On Saturday the strain became too great for the women," Merritt observed, "and several of them broke down and cried. This was too much for the men in the crowd, and all left the car for the tall timbers."

The women's growing alarm was only deepened several hours later when the foreign snow shovelers began walking off the job. The mail clerk A. B. Hensel first noticed their retreat late on Saturday afternoon. The shovelers were leaving in groups of three and four, packs and bedrolls flung over their shoulders in the swirling snow. As they passed the passenger train, some of them paid back the ridicule they'd earlier received from the passengers. "They bade us goodbye as they walked along," Henry White admitted, "and they said, 'Goodbye, boys; God only knows when you will get out of there—we are going now.'"

The main cause of this impromptu job action was discontent over wages, which were beginning to seem ridiculously low to many of the laborers. White had been surprised to learn that these men were making only fifteen cents an hour. (Longcoy—who seems to have resorted to flagrant and frequent lying to keep the passengers in line—had told him that the shovelers were being paid twice that.) This already low wage was further reduced by deductions for board. "One or two of them told me [that] if he worked a week, often getting wet through, and his clothes all wet, he could manage to pull down about two dollars for himself. He said it didn't look good to him and he was going."

With the example of the retreating gangmen before them, some passengers began to think along similar lines. One particularly impatient man—Solomon Cohen, a mine speculator and former shopkeeper from Everett—began to openly advocate the idea of escaping on foot. "Those men will make a pretty good trail," he announced on Saturday afternoon, "and it will be a good idea to follow them." Unfortunately, it was already too late for the passengers to pack up their things and start out for Scenic. No one wanted to be stuck halfway down the mountain when night fell. "The feeling prevailed," White recalled, "that if we wanted to make a start it ought to be in the morning."

So nothing further was done that day. Tentative plans were made to leave the next morning, but many people seemed to lack conviction. The storm was still blowing hard, and now, seemingly as they watched, the dense snowfall began to turn into a hard, driving rain. A warming Chinook wind had blown in sometime after noon, pushing temperatures even further above the freezing point. Water was beginning to streak down the sides of the railroad cars and puddle in the impressions left by dirty boots in the snow. This was a discouragement for some— the hike down the mountain was bound to be more slippery and uncomfortable in the rain. For others, it was something more ominous. What would this rain do to the snow covering on the mountainside above them? No one seemed to know for sure. But for many of those aboard—particularly those for whom escape on foot would not be possible—the determination grew to find someone in authority and get those trains backed away from the flank of Windy Mountain. Whatever the high cost in time and manpower, they wanted to be moved.

✧

Situation 8:00 P.M. Raining hard on west slope with a strong Chinook wind. . . . Mr. O'Neill with double rotary still working about 3 miles west of Wellington. Have had no late news of him. Slides are numerous and continually coming down on west slope.

No wires east of Berne. People at Wellington very much alarmed over slides.

—G. W. Turner,
telegram to W. C. Watrous et al.

On the Line
Early Saturday Evening

In the mountains east and west of Wellington, the railroad's battle against the storm pressed on. To the east, Harrington and the X801 had spent all of Friday night drilling through a big slide encountered just east of Berne. By Saturday noon they had broken through it, but at a cost—twelve hours of almost constant rotary work had dangerously depleted the coal supply of both plow and pusher engines. It had thus become absolutely essential for them to reach the coal cars at Merritt before too much longer.

At first it had looked as if they might actually succeed. For a mile or two beyond Berne, they'd encountered only drifted snow on the tracks, which the rotary handled easily. But just as they were clearing Gaynor, a small station about nine miles east of the Cascade Tunnel, an avalanche had let loose on the mountainside across the river from the train tracks. It was a powerful, fast-moving slide, and before Harrington and his men fully grasped what was happening, the onrushing snow had surged across the thousand-foot-wide valley and raced up the slope on the other side, covering the tracks right in front of the still-moving rotary. Though the crew managed to stop the plow train in time to avoid being engulfed, the slide at Gaynor put a quick and certain end to any plans for reaching the coal at Merritt. Harrington and his men did continue to work at the new slide until they were down to their last ton of coal, but they found there was no way to get through that vast escarpment of snow before running out of fuel. Nor could they back up and return the way they had come, since other slides had come down behind them in the interim since they'd left Berne.

With so little fuel remaining and only a single east-facing rotary in his train, Harrington understood that he must abandon the X801. Leaving J. J. Mackey and a small crew of five to keep the rotary alive (since large steam engines could take up to twelve hours to start up once they'd gone cold, it was wise to avoid letting them "die" entirely), Harrington took the remainder of his men and started on the nine-mile hike back to Cascade Tunnel Station. For the moment, at least, the eastern front of this battle against the storm would have to be relinquished.

✧

The outlook was only somewhat brighter on the western front. Since discovering the third slide at Snowshed 3.3 that morning, O'Neill and the double rotary had been making slow but significant progress digging through it. Even so, every foot of cleared track had been hard-won. The wind, after tapering off for much of the day, had returned in full force, sweeping up drifts and making a chore of just standing upright. ("When the wind was blowing its hardest," one fireman would later recall, "it was . . . strong enough to blow a chew of tobacco out of a man's face.") The "Cascades cement" deposited by this new slide was also proving to be particularly intractable. An excerpt from the court testimony of engineer J. C. Wright describes the agonizingly deliberate procedure required to make headway in such a difficult slide.

A: The knives will not cut the snow [in a hard-snow slide], and the engine, if she is being pushed gradually against this, the knives won't take hold—you have to put her into it hard.

Q: What do you mean by putting her into it hard?

A: Well, you have to back away from the face of the slide, probably eight or ten or fifteen feet, and then when you are ready . . . [the engineer] just pushes the rotary against the face of the slide as hard as he can.

Q: It goes into it with a jolt?

A: Yes sir. And then when the wheel quits throwing the snow out, he will back away from it again, and then go at it the same way again.

Even this dogged approach, painstaking as it was, yielded only limited results. "The progress was so slow," fireman Floyd Stanley Funderburk later reported, "that we only made six to eight inches in the drift every time the rotary would come in."

This was hard, brutal, unrelenting work. Choked by steam and coal smoke, deafened by the roar of the engines, and buffeted this way and that by the repeated collision of unstoppable force and immovable object, crews would be worn out after a few hours of this grueling labor. And yet they had been at it for days on end. O'Neill had to be wondering how much longer they could all go on.

For at least the temporary snow shovelers, the answer to that question was becoming obvious. "Almost impossible to get them to work," O'Neill would report of the shovelers in one of his Saturday telegrams. The going rate of fifteen cents an hour for temporary gang work apparently did not inspire these men with much company loyalty, and they were at times pointedly refusing to lift a shovel, forcing the trainmen to shovel down the slides on their own. Left to his own judgment, O'Neill might have been willing to hike their wages at least temporarily, but he was familiar with Chairman Hill's well-publicized feelings about worker blackmail. So he knew that handling this situation would require considerable delicacy. If pushed too far, these temporary employees would be gone in an instant. Unfortunately, this meant pushing his more loyal employees even harder.

Toward evening, when they had worked through about half of the slide at Snowshed 3.3, the engines and the west-facing rotary began to

A view of Wellington in summer, around 1910, with the avalanche slope visible straight ahead. Established in the early 1890s, when the Great Northern first built its line through the wilds of the Cascade Mountains, the town existed solely to serve trains coming through the Cascade Tunnel on their way to and from Seattle. *(Courtesy of the Museum of History & Industry, Seattle)*

James H. O'Neill, superintendent of the Great Northern's Cascade Division, in 1910. A railroader through and through, he had begun his career as a thirteen-year-old water boy and had since worked his way up through the ranks. At the time of this photo, he was thirty-seven years old and in charge of all GN operations in the western half of Washington State. He was directly responsible for the fate of the two trains stranded at Wellington. *(Courtesy of the University of Washington Libraries, Special Collections, Curtis17474)*

O'Neill, in white shirt and vest, as a water boy with a railroad work gang in the Dakota Territory, circa 1886. *(Courtesy of Jeanne Patricia May)*

BELOW LEFT: O'Neill as a youth. In order for the underaged boy to work as a brakeman, his parents had to formally indemnify the railroad of all liability in case of accident. *(Courtesy of Jeanne Patricia May)*

BELOW RIGHT: Berenice McKnight, whom O'Neill married in October 1908. A gifted painter and pianist from a prominent Montana family, Berenice was better educated, better connected, and fourteen years younger than her husband, but their marriage was one of unusual closeness. *(Courtesy of Jeanne Patricia May)*

The Great Northern's founder and chairman, James J. Hill, was called the Empire Builder of the Northwest. Often regarded as the last of the great railroad barons, the irascible, indomitable Hill had taken a small, bankrupt Minnesota railway line and turned it into one of the premier railroad empires in the country. *(Courtesy of the James J. Hill Reference Library, Louis W. Hill Papers)*

A rotary snowplow and its crew. Pushed by one or two trailing locomotives, rotaries were the state-of-the-art snow-fighting machines of their day. Under normal winter conditions, a fleet of six could usually keep even the GN's notoriously snowy Cascade crossing open to traffic. *(J. D. Wheeler Photograph, courtesy of the Robert Kelly Collection)*

A rotary on the job in Tumwater Canyon, east of the Cascade Tunnel. Work gangs accompanying the plow would often have to shovel snow by hand down to a depth of thirteen feet, the maximum that the plow's rotating blades could handle. *(Courtesy of the Robert Kelly Collection)*

Edward "Ned" Topping, a traveling salesman for an Ohio-based hardware manufacturer, was a passenger aboard the ill-fated Seattle Express. Still mourning the recent deaths of his wife and unborn daughter, he was writing a day-by-day account of the Wellington crisis for his mother. The letter was found in the wreckage of the train after the avalanche. *(Courtesy of John Topping)*

Alfred B. Hensel, known as "A.B." to family and friends, was one of the mail clerks on the trapped Fast Mail train. On the early morning of March 1, shortly before the avalanche, he moved his bedding from one end of the second-class mail car to the other to find a more comfortable sleeping place. As a result, he was the only mail clerk to survive. *(Courtesy of Dolores Hensel Yates)*

"Dead Man's Slide," with the Scenic Hot Springs Hotel visible below. In the two days before the avalanche, several groups of passengers and railroaders escaped by sliding—at great risk to themselves—from the upper rail line to the hotel. Later, the dead and some of the injured were evacuated from Wellington down this slope. *(Courtesy of John Topping and the Robert Kelly Collection)*

Hotel Bailets → The morning after the avalanche at Wellington, Wash.

The Hotel Bailets (a.k.a. Bailets Hotel), where the passengers ate their meals while stranded at Wellington. Although its location was considered more vulnerable to avalanches than that of the passing tracks on which the trains stood, the hotel was left undamaged by the slide. (Note: The words "Hotel Bailets" on the roof were physically added to the photograph.) *(Courtesy of the Robert Kelly Collection)*

Wellington, just after the avalanche. The overhead catenary wires, badly damaged in the slide, were what powered Wellington's four GE electric locomotives. The smokeless "electrics" could pull trains through the Cascade Tunnel without the asphyxiation danger created by the polluting steam engines. *(Courtesy of the University of Washington Libraries, Special Collections, Curtis17481-1)*

Superintendent O'Neill inspects the wreckage of a railroad car at the avalanche scene. Many of the cars were deeply buried, but the remnants of a few lay near the surface, scattered over acres and acres of steep, treacherous terrain. *(Courtesy of the University of Washington Libraries, Special Collections, Curtis17469)*

Workers among the wreckage. Rescue and recovery efforts were complicated by the vast amount of timber and other debris brought down by the avalanche. At times, rescuers had to dive into the wreckage to pull victims out "as if taking them from a river." (PHOTOGRAPH ABOVE: *J. D. Wheeler Photograph, courtesy of the Robert Kelly Collection;* PHOTOGRAPH BELOW: *J. A. Juleen Photograph, courtesy of the Everett Public Library)*

Avalanche fatalities lying in the snow. Once recovered and—if possible—identified, the bodies of the dead were wrapped in brown-and-white checked GN blankets and lined up to await removal. *(Courtesy of the Museum of History & Industry, Seattle)*

Tied to rugged Alaskan sleds, bodies were evacuated down the right-of-way in groups of a dozen at a time. Each sled was maneuvered by four men with ropes, two ahead and two behind. Once they reached the top of Dead Man's Slide near Windy Point, they were lowered by rope to a train waiting at Scenic below. *(J. D. Wheeler Photograph, courtesy of the Robert Kelly Collection)*

Some injured survivors were able to hike down to Scenic. Here, several injured men, their heads heavily bandaged, emerge from a nearly buried snow shed, led by rescuers and what appear to be newspapermen. The figure near the center of the group (with crooked arm holding a walking stick) may be Superintendent O'Neill. *(Courtesy of the Jerry Quinn Collection)*

A view looking northeast from the avalanche track back to Wellington, showing how the depot (center) and the hotel (left) narrowly escaped destruction. The wrecked structure to the west of the depot is probably part of an electrician's cabin. *(J. A. Juleen Photograph, courtesy of the Everett Public Library)*

Several of the injured survivors, along with their nurses and assorted Wellington residents, gather for a group portrait outside the enginemen's bunkhouse, which served as a makeshift hospital after the avalanche. *(Courtesy of the Wenatchee Valley Museum & Cultural Center)*

Dr. A. W. Stockwell, the physician in charge of the bunkhouse hospital, holds seven-year-old Raymond Starrett. When pulled from the wreckage, the boy had a thirty-inch wood splinter lodged in the skin of his forehead. Since Dr. Stockwell was not yet present on the night of the avalanche, Wellington telegrapher Basil Sherlock removed the splinter with a shaving razor. *(Courtesy of the Wenatchee Valley Museum & Cultural Center)*

The first through train reached Wellington on March 12, eleven days after the avalanche. Another slide early the next morning toppled a rotary off the mountain, killing a workman and closing the line yet again. Regular traffic did not resume until March 15. *(J. D. Wheeler Photograph, courtesy of the Robert Kelly Collection)*

The Wellington passing tracks after being cleared by a rotary plow. The height of the walls on either side gives some indication of the sheer volume of snow that had to be removed to open the line. *(J. D. Wheeler Photograph, courtesy of the Robert Kelly Collection)*

Salvage efforts went on for months after the avalanche. Most of the wooden train cars were totally annihilated ("as if an elephant had stepped on a cigar box," as one witness put it), but the much heavier locomotives suffered surprisingly little damage. *(Courtesy of the Jerry Quinn Collection)*

An older James H. O'Neill (second from left) joins other officials for the opening of the GN's New Cascade Tunnel on January 12, 1929. This much lower tunnel enabled the Great Northern to eliminate miles and miles of steep, avalanche-prone track between Berne in the east and Scenic in the west. Stations like Wellington (renamed "Tye" after the disaster) and the old Cascade Tunnel Station were dismantled and allowed to return to their natural state. *(Courtesy of the University of Washington Libraries, Special Collections, Pickett4203)*

The abandoned Wellington site, circa 1930, with only the depot and the concrete snow shed (built after the slide) remaining to mark the spot. Today, the depot is long gone and the site is deeply forested once again. The concrete snow shed remains, a fitting monument to the Wellington dead. *(Courtesy of Warren Wing and the Robert Kelly Collection)*

run low on coal and water. Stopping work, O'Neill ordered the plow train back to Wellington to refuel. This would at least allow some of the men to flop down on the floor of the rotary and doze. But whether they'd be able to scrape up enough coal in Wellington to refill the tenders was very much an open question. With the coal chute now all but empty and the extra engines on the sidetrack already plundered at least once, O'Neill was running out of places to look for extra fuel.

Then, halfway back to Wellington, about a mile and a half from the coal chute, the rotary ran into yet another problem—and it was a major one. "We started back toward Wellington to get more coal," brakeman Earl Duncan recalled, "and found a slide behind us, just west of [Snowshed 2.2]. This was about 900 feet long and 30 feet deep, and full of snags and green timber."

This latest slide, as O'Neill understood instantly, was a truly devastating blow. Even if they'd had enough coal left on the rotaries, a slide so large and so thickly littered with timber would take at least forty-eight hours to work through. Without access to more fuel, this was clearly going to be impossible.

For the first time that week, superintendent O'Neill had to admit that he was beaten. The double rotary—his last real hope for clearing the main line off the mountain—had become useless. It was now obvious to him that those two trains at Wellington weren't going anywhere until outside help arrived. After days and days of punishing, nonstop work, those trains, and all the people aboard them, were now truly stranded, and for how long he could not even guess.

Ordering the double rotary back to a safe place on the mountain, O'Neill assigned four men to remain behind and keep the engines alive. Then he and the rest of the crews headed back to Wellington on foot, trudging wearily through the rain and the shrieking wind.

✧

Q: Was there ever a time, up to the evening of the 26th, when you did not expect to get the train through within twelve to twenty-four hours?

A: No sir, [there] was not a time.

Q: When did you first give up hope of getting it through in some such time as that?

A: On the night of the 26th. . . . That was the night that tied us up.

—James H. O'Neill

Wellington
Saturday Evening

Sometime after supper on Saturday, several of the passengers decided to call another meeting in the observation car. The impetus this time came from the attorney Edgar Lemman. His wife Ada's condition was only getting worse, and he was eager to do whatever he could to relieve her anxiety.

"Mr. Lemman came back [to the observation car] with a solemn look on his face and a number of people following him," John Rogers would later recall. "They seated themselves, and [Lemman] gravely arose and said, 'Now, to the point, gentlemen. . . .'"

What followed was, in Rogers's words, "a very peculiar meeting"—a curiously formal proceeding amid the cigar smoke and boardroom-like appointments of the observation car—during which little was ultimately decided. According to accounts by several men who were playing cards there that night, the discussion focused mainly on the issue of moving the train back into the tunnel. Some members of the group also wanted to ask O'Neill about the feasibility of transporting a doctor up from Scenic to look after the sick passengers. At one point the men tried to elect Solomon Cohen as their chairman, but he refused to serve. "With that refusal," Rogers observed, "the meeting seemed to pass away into nothing, and so nothing was accomplished."

The appearance of Joseph Pettit in the observation car seems to have revived the conversation. The conductor had been trying to accommodate the passengers as best he could, bringing them buckets full of melted snow for their drinking water and carrying hot food from the hotel to the shut-ins on board, but this time he had bad news to impart—namely, that the coal supply had now run out entirely. In other words, even if the tracks behind the train could be cleared (which they couldn't), even if the tunnel were a better, safer place for the train (which it wasn't), and even if the single engine remaining on the Seattle Express could manage to haul the train upgrade to the tunnel (which it couldn't), there was now insufficient fuel available at Wellington to accomplish the job. According to one eyewitness, Pettit claimed that "if they burned up the coal to get up steam enough to push the train back there, why, he was afraid that they would not have enough to heat the coaches."

This argument still failed to persuade some members of the passenger committee. It seemed preposterous to them that there was not enough coal in all of Wellington to move a single train several hundred yards upgrade. Again they requested to see superintendent O'Neill. Pettit agreed to go and look for him, but he returned a short time later, saying that the superintendent was still out working with the double rotary. By this time, moreover, the lawyers Jesseph and Merritt had joined the meeting, and both of them were adamantly against bothering O'Neill with these grievances. "I did all I could to keep down any protest that was attempted once or twice to get out and send to the Superintendent," Jesseph admitted. "I did not believe that the Superintendent or the trainmen or the shovelers or anybody else in there could have done any more than they were doing under the circumstances."

This second meeting therefore trailed off as inconclusively as the first had. No one seemed capable of settling on any definite course of action whatsoever. It was as if time itself had come to a halt, stranding the passengers in a limbo of helplessness. "Everyone who was on the trains was in a state of quandary," Rogers would later recall. "Their minds seemed to be bewitched, as . . . in the legend of Sleepy Hollow. I know that I myself scarcely knew what to do."

In truth, there was nothing that the passengers realistically could do—at least not until morning, when they would have a full day in which to act. Some were determined to follow the striking laborers off the mountain on foot, no matter how dangerous the trip might be. Others were content to trust the judgment of the Great Northern Railway and stay put. A few still clung to hopes of somehow getting the train moved back to the tunnel. Perhaps the only thing they all agreed on at that moment was the sentiment expressed by Ned Topping in his letter that night. "If I ever make this [*indecipherable*] trip again it will be in the summer or fall," he wrote, the strain of imprisonment apparently affecting even the legibility of his handwriting. "This is the fourth day and it seems like a month."

9

The Empire Builder Looks On

He is a calculating machine. He knows nothing of sentiment in business. Susceptible as he is to appeals to his own pocket, he never permits an invested nickel to be diverted from its duty of making more nickels.

—Seattle Post-Intelligencer
on James J. Hill

Sunday, February 27, 1910
St. Paul, Minnesota

The events unfolding in the Cascade Mountains were not meanwhile going unnoticed in the rest of the country. The massive storm system terrorizing the entire Pacific Northwest had become national news, monitored by newspaper readers from the East Coast to California. One person in particular was following the developments with a uniquely proprietary eye. James J. Hill, now seventy-one years of age, was no longer president of the railroad he'd created, but he was still its chairman. Already fabled in the industry for taking an active part in the daily operations of his company, he was now preparing to take an even more hands-on role than usual. Just the night before, his son Louis, the Great Northern's president ever since the elder Hill's resignation in 1907, had left with his family on a six-week vacation to California. In Louis's absence, the Empire Builder himself was going to sit in for him. With the railroad's main line to the West Coast locked down for the foreseeable future—disrupting freight and passenger traffic as well as delivery of the all-important U.S. mail—Hill was doubtless anticipating a rough few weeks.

The seventeen years since the completion of the Great Northern's transcontinental line had been good to James J. Hill. His railroad empire had expanded steadily and inexorably, growing into one of the half dozen or so largest railroad networks in the country. Thanks to a frugal management philosophy and an unerring instinct for strategic acquisition, the former steamship clerk now controlled upwards of 20,000 miles of track in three major American railway systems (including roughly 7,000 in the Great Northern, 5,000 in the Northern Pacific, and 8,000 in the Burlington system). As one writer put it in 1907, "If the three [Hill] lines were placed end to end in a single track, they would reach from Seattle, across the continent, across the Atlantic, across Europe and Asia, to the eastern shores of China, where one might take one of Hill's big Pacific line steamers and complete the trip to Seattle."

By 1910, moreover, Hill's fame and influence had reached far beyond the realm of transportation. He was practically an American institution by now. One of the last of the great railroad titans, he consulted with presidents, influenced trade and agricultural policy, and expounded regularly in the national media on everything from animal husbandry to international politics.

Yet for all his eminence, in recent years Hill had been finding it necessary to defend his achievements against an increasingly hostile American public. As Hill saw it, the nineteenth century's noble virtues of individual enterprise and bold, visionary entrepreneurship had come under broad attack in the new century. Average Americans seemed to find only fault with the railroad industry and its leaders. Where once the Great Northern had been hailed as the economic savior of an entire region, it was now being reviled as something more like its economic demon.

Considering the enthusiasm with which railroads were first welcomed in many parts of the country—particularly in the West—the story of their fall from grace is especially disheartening. Once the general public had realized that railroads were not a ticket to automatic economic success, disenchantment had set in with a vengeance. As late as 1872, a railway brakeman could still make the claim that "any railroad man was popular. The railroad meant prosperity to the community, and this reflected back in goodwill upon all railroad employees." But by the end of the following decade, the romance with the rails had largely soured. As historian Robert H. Wiebe has written: "By the eighties [the railroads] had alienated a remarkable range of Americans: the farmer saw them as the arrogant manipulator of his profit, the small-town entrepreneur as the destroyer of his dreams, the city businessman as the sinister ally of his competitors, the labor leader as a model of the callous, distant employer, and the principled gentleman as the source of unscrupulous wealth and political corruption."

For this alienation of affection the railroads had no one to blame but themselves. Numerous financial scandals in the mid- to late nineteenth century, combined with rate and fare structures that struck many as arbitrary, inconsistent, exorbitant, and often downright vindictive, had eroded the public's initial goodwill. The railroad barons themselves, meanwhile, were increasingly often perceived as arrogant opportunists who had enriched themselves at the expense of the communities their railroads were supposed to serve. As one dyspeptic latter-day observer would put it, the men who ran the railroads were little more than "buccaneers who took a positive delight in throttling the public interest, dragging it down a dark alley, raping it, and leaving it for dead."

Whether this depiction of the so-called robber barons is accurate or hopelessly wrongheaded and biased (as some revisionist historians now claim), it is undeniably true that they were, as Stewart Holbrook has deftly suggested, men more noteworthy for their abilities than for their morals. In any case, the resentment against them eventually reached epidemic proportions, culminating most vividly in the publication of that orgy of anti-railroad indignation, Frank Norris's 1901 novel *The Octopus*. According to Norris, the railroad was "a vast power, huge, terrible . . . leaving blood and destruction in its path." The fact that the novel's sensationalistic plot was based on actual historical events—the Southern Pacific's bloody conflict with wheat farmers in the 1880 Mussel Slough tragedy—lent an air of credence to this indictment. To Norris—and to an increasing number of disillusioned Americans—the railroad had become nothing less than "the soulless force, the ironhearted power, the monster, the colossus, the octopus."

This was, needless to say, an exaggeration. And certainly there had been plenty of attempts over the years to fight the railroads' growing power. Not long after the Civil War, several state and local legislatures had taken arms against the industry, using a weapon rarely employed in that laissez-faire era: governmental regulation. With the passage of the Granger Laws of the 1870s, legislators had tried to impose controls on railroad operations and end discriminatory practices.

These attempts, however, had proved short-lived. As an inherently interstate business (and one rich enough to hire very able lawyers), the railroad industry had been successful in overturning these early laws in the courts. The first real federal attempts at regulation—in particular, the creation of the Interstate Commerce Commission in 1887—had also been hampered by well-funded legal harassments. ("Hoh, yes, the Interstate Commerce Commission," an anti-railroad farmer remarks scornfully in The Octopus. "The greatest Punch and Judy show on earth.") But as the new century began, laws to give the ICC some bite were eventually passed. The Hepburn Act of 1906 empowered the agency not only to regulate but also, to an extent, to set actual rates and fares, a power that was further augmented by the Mann-Elkins Act of 1910 (which was a few months from passage as the Seattle Express stood stranded in the snow at Wellington).

Naturally, such laws infuriated Jim Hill, who attributed their passage to the influence of "a lot of doctrinaires . . . mainly either politicians seeking office or college tack-head philosophers and preachers." To his way of thinking, all of this hostility toward the railroads was just so much political grandstanding. "It really seems hard," he wrote in 1902, "when we look back at what we have done in opening the country and carrying at the lowest rates, that we should be compelled to fight political adventurers who have never done anything but pose and draw a salary."

One such political adventurer was Hill's special nemesis. President Theodore Roosevelt, a man with a strength of personality to match even that of the Empire Builder himself, clashed with Hill in a confrontation that came to be emblematic of this new attitude toward the railroads and other big businesses. Shortly after rising to the presidency upon William McKinley's assassination in 1901, Roosevelt had decided that it was time to do something about the increasing power of the enormous trusts and holding companies that had been multiplying at an alarming rate in the final years of the Gilded Age. "The conscience of business had to be aroused," Roosevelt would later explain. "The authority of the government over big as well as small had to be asserted." Whether his subsequent efforts were motivated by true moral rectitude or by cynical political opportunism, the results were to be enormously troublesome for the so-called Moses of the Northwestern Wilderness. For the trust that Roosevelt chose to bust first was that great octopus of the Northwest—the vast and ever-growing railway empire of James J. Hill.

Roosevelt's attack took the form of a federal lawsuit against an attempted combination of Hill's three major railroad systems—the Great Northern, the Northern Pacific, and the Burlington—under the umbrella of a separate entity called the Northern Securities Company. This combination, which was the brainchild of Hill, E. H. Harriman, J. Pierpont Morgan, and the Rockefeller interests, would have created a holding company so enormous (second in size only to U.S. Steel) as to be all but impervious to corporate raiding. The deal was hardly easy in the making. In a struggle between Hill and Harriman over the Northern Pacific and the Burlington early in 1901, the two titans caused a stock-market panic that only Morgan's millions were able to reverse. Compromise was eventually reached, however, and on November 13, 1901, the world first learned of this mighty thing that Hill and his associates had made. As a writer subsequently quipped in the magazine *Life*: "God made the World in 4004 B.C., but it was reorganized in 1901 by James J. Hill, J. Pierpont Morgan, and John D. Rockefeller."

Even if God had no objection to this reorganization of His world, however, Theodore Roosevelt did. Believing Northern Securities vulnerable to attack, the president instructed his attorney general to file suit against the combination under the auspices of the Sherman Anti-Trust Act. The reaction from Hill was predictable: He wanted to fight. The barbarian hordes of government regulators, led by their yawping chieftain in the White House, were not about to tell Jim Hill how to run his own railroads. So whereas Morgan and Harriman were inclined to settle the case, the Empire Builder was adamant, determined to do battle with what he regarded as "the newly established court at Washington, with all its tinsel and red-stockinged and gilded flunkies."

The Northern Securities case ultimately went on for two years, occupying so much of Hill's attention that his family and associates began to worry aloud about his obsessive preoccupation with it. But his long fight was to no avail. The suit was eventually upheld by the Supreme Court, and the combination was duly undone. Hill, chastened but unbowed, tried to make light of the setback. ("The three railroads are still there," he would later say, "earning good money.") And there are some historians—Hill's biographer Albro Martin among them—who maintain that Roosevelt chose Northern Securities as a target since busting it would make him look like a crusading reformer while not doing much actual harm to capitalist interests. Still, the suit did achieve at least one objective: encouraging the nation, as Richard Hofstadter has put it, "to feel at last that the President of the United States was really bigger and more powerful than Morgan and the Morgan interests, that the country was governed from Washington and not from Wall Street."

For Hill, the case was a grim lesson in the new politics of the Progressive Era. He still had control of his three railroads, but (to quote railroad historian Kurt Armbruster) "he would henceforth find Uncle Sam in the fireman's seat." At least Hill could console himself with the thought that the much-despised Roosevelt was finally gone from the White House. By February 1910, the ex-president was about as safely out of the way as he could be, on a hunting safari in Africa (where, as Morgan famously remarked, "I trust some lion will do its duty").

Not that Roosevelt's successor was much better. William Howard Taft, who had assumed the presidency in 1909, may have been a man more to Hill's conservative tastes, but he was, by Hill's lights, "a platter of mush, a jellyfish," too likely to be influenced by grandstanding reformers unfriendly to big business. This new president was also proving dangerously susceptible to foolishness in a matter that was to turn quite troublesome for Hill over the next few weeks—namely, a three-month-old strike of railway switchmen that may have played a larger role in creating the Wellington crisis than anyone in the company would ever afterward admit.

✧

Their strike is a modern repetition, in the industrial field, of the little band of 300 Greeks of ancient times, standing off the countless hordes of Persians at the Pass of Thermopylae.

—Seattle Union Record,
on the switchmen's strike

The ongoing switchmen's strike was probably not the main thing on Hill's mind as he took up the reins of the company in his son's absence. Certainly there was plenty of other pressing business for him to be thinking about (including talk of a possible firemen's strike that would make the switchmen's walkout look like a mere inconvenience). Whether or not Hill realized it, though, the controversy with the switchmen was soon to provoke—or at least exacerbate—a major public relations fiasco connected to the mess at Stevens Pass. With the idling of those four rotaries and the near-total exhaustion of the coal supply at Wellington, certain questions would inevitably be raised about the company's preparedness for such a crisis. Specifically, the missed delivery of extra coal that now sat in the Leavenworth yard was bound to be cited as an indication of how the railroad's refusal to deal fairly with the switchmen had hindered its operations. After all, while the responsibility for getting those four cars of coal to Wellington may have been that of the chief dispatcher, the actual work of attaching them to a westbound train would have been a switchman's job.

The strike had begun some three months earlier, on November 30, 1909. The switchmen's demands had been relatively modest—a six-cent-per-hour raise, along with a few other concessions. From the very start, though, the Great Northern had been rigid in its refusal to entertain such a notion. "We will fight," president Louis Hill had announced at the outset of the conflict. "We carried the men through the financial depression [of 1907] without a cut in pay. Every five years or so we have to meet this question and now it is time to settle."

Negotiations were energetic, but neither side proved willing to compromise, and so the union went out. Not all of the GN's switchmen honored the strike, but enough did to force high company officials— including superintendent O'Neill himself—to leave their offices and help out in yards throughout the western divisions. And though rail traffic throughout the West was severely crippled for several days, the Great Northern soon had matters well in hand.

"We are getting in better shape every hour," general manager J. M. Gruber announced to the papers on December 4. "New men are going to work right along. In fact, we now have more men in St. Paul and Minneapolis than we need. We will ship some of them tonight to Seattle and Tacoma, the only two points on the system where they are needed. The paralysis of traffic is practically over."

In the months since then, the striking switchmen had been hanging on, but barely. Sporadic violence had broken out, once even in Leavenworth, but the railroad was making do, using strikebreakers and other scab labor to get the job done. Chairman Hill, for his part, was adding fuel to the conflagration by mocking the alleged inadequacy of workers' wages: "Half the problem of the high cost of living lies in the discretion of the housewife," he told reporters in New York in January. "If a housewife, instead of standing in front of the telephone to order the family supplies, would go to market and learn what foods are cheapest and what are dear, there would be less of this kind of talk. As I have said before, the high cost of living is the cost of living high." This comment may not quite qualify as a 1910 version of "Let them eat cake," but it does show a distinctly unsympathetic attitude toward labor in a season of suddenly rising prices (and at a time when the GN was experiencing its most profitable year ever).

Certainly Hill's railroad had throughout its history earned a reputation as a less than generous employer. The Great Northern was reviled among railroaders for charging high boarding rates while at the same time paying below-average wages. Hill, who claimed to believe that "organized labor is socialistic," had a straightforward philosophy about wages: they were to be set at the sole discretion of management, with absolutely no interference from outside sources such as national unions. "Why," he once famously remarked, "should I have to pay a fireman six dollars a day for work that a Chinaman would do for fifty cents?"

Hill had paid for this anti-labor attitude more than once over the years. Shortly after the line through Stevens Pass had been completed in 1893, for instance, Hill had used a spreading nationwide depression as an opportunity to cut wages no fewer than three times over the space of seven months. This had prompted a strike against the Great Northern that eventually became so disruptive that Hill called on President Grover Cleveland to send in federal troops to restore order. Cleveland refused (unlike in the soon-to-follow Pullman strike) and the issues at stake were eventually resolved by arbitration, but not before the strike had generated plenty of animosity toward the defiant Hill. "It would be a fitting climax," one bitter correspondent wrote to him afterward, "if you should be taken by your employees and *hung* by the neck till dead, from one of the triumphal arches so recently erected at the expense of the very people you are now defrauding of their hard earnings. . . . I send this to your wife in order that it may strike you in your home."

By 1910, of course, Hill was no longer as closely involved in the GN's labor conflicts, having given up the president's post three years earlier. But with the current president now making his way toward the Casa Lomo Hotel in Redmond, California, the aging chairman would find himself once again dealing with the labor problems his policies had created. Although there had been signs in recent weeks that the switchmen were near capitulation in their strike, the current crisis in the Cascades was apparently giving them a new issue with which to rejuvenate their cause. Within days, the press committee of the switchmen's union would be taking advantage of the situation, publishing broadsides in the Seattle *Union Record* attributing the long entrapment of train No. 25's passengers to the deranging effects of the strike. In an attempt to lift the blockade before it got any worse, general manager J. M. Gruber was planning to head west to Washington

State that very morning to try to assist superintendent O'Neill in person. With him would go some of the top operating officials in the company, including G. H. Emerson, the superintendent of traffic and motive power. Along the way, they would also pick up scores of extra men and several trainloads of extra equipment—whatever was required to get the railroad moving again.

Regardless of how the crisis was eventually resolved, however, the Great Northern was not likely to emerge from the situation in the Cascades with its reputation unscathed, and this could not have been a pleasant prospect to the old man at 240 Summit Avenue in St. Paul. At seventy-one, James J. Hill had to be thinking about the legacy he would be leaving upon his death. That legacy, while certainly as impressive as ever, had been damaged more than once recently in the eyes of the public. He would not have wanted his railroad's name—or its sacred bottom line—to sustain any more harm.

10

Ways of Escape

PASSENGERS ARE STILL HELD FAST

An additional twenty men were dispatched from Everett today to fight the snow that continues blockading traffic on the Cascade Division of the Great Northern, making an army of more than 400 laborers and skilled rotary plowmen now pitting their strength against the worst storm that has visited the Cascade Range for years.

—Everett Daily Herald

Sunday, February 27, 1910
Wellington
Morning

On Sunday morning the Reverend James M. Thomson, an Irish-born Presbyterian minister from Bellingham, held a church service on one of the day coaches of the Seattle Express. Understandably, the impromptu worship drew a large congregation of both passengers and railroaders, packed shoulder to shoulder in the airless, much-lived-in coach.

"Quite a number present," old Mrs. Covington wrote with approval in her diary, taking note of "the reading of Psalm 17 and 27, songs and preaching." That the reverend chose to organize his service around two such fortifying Psalms ("The Lord is my light and salvation; whom shall I fear? The Lord is the strength of my life; of whom shall I be afraid?") is perhaps significant. With the storm howling outside as wildly as ever, some spiritual reinforcement among those trapped at Wellington was certainly in order. And when the service culminated with a strangely beautiful rendition of "To the Holy City"—sung by what one Pullman porter called "a rough-looking fellow with a fine bass voice"—the effect was cathartic. "It helped those in need," brakeman Ross Phillips later recalled of the service, "for a time."

For a time. But that time was soon past, and it wasn't long before discontent was again seething among the passengers. Edgar Lemman and several other men went looking for O'Neill after the service, but the superintendent had disappeared yet again. The previous night's slide at Snowshed 2.2 had taken down the telegraph wires, so O'Neill had been forced to hike down to Scenic early that morning to find a working key. Although the superintendent's trip had been unavoidable, the passenger delegation couldn't help feeling that their concerns were simply not being taken seriously by those in charge.

Meanwhile, news of the failure of rotaries both east and west had by now reached the passengers. Sometime on Saturday night they'd learned of the trapping of the double on the west slope near Snowshed 2.2; but by this morning they'd also heard about the stranding of the single rotary on the east slope. Harrington, Clary, and a dozen other men from the X801 were now at Wellington, having spent most of Saturday on a monstrously arduous trek back from Gaynor to Cascade Tunnel Station. A trip of only nine miles, it had consumed hours in the storm-lashed night, each man taking turns breaking trail in the deep snow that had fallen in the brief interval since their own rotary's last run. The effort had nearly finished the already fatigued men. "As soon as I got into the depot [at Cascade Tunnel Station] I was completely exhausted," Clary would later recall. "I just fell on the floor and I slept there for about 8 hours with my rain clothes on, boots and everything else." For the passengers, the presence of these men at Wellington this morning was an ominous sign, bearing mute testimony to the hopeless blockage of the line in both directions. Even conductor Pettit was no longer talking about an imminent escape from the mountain.

These new setbacks seemed to call for some sort of concerted response from the passengers, but no one could decide what that response should be. "Everybody was making suggestions and plans of their own," Henry White would later recall. They were "talking over the matter independent[ly] with the conductor and anybody they could meet—it was the only topic of conversation."

One female passenger—Libby Latsch, the fashionable young hair-accessories entrepreneur—came up with the idea of going over O'Neill's head. According to White, "She made the suggestion that we wire the Chamber of Commerce, or the newspapers, or somebody of importance in Seattle. . . . She thought if there was anybody who was influential enough on the train, we ought to do that." There were no immediate volunteers, and in any case the telegraph wires were down at the time. So White merely patronized her: "I assured her, more to calm her than anything else, that just the minute the wires were up . . . I would wire my house and get them busy in the matter."

Other passengers, less willing to wait for outside assistance, began exploring further the possibility of hiking out. Solomon Cohen, who had originated the idea, talked about it with locomotive engineer Antony Blomeke. The engineer offered to guide Cohen and another passenger down the mountain, but insisted that the trip would require significant effort on their part. "I told them I would not carry them out," Blomeke later explained. He also assured Cohen that they were perfectly safe on the passing tracks, but "if they wanted to come up and sleep in the bunkhouse at Wellington where I stayed, that they were welcome to it."

Certain Wellington residents were more emphatic in discouraging any exodus on foot, convinced that spending several hours out on the trail would be far more dangerous than staying put. When asked by passenger George Davis whether it was worth trying to walk out with three-year-old Thelma, one of the engineers on the electric motors, Charles Andrews, advised him not to attempt it. "His chances with the kid," Andrews insisted, "would have been poor."

George Loveberry, the owner of a hay and feed store in Georgetown, Washington, even offered $20 to a local trapper named Robert Schwartz to serve as mountain guide on the trip down. Schwartz demurred, citing a very persuasive reason: Unless the hikers wanted to follow the gradual descent of the railroad tracks the whole way down, which would involve taking a seven-mile detour loop through a long, lightless tunnel, they would have to leave the right-of-way at Windy Point and make a sharp one-thousand-foot descent to Scenic below. The slope in question was too steep to hike down, so they would have to slide to the bottom on their backsides—and probably kill themselves in the process. According to Loveberry, the trapper claimed that "he would not take a bunch of tenderfoots down there for anything."

The urgency of these efforts only increased when the shortage of coal began to hit closer to home. By late Sunday morning it was announced that the remaining locomotive on train No. 25 was down to its very last ton of fuel. If that supply ran out, there would be no heat on the train, and so it was decided that some of the coal from the Fast Mail's engine should be transferred to the Seattle Express. After much digging out of the second passing track, the shorter mail train was shifted just enough so that coal could be shoveled from one engine's tender to the other. This expedient would alleviate the problem for a time, but the implication was clear: The coal would not last forever, and soon the passengers and railroaders might have to scavenge the surrounding mountainside for wood to heat the coaches.

John Merritt, weighing all of these new developments, decided that he didn't like the looks of the situation. He and Lewis Jesseph had been tramping around in the storm all morning, checking the line down the mountain, and had been struck by the extent of the blockage. "I did not figure that they would open that track for three or four weeks," Merritt would later testify. Faced with the prospect of being out of commission for so long, the two lawyers began to feel unbearably restless. Their supreme court hearing may have been history but, as Jesseph explained, "we had a March term of court on at home. . . . I had several [other] cases for trial and I was not prepared to try those cases."

The two lawyers decided, therefore—against all advice to the contrary—to organize an escape party. Over the course of their five-day imprisonment they had become quite intimate with several of their trainmates. According to Merritt, "Mr. Jesseph and I and Mr. Loveberry and a young boy who was going to school at Portland, Mr. Horn, had got very well acquainted with a number of passengers on the train: Mrs. Latsch, and Mr. Barnhart I had known a number of years, and I knew Miss O'Reilly who was a nurse, and we were joking around with them a good deal." This group—probably the "smart set" whose drinking and slang talk Mrs. Covington disapproved of—had often played cards together during the long hours of waiting. They had even started calling each other by nicknames. Libby Latsch was dubbed "the Merry Widow" (probably because her husband, a traveling salesman, was gone so frequently), while Nellie Sharp, the would-be chronicler of the West for *McClure's* magazine, was "the Wild West Girl." John Rogers became known as "Seattle" and R. H. Bethel, with his small white beard, was playfully referred to as "Colonel Cody." Soliciting this group for like-minded others, the lawyers found in Loveberry, at least, a man as desperate to get away as they were. Their resolve was only strengthened when they heard that O'Neill himself had started out on a hike down to Scenic. So while the superintendent would surely have discouraged them if he'd known, the three men decided to follow him down the mountain.

"All the passengers on the train laughed at us," Merritt later reported. "[But] when they saw we were in earnest, they urged us to stay." Some of the women begged the lawyers not to leave, convinced that they would never make it to Scenic. After five days of inaction, though, the men would not be dissuaded. They were getting out: "We returned to the train, packed our bags, delivered them to the porter, instructed him what to do with them on reaching Seattle, and quietly left the train."

✧

Q: Did you have any difficulty in walking to Scenic yourself?
A: Yes sir, we had considerable difficulty.

　　　　　　　　　　　　　　　　　　　　　　　—*James H. O'Neill*

On the Trail to Windy Point
Sunday Morning

At the very least, he had gotten some sleep. In the small hours of Sunday morning—for the first time since the storm had begun on Tuesday—James H. O'Neill had actually been able to peel off his boots and climb into bed for more than a quick hour's nap. In the comfort of his snow-swaddled business car on the coal-chute track, he'd attempted to disengage from the ongoing crisis and retreat for a few hours into oblivion.

Exhausted as O'Neill was, however, he could not have had an easy night's rest. The situation was simply too dire. The stranding of the double rotary on Saturday night, he knew, would require a radical rethinking of his entire time frame for getting the trains to safety. With only one rotary still working on the mountain, freeing the line would now be a matter of days or even longer. Other rotaries were on their way—one from the Northern Pacific's fleet and one from the GN's own Kalispell Division—but until they arrived, the X808 was all he had left to work with.

To make matters even more desperate, O'Neill now had a full-scale revolt of snow shovelers to complicate his calculations. On Saturday night—at his lowest moment, right after losing the double rotary—the extra gangmen had decided to give the superintendent an ultimatum: Either O'Neill would begin paying them fifty cents per hour (an exceedingly high rate for unskilled day labor in 1910) or they would all walk out.

It was a foolish demand, and foolishly timed. Without a working rotary anywhere near Stevens Pass, there was little of significance that the shovelers could do to affect the situation of the two trains at Wellington. They couldn't very well dig out the snowslides by hand, and anything short of that would have made little appreciable difference. Nor was O'Neill—a man who had once faced down three armed robbers on a day coach in Idaho, tossing them bodily off the train—the type of person to back down in a confrontation like this. Although he had later walked into their camp and offered them a raise to twenty cents per hour plus free board, the laborers had stood firm in their demand. "I told them I would not pay it," O'Neill would later report, "and told them to get out."

They had obliged. All but about ten or a dozen laborers had walked off the job, leaving O'Neill with a force barely large enough to keep the switches clear in the Wellington yard.

This walkout of useless snow shovelers, however, was something that O'Neill would have to worry about later. He now had more pressing business down at Scenic, and so, leaving trainmaster Blackburn in charge at Wellington, he buttoned up his heavy cardigan sweater, shouldered into his waterproof slicker, and started off down the mountain. With no prospect of freeing the trains for at least several more days, he knew he had to get emergency supplies up to Wellington to keep the stranded passengers warm and well fed. The relief train from the coast was due to arrive at Scenic that morning, but since there was no working telegraph connection, O'Neill would have to be physically present to deploy its cargo of food, fuel, and men. He would also want to check in with master mechanic J. J. Dowling, to be sure that the all-important X808—his last operational rotary on the mountain— kept working.

These two tasks were mission enough, but there was probably one other objective to O'Neill's Sunday morning journey to Scenic. With no hope of opening the line soon, the superintendent had to be at least considering the drastic measure of evacuating the passengers off the mountain on foot. Obviously, this would be a dangerous proposition, considering the instability of the snow on Windy Mountain and the number of women, children, older people, and invalids to be carried. But the alternative—leaving them all at Wellington for days or even weeks more—was also unthinkable. So O'Neill would surely have wanted to get an idea of the feasibility of a full-scale evacuation. When the storm passed—as it must, eventually—it might be possible, with enough manpower and equipment, to get those people down to safety over the trail.

What O'Neill was experiencing on his own trip down the right-of-way, though, was hardly encouraging. The storm was still howling, its seemingly endless supply of precipitation falling now as a drenching mixture of sleet and rain that rendered the snow slushy and slick beneath his feet. The superintendent had enlisted two men to accompany him, a brakeman named Churchill and a bruiser of a trainman called "Big Jerry" Wickham. Thanks to the latter's prodigious size (he was, as one witness later put it, "a giant . . . broad as a barn door"), Big Jerry was able to cruise through the high drifts with little trouble, but O'Neill and Churchill struggled along behind him. At times they could make no progress at all without scrambling. As O'Neill later explained, "I guess we crawled on our hands and knees for two thousand feet in the soft, heavy snow."

But the newly moistened snowpack was not just more difficult to navigate—it was also more treacherous. Not long after they passed the stalled double rotary, the snowfield above the three men disintegrated into a fast-moving avalanche that came careening down the mountainside without warning. O'Neill and Churchill watched in horror as the slide engulfed the form of Big Jerry Wickham a short distance ahead. Acting quickly, O'Neill sent a man (either Churchill or one of the men from the rotary) scrambling over the slide to see if Wickham had perhaps outrun the falling snow and gotten safely to the other side of the avalanche track. When no trace of the man could be found, they assumed that he must have been knocked from the right-of-way and carried down the side of the mountain. The superintendent was certain the man couldn't have survived.

For O'Neill, this was another hope dashed, another possibility closed. Whatever options he had left for getting those people off the mountain, bringing them down on foot—at least until the rain stopped and the snowpack had stabilized—was not going to be one of them.

✧

That was the most thrilling experience of my life. I was afraid I would never live to tell the story of that journey.

—*John Merritt,*
on the hike down to Scenic

On the Trail to Windy Point
Midmorning Sunday

Shortly after 9:30 A.M. John Merritt, Lewis Jesseph, and George Love-berry set off westward down the railroad right-of-way. With their hats pulled down over their ears and the collars of their overcoats drawn tight around their necks, they at first found the going relatively easy. The rotaries had last cleared these tracks the night before, and only two feet of wet, slushy snow had fallen since. Not far down the line, they came across two other passengers. Edward Rea and Milton Horn, both eighteen, had been on an excursion to see the snowslides and were now on their way back to the trains. When they heard that the three older men were going to attempt to hike out, they decided to go with them. Horn was overdue back at his school in Portland and, according to a let-ter he wrote to his mother, was afraid that if he didn't get out soon, "I never would get there."

Now five in number, the party continued down the mountain, straight into a strong, piercing wind. "The snow was wet and heavy," Jesseph would later report. "It stung our faces and clung to our clothes." When they reached the shelter of the first major snowshed—probably Shed 2—they began to reconsider their decision to leave. "Silently, we stood there [at the far end of the shed], watching the snowflakes fall, and listening to the wind chanting a dirge in the tops of the evergreens. We were debating, each with himself, whether to proceed or return to the train."

"This doesn't look too good to me," Merritt said.

Jesseph was inclined to agree. But Loveberry was absolutely deter-mined to continue, and so they went on, leaving the shelter of the snowshed and stepping out again into the furious storm.

Before long, the five men reached the first of the snowslides blocking the tracks, and it was here that the real difficulties began: "Many times we sank up to our waists," Jesseph later wrote, "struggling desperately to get out and on our way again. Twice Merritt sank up to his armpits. Then his age and weight were heavily against him, but putting up a heroic battle each time, he succeeded. Once, in helping him, I broke through, and we both wallowed in the snow in search of a better footing." Now that they were out in an actual slide, they could understand why the rotaries had had so much trouble clearing them. The snow was ridiculously deep in places, with windblown drifts as high as thirty-five feet. At one place, the men stepped around what they thought was a stump but then recognized, with amazement, as the top of a buried telegraph pole.

On the other side of the avalanche track they encountered the trapped double rotary, its skeleton crew of men keeping the steam engines alive with scavenged wood and melted snow. Here the hikers heard about Big Jerry Wickham's mishap with the avalanche, a story that left them "feeling pretty sad—and, to be honest, pretty thoroughly scared." According to Merritt: "We could look up the mountain as far as we could see . . . and we could look down below, and we did not know what minute the weight of ourselves was going to start a slide that would take us off the side of the mountain and bury the whole bunch of us."

A little farther down the right-of-way, they encountered two linemen who were attempting to repair the telegraph and telephone wires. Refusing to mince words, the linemen warned them that it would mean "instant death" to go any farther. So again the hikers considered turning around, but only for a moment: "Slides that fell after we had passed made it as impossible . . . for us to go back as to go ahead," Merritt explained. "And [so] we took our lives in our hands and started on."

Finally, after almost four hours on the trail, they reached a long snowshed over the tracks near Windy Point. They entered it—the abrupt transition from stormy clangor to cavelike quiet as eerie as a sudden dive underwater—and hiked through the dim, dripping shed to a place where a small escape hole had been cut high on the wall facing the canyon. Rolling up their trouser cuffs, they climbed the wooden scaffolding and peered out of the hole. Far below, the lights of Scenic glowed faintly through the falling snow. The slope seemed even steeper than they had feared, following an avalanche path almost one thousand feet down the side of Windy Mountain. But they knew that this was their only way out, their only feasible escape from the paralysis of the past five days. So they plunged ahead. "We drew our overcoats between our legs," Jesseph wrote, "squatted on our heels, and let go."

Their descent was fast, wet, and anything but controlled and orderly. Partway down, Jesseph and Merritt both lost their balance and began tumbling. If not for the covering of deep avalanche snow that had buried all obstacles, they would surely have collided with a tree or a stump.

After a minute or two of helpless thrashing and rolling, all five slid to a stop at the bottom of the slope—battered and plastered with snow but safe. Getting to their feet, they took a few "thumping drinks" of whiskey from Merritt's hip flask. "Here's to happier days," Merritt toasted grimly, and then they brushed themselves off and trudged the last few hundred yards to the Scenic Hot Springs Hotel.

At the chalet-style resort they found a scene of hectic activity. The relief train from the coast had arrived late that morning, and O'Neill, who had reached Scenic himself by now, was frantically arranging to deploy its cargo of men and supplies. The passengers were also amazed to find Big Jerry Wickham at the hotel—alive, if not quite well. The brawny trainman had somehow survived his fall into the canyon with little more than some cuts and bruises and a dislocated knee, but the story he told of his fall was harrowing.

"I thought, as I was going down, that if I hit one of those trees a little further down it would be the end of Jerry," he said. "But I guess luck was with me, for I sailed between them as clean as a pin, and the next thing I knew I was hanging on the trunk of a tree while the snow and rocks and trees were sliding by me. My clothes were pretty well torn off. I had a knee out of joint and I felt a bit dizzy, but otherwise seemed to be none the worse for the journey."

As soon as he caught his breath, Jerry crawled on hands and knees down to the creek at the foot of the slope. Then he slowly and agonizingly made his way to Scenic. "My knee bothered me a bit, but I put my foot in the crotch of a tree and wrenched it back in shape to go on again."

This tale (particularly the last part of it) may have been embroidered for effect, but it was frightening enough to drive home to Jesseph's group just how lucky they themselves had been. Knowing now the considerable perils of the trip, Merritt found a telegram form and wrote out a message for the people who'd remained behind in Wellington—a message that, because of the downed telegraph wires, would never reach them. Addressed to "Colonel Cody, Wellington," it contained a terse but unambiguous warning: "ARRIVED SAFE. DON'T COME."

For the two lawyers and their companions, however, the ordeal was over. Before dark all five had boarded a small work train headed back toward Skykomish, where they caught another train to the coast. "After a long delay from mudslides caused by coastal rains," Jesseph later wrote, "we arrived in Seattle at midnight Sunday, fourteen hours after leaving the train." He and Merritt would learn the fate of those they'd left behind only later, after the rest of the world did—when the news reached them on a train in Vancouver, Washington, some thirty-six hours later.

✧

4:30 P.M. Cas. Tunnel reports worst day we have had so far: 32°
above, snowing hard all day, about 2' of snow and it is wet snow;
wind has been blowing hard and trees falling all around; can hear
slides coming down.

—J. C. Devery,
Operations Diary

Wellington
Early Sunday Evening

Sometime around 4:30 P.M. the linemen working on the wires near Windy Point restored telegraph and telephone service to Wellington, reconnecting the small station with the outside world. Second-trick operator Basil Sherlock, who had come on duty at 4:00, took the opportunity to make contact with division headquarters. While working at the telegraph key with an Everett-based dispatcher named Carl Johnson, Sherlock saw—through the rain-blurred windows of the small telegraph office—a snowslide roaring down the mountain west of the old switchback. It was the first avalanche Sherlock had ever witnessed as it occurred, and the spectacle alarmed him. He was especially concerned since the slide had come down a slope similar in steepness and forest cover to the one standing above the two trapped trains. "I told dispatcher Johnson about it," Sherlock would later write, "and that I thought the trains were in a bad place."

It should be noted that Sherlock is not the most reliable of witnesses. His unpublished Wellington memoir was written fifty years after the events described, and in it he tends to attribute to himself a heroic competence that strains credibility. But if his account is to be believed, Johnson, after hearing Sherlock's concerns, left the wire open for several minutes and then returned with a message for conductor Joseph Pettit, signed by chief dispatcher G. W. Turner. The telegram, a handwritten version of which still exists, read: "PETTIT: USE EVERY PRECAUTION NECESSARY FOR SAFETY OF PASSENGERS AND IF NECESSARY BACK TRAINS INTO TUNNEL."

This was all but useless advice under the circumstances. There was at this time so much drifted snow on the tracks between the trains and the tunnel that it would have been almost impossible to move the trains even a few hundred feet back from their current position. But Sherlock carried the message to Pettit anyway. Finding him in conversation with several passengers, he pulled the conductor aside and handed him the telegram. "We both walked down the track," Sherlock later reported, "and looked up [at] the mountain [above the trains]. . . . Mr. Pettit said, 'This is putting it right up to me. If I do not move the train and they have a slide, I will be to blame for it. And if I do move the train and they do not have a slide, and I use up all the coal we have moving the train . . . I will be to blame for that."

For Pettit, a man not likely to take such a responsibility lightly, this was an agonizing conundrum. Assessing avalanche danger was well beyond a conductor's normal scope of duty. Even so, the conductor could take comfort in the fact that it was trainmaster Blackburn who was the ranking GN official at Wellington in O'Neill's absence. Any decision to move the train would ultimately have to lie with him and superintendent O'Neill.

It was Blackburn himself who came to the telegraph office later that evening to talk to O'Neill on the telephone. Sherlock heard only Blackburn's side of the conversation, in which (he claims) the trainmaster informed his superior about the passengers' fears of remaining where they were—without mentioning a word about the recent slide on the switchback slope. After some further discussion, the two seemed to come to a decision: "I assume Mr. O'Neill said leave the train where it was," Sherlock wrote. He added, however, that the superintendent was "making his decision when not on the ground, [judging solely] from the way it was put up to him. . . . [I] have often regretted I did not call him back on the telephone and give him my version of the situation."

Even if Sherlock had called O'Neill—not a very plausible scenario, given the relative insignificance of a second-trick telegrapher—the same arguments for keeping the trains on the passing tracks still applied. And the whole issue was largely academic. There was simply too little coal, too little motive power, and too little manpower to make that course of action feasible. For better or worse, the trains were staying where they were.

Back on the cars of the Seattle Express, meanwhile, morale was reaching new lows. "A lady borrowed a phonograph and we had some music," Mrs. Covington wrote in her diary, "but people are getting very blue." Judging from several letters she was writing, the old woman's sense of unease had returned in recent days, stoked by the increasing frequency of slides around them. She was nonetheless putting on a brave front, even comforting Anna Gray and Ada Lemman when they threatened to become hysterical. Only in her diary and letters did she reveal her growing sense of fear and loneliness: "Some of the ladies have children," she wrote, "and I am practically alone."

It did not ease her mind when a second group of passengers started talking of escape on foot. Earlier that evening John Rogers had witnessed the same snowslide that Basil Sherlock had seen. Although it had been a minor slide—one that extinguished itself harmlessly on the empty flat below—it had been impressive enough to convince him of the awesome power of a Cascades avalanche. And there were now other worrying developments to think about. "It was getting warmer,"

Rogers later testified, "and on Sunday night I heard the quaking of timbers. . . . I called my friend's attention to the fact that a slide might occur anywhere."

Perhaps the most ominous portent was a white cornice hanging near the top of one of the surrounding peaks—"an enormous cap of snow hanging precariously on the side and clinging to the sparse timber. . . . The menace of that immense snow cap was a pall on all our spirits," Rogers noted. Although the cornice was not hanging directly above the trains, it was causing serious misgivings among many of the passengers. "It didn't look to me that there was any safe place there [at Wellington]," he concluded. "I knew it was time to act."

So he decided to follow Jesseph and Merritt's lead and hike out the next day. Several others agreed to go with him, but James McNeny, the man he was traveling with, refused. And there were people like Mrs. Covington who had no choice but to remain on the train. Her only conceivable course of action was to pray, which, in her own way, she did, scrawling a few lines of a familiar prayer in her diary: "If I should die before the night, I pray the Lord my work's all right . . ."

Toward midnight, conductor Pettit announced that he himself would be attempting the trip down to Scenic the next morning. Food was running short, and he wanted to personally oversee the delivery of supplies brought in by the relief train. The trip would also give him firsthand knowledge of the condition of the trail, enabling him to judge the feasibility of evacuating the other passengers that way. Lest anyone think he was abandoning them, though, he would attempt to go and return on the same day, so as not to leave his charges alone for a night.

One passenger—R. M. Laville, an electrician from Missoula, Montana—had been trying to decide whether to go out over the trail with the next day's group. After most of the other passengers had already gone to bed, he approached Pettit in the observation car to solicit his advice. The conductor responded by asking him to step outside to the vestibule of the car. As the two men stood together in the cold, rainy night, Pettit gestured toward an ominous-looking break in the snowfield about twenty or thirty feet above the train. He assured Laville, first of all, that the specific break they were looking at was not a serious threat to the train, but said that it was an indication in miniature of what they were likely to encounter on the way down to Scenic. "You can judge from this," he said, "what may be expected out on the trail, where slides usually occur."

No record exists of Laville's reaction to the sight. It's known only that, by the next morning, when Pettit and his party were making ready to leave, Laville was not among them. For whatever reason, the electrician had decided to remain with the train.

11

Last Chances

I felt for quite a while that we were going to get out; we were battling the snow to get out, but I began to see that they could not
battle the clouds away, and I knew, the way my eyes and ears told
me, that I was in a very unsafe place.

—*John Rogers*

Monday, February 28, 1910
Wellington
Morning

For many it was the sound that was most unsettling. Few of the passengers had slept well on Sunday night, and one reason was the eerie,
increasingly frequent rumble of avalanches in the distance. After six
days of heavy precipitation, the surrounding mountains had simply
reached the limit of their capacity to hold any more, and whole snowfields were now losing their grip on the slopes and plummeting into
the canyons below. "All day and night you could hear the reports of
trees being snapped off by snowslides," John Rogers recalled. "And on
Monday morning the overhanging ledge of snow looked almost ready
to tumble."

His resolve of the previous night shaken, Rogers again sought advice
on the pros and cons of braving a hike along the ever more unstable side
of Windy Mountain. It had not escaped him that the increasing danger
of snowslides cut both ways—it magnified the potential danger of either

going or staying. But Rogers could find no consensus among the passengers. One group of Irish mill hands was especially resolute about staying on the train. Having worked in the mountains of Alaska and British Columbia, they felt confident that the trains were in the safest place on the mountain. The fact that scores of railway workers had elected to sleep on the trains' day coaches and mail cars, rather than in their usual quarters east of the station, lent significant weight to this argument. On the other hand, the apparent success of the previous day's hikers was a compelling argument for leaving, and so Rogers wavered. "There were so many different opinions," he said, "a fellow didn't hardly know what to think."

His decision was complicated by the lack of any news about weather and trail conditions elsewhere on the mountain. At 9:40 P.M. the previous night, after being operational for only five short hours, the telegraph wires had gone down again. Without a line of communication to the stations at Scenic and Alvin, the people at Wellington were once more on their own. Anyone hiking down the mountain would be heading out into an unknown situation, with no recent information about what to expect on the trail.

By the end of the morning—perhaps because of the determination of conductor Pettit, whom Rogers knew quite well from previous trips over the Cascades—the real estate man finally made his decision: He would go ahead with his original plan to hike out. Although his companion McNeny disagreed, Rogers felt it futile to wait around for the Great Northern to win its fight against the storm. "The only way to get out of there," he concluded, "was to get out."

At noon a group consisting of Rogers, Pettit, several of the younger passengers, and a handful of other GN employees set out from the trains into the storm. As they were leaving, the ever-professional Libby Latsch handed Rogers a letter, which she asked him to post once he reached "civilization." He agreed, and the letter—addressed to the manager of her hair-accessories business, informing him that she was going to be delayed at least several more days—was tucked away in his pocket to be mailed at Skykomish or Seattle. It would arrive at its destination several days later, its terse, businesslike message tragically obsolete.

Once out on the trail, the group encountered another passenger. Edward W. Boles, a railroad construction worker from Ontario, had been traveling on train No. 25 with his brother Albert and was now trudging around the Wellington yard, trying to expend some restless energy. Seeing the Rogers party heading off, Boles decided to tag along with them, at least for a while. He was eager to get a look at the slides that had been causing the railroad such trouble. So he joined the hikers, intending to return to his brother on the train after a few hours at the most.

Unfortunately, the weather on the trail was even more forbidding than it had been the day before. "It was snowing so badly," according to Rogers, "that I could see only with my right eye." Sunday's late rain and warmer temperatures, however, had apparently melted or washed away enough snow to make passage easier. With conductor Pettit breaking trail for much of the way, this group made much better time over the slides. Even so, it was a frightening experience, with trees cracking in the wind and snow slipping on the slopes all around them. "I did not realize when I started that there was as much danger in going to Scenic as there was," said one of the hikers, H. L. Wertz, who soon regretted his decision to leave the train. "But after I got two-thirds of the way, it was easier to go the other third than to go back."

Here again the most harrowing part of the journey came at the very end—when the hikers had to slide down an avalanche track to Scenic. Leaping from the railroad right-of-way, they dropped down the sheer slope at the speed of a toboggan. One person hit a rock on the way down, and Rogers thought at first that the man had been killed, but the collision was not as serious as it looked: "We all landed in a heap, picked ourselves up, and ran as fast as we could down the road, to avoid the boulders and gigantic snowballs that followed us."

When they reached the Scenic Hot Springs Hotel (Edward Boles still among them, despite his earlier intention not to leave his brother), they were amazed to find that less than an hour and a half had passed since they'd left the trains. This was about one-third as long as it had taken Jesseph's group to cover the same ground, convincing Rogers that conditions on the trail had improved sufficiently over the past twenty-four hours to make a passenger evacuation feasible. The able-bodied men could certainly have gotten out, Rogers later testified, "and I believe that they could have carried out the others"—a notion on which Pettit apparently concurred. Accompanying the conductor to the telegraph office, Rogers watched Pettit write out a telegram to the operator at Wellington: "TELL THE PASSENGERS THEY CAN COME OUT OVER THE TRAIL."

This message, however, did not go through. The wires to Wellington, which had been going in and out of service with maddening frequency, went down just as the Scenic operator was preparing to transmit. Whether or not the telegram's encouraging message would actually have convinced other passengers to make the hike that day is impossible to say. If so, then the failure of the wires at this critical moment was truly fateful for many of those aboard. For by the time conductor Pettit was able to deliver the same message in person, it was already too late in the day for any further evacuation attempts. Anyone wanting to leave would have to wait until Tuesday morning.

As he arranged for the packing in of supplies to Wellington that afternoon, Joseph Pettit's own fate was also in the balance. He was at Scenic now, out of danger and a mere hour or two by train from his home near Everett. With the welfare of a wife and five young children to think about, he could surely have justified at least remaining at Scenic for the duration of the crisis, or even heading home. He had been on duty and under enormous stress for six long days now. If anyone could be said to have done his part in this situation already, it was he.

However, Pettit made his difficult choice with no apparent hesitation: After finishing with his arrangements at Scenic, he left the hotel and started off toward the trail. Rogers accompanied him for a few minutes but soon had to turn back. "I told him that I sympathized with him, because he had a difficult task before him," Rogers remembered. The two men shook hands, and then Rogers watched as his friend began the long, hard climb back up the mountain in the storm.

✧

Q: When did you reach it [the X808]?

A: About noon of the 27th.

Q: And what did you do from then on until the night of the 28th?

A: I rode that machine all that day and all night of the 27th and
the day of the 28th.

—James H. O'Neill

Above Scenic
Monday Afternoon

Sometime on the afternoon of February 28, the X808—the last surviving rotary on the west slope of the GN's Cascade line—stopped working. The problem this time was not coal; with an extra two carloads in
tow, the rotary had fuel enough to last for days. Because of slides that
had come down behind the single rotary on Sunday, however, the plow
had not been able to get back to Scenic for water. Instead, O'Neill and
master mechanic Dowling had ordered the crews to shovel snow into
the tank, where it could be melted with a steam hose. While this
method had worked for a time, the dirt and debris in the melting slush
had eventually clogged the steam engine's injectors. Now the entire
plow had to be idled so that the tank and the injectors could be
cleaned—a job that would take at least several hours.

During those several hours, however, the snow continued falling.
"Wellington, blowing hard, snowing," read the 1:00 P.M. weather report
in the division's operations diary. "2' of new snow." Over the past six days,
in other words, enough new snow had fallen to bury a two-story house. In
places the gusting winds had actually drifted the snow far higher.

For O'Neill, this was now a nightmare that simply refused to end.
Nothing he had seen in his quarter century of railroading in the Rockies
and Cascades had prepared him for such a concentrated and relentless
snowfall. This storm had already utterly overwhelmed five of his rotary
plows and the efforts of hundreds of men. It had killed two people, had
nearly killed a third, and was now threatening the lives of everyone on

the line between Leavenworth and Skykomish. Yet still the snow kept falling.

So still James H. O'Neill kept working. The superintendent had been on the rotary for about thirty hours now, trying to give some relief to Dowling, who had been actively plowing since Thursday. After ninety-six straight hours of work, though, Dowling and his crew needed something more than a quick nap on the floor of the rotary to keep going, and so O'Neill had called in replacements from the idled double rotary at Snowshed 2.2. He got a message to Irving Tegtmeier by runner, and now the traveling engineer was heading down the mountain with a crew including Walter Vogel, the conductor of the Fast Mail, and several engineers.

Meanwhile, the rotary he'd called in from the Kalispell Division had finally arrived at Leavenworth and was at work on the east slope. The plow was making extremely slow progress—about a mile every hour, clearing slides as it went—but once it reached Gaynor, it could revive and hook up with Harrington's abandoned X801, giving them a double rotary to work with again. There was also help of a different sort on the way from the east. On Sunday O'Neill had wired the equivalent of an SOS to company headquarters in St. Paul, only to discover that the general manager of the entire Great Northern Railway, J. M. Gruber, had already left for Washington State. He was reportedly bringing with him some of the highest operations officers in the company, and though O'Neill may have felt some loss of face in having to issue such a cry for help, he had to be feeling relief as well. Once Gruber and the others arrived, O'Neill would no longer be the commander of this operation. Gruber would be the ultimate decision maker—and the person responsible for the consequences of those decisions.

For at this point—sleep deprived and as weary as a man can be—O'Neill would have been well advised to ask himself whether he was indeed making the correct decisions. Certainly the opinion of most of those on the mountain was that his actions in battling the storm were impeccable. "He is a prince," John Merritt had told a reporter from the *Post-Intelligencer* after reaching Seattle. Other escaped passengers had seconded the judgment, describing O'Neill's fight as "little less than heroic." But in hindsight, one can legitimately question whether the sleep-deprived O'Neill was really thinking as clearly as he should have been. Letting the snow shovelers walk out on Saturday night (when he'd gone five days without a decent sleep) had clearly been a mistake. At that point in the crisis, given the ongoing switchmen's strike, the Great Northern could ill afford the appearance of putting financial concerns ahead of passenger safety, particularly on a labor issue.

Now O'Neill seemed to be making another questionable choice. With the two trains hopelessly trapped for at least the next several days, he had just spent over thirty hours with Dowling on the X808—time that arguably would have been better used attempting to get the passengers off the mountain on foot. The mishap with Big Jerry Wickham may indeed have soured O'Neill on the idea of evacuation, but conditions on the trail had improved significantly in the thirty hours since then, as demonstrated by Pettit's ninety-minute journey that morning. An evacuation effort that had seemed impossible on Sunday might have been much easier to accomplish on Monday.

Moreover, O'Neill now had enough manpower at his disposal to at least attempt a Plan B for getting the passengers to safety. Many of the idling snow shovelers, while persistent in their demands for unreasonably high wages, were still hanging on at Scenic and Skykomish. ("We only get one chance to make a little money," John Rogers overheard one of them saying. "Now it will take you about fifty or seventy-five cents an hour if you want to get me.") He also had the extra men at Scenic who'd arrived on the first relief train on Sunday. And while even a large force of men might not have been able to evacuate the passengers safely through the ever more frequent slides, O'Neill could at least have been exploring this and other options with Pettit and the passengers who so desperately wanted to see him. Instead, he seems to have been entirely focused on the work of this single rotary, which was still, by any realistic estimate, days away from reaching Wellington. This was one situation, then, in which O'Neill's hands-on, detail-oriented style of command may actually have been working against him.

But there can be no doubt that the superintendent was doing what he thought was right at the time, considering that the X808 was the only part of his fighting force left in the vicinity. The plow would clearly have to be put back into action as soon as possible. Once Tegtmeier arrived with the replacement crew, O'Neill could turn over the rotary to them and move on to the next problem. Until then, he would focus on the problem at hand. There was a tank to be cleaned, an injector to be repaired. If there was one thing O'Neill had learned in his twenty-five years of railroading, it was that even the largest operational challenge had to be broken down and attacked step by step.

✧

The train was warm and we were getting enough to eat, such as it was. . . . It was beef every day, but that was all right—a man can't starve to death with beef. . . . Of course, it was very monotonous, but as soon as it would become dusk in the afternoon, then the fear would begin.

—*Henry White*

Wellington
Monday Evening

For much of the long day on Monday, as they anxiously awaited word from Pettit, the forty-four passengers remaining on the Seattle Express wandered the coaches in a distracted, irritable state of mind. In an attempt to lighten the mood, a couple of the women had started on a project: "My baby was getting so dirty," Anna Gray would later write, "so Mrs. Covington told me if I would go to the little [hotel] store and buy some cloth, she would help me make Baby some clothes." Mrs. Gray had found something suitable, and soon the two women were busily sewing a dress and underskirt for little Varden, trying to make the task a source of cheerful interest for everyone on the train.

Despite such efforts, however, many passengers remained morose. Over the past two days the atmosphere on the train had shown signs of turning ugly, even a little surreal. One father apparently lost patience with his fidgety daughter. According to Mrs. Covington's diary: "A man said to his little girl, you sit right there, you're crippled, you're crippled in the head where you can't wear crutches." One man said wistfully that he had dreamed he was in Seattle, "and another said if he had that dream he'd never want to wake up."

Inevitable minor annoyances just heightened the uneasiness. After days of immobility, the Seattle Express was becoming more than a little malodorous. Sanitation was a worsening problem, and even the luxurious Pullman sleepers had grown rank and dirty. For drinking water, the passengers had resorted to melting snow on their own ("snow that was taken up right alongside the trail where all those laboring men [were] expectorating," as Henry White complained). There was a spring in town where Wellington residents got their own water, but somehow the passengers had never been told of it.

Claustrophobia was also a problem for some, since by now the trains were all but completely entombed in snow: "There was a space not over a foot that you could see of the trains . . . along the windows," mail clerk A. B. Hensel would later report. "The balance of the trains were buried." He and his fellow clerks had been keeping informal tabs on the amount of snow that fell every day—in the morning they'd toss an empty mail sack outside the train door and then later dig it up again. They'd been amazed to find that it was consistently snowing as much as three feet a day. The snowfield above the trains was by now a total blank; even the burned trees had been buried under the whiteness. "It was mighty deep," Hensel remarked. "It looked . . . to me that it could not stay up there."

Ida Starrett was particularly distressed about the buildup of snow above the trains, and the coming of rain had only sharpened her distress. She knew nothing of the physics of snowslides, but it seemed clear to her that the weight of extra moisture on those slopes would make them much more likely to slide. Holding tight to the eight-month-old baby in her arms to ward off her growing despondency, she began to speak in almost fatalistic terms about the possibility of a snowslide. Mrs. Covington, too, was succumbing to despair. "I think we are here to stay until spring," the old woman wrote to her husband. "I am trusting in God to save us."

This fretful atmosphere eased somewhat with the return of Joe

Pettit that afternoon. True to his word, the conductor had made the trip to Scenic and back in a single day, and the news he brought was heartening: the trail was passable, at least for those in reasonable physical condition. This intelligence came too late to be acted upon that day, but many passengers began making plans to leave first thing in the morning. R. M. Barnhart, an attorney, and Charles Eltinge, the former bank vice president, went to the Bailets Hotel and bought rough leggings and a three-days' supply of food. "We're going to get out of this," they told the proprietor, and then carried the leggings back to the Pullman to try on for size. Customs official H. D. Chantrell started asking around for a personal mountain guide (he was referred—one assumes fruitlessly—to trapper Robert Schwartz, the disparager of tenderfeet).

Even Ned Topping had decided to escape. "Still in this snow," he wrote to his mother on Monday night. "If nothing happens, I expect to leave in the morning for Scenic—down the track for 2 or 3 miles, then down the side of the mountain. There are numbers of people going out, so I'll have company. Oh, if I ever get out of this place, how happy I will be."

Henry White, though, was skeptical of the plans afoot. After learning from Pettit that there was no chance of the rotaries reaching them anytime soon, the salesman grew angry that the railroad had not come up with any official alternative plan. Ad hoc preparations among the passengers were all very well, but White realized that getting the old and infirm down that trail would require a massive effort involving ropes, a throng of trailbreakers, and perhaps even some sort of sled or stretcher for certain individuals. Sixty-nine-year-old Mrs. Covington, for one, was not about to hike off the mountain with nothing more than a pair of men's trousers and a walking stick. For her and for some others aboard (such as J. R. Vail, whose carbuncle, according to Nurse O'Reilly, was now life-threatening), the idea of evacuation on foot was patently far-fetched. In White's opinion, the only workable plan was to get enough shovelers up from Scenic to move the train to a safer place.

At this point, though, he realized that Joseph Pettit could do nothing more for them. While the conductor implied that the train would indeed be safer near the tunnel, he clearly didn't want to contradict his superiors. So White and his contingent again began agitating for a personal interview with the superintendent. The clearing of the line could no longer be considered in any way imminent, so there was nothing to prevent O'Neill from sparing a few moments to see them. To emphasize the seriousness of their resolve, they decided to draw up a petition, which would be signed by every passenger willing to do so. The petition, a copy of which still exists, read as follows:

Feb. 28th, 1910

Mr. J. H. O'Neill
Sup't. Cascade Div. Gt. N. R.R.

Dear Sir:—

We, the undersigned, passengers on train #25, after waiting here six (6) days, and believing it will be impossible to move this train for many days, request that you meet us here, on train tonight, to the end that some means [may be found] by which the passengers can make their way over to Skykomish or to some point this side of there, where they may take trains for their respective destinations.

Passenger Bert Matthews, a traveling salesman from Cincinnati, carried the document over to O'Neill's business car and typed it up on the superintendent's own typewriter, probably under the fretful eye of the stenographer Earl Longcoy. The petition was then brought back to the Seattle Express, where it was signed by thirty-four passengers. A carbon copy was given to attorney James McNeny for safekeeping, while the typed original was sent over to the A-16. Having thus made their request official, the passengers retired to the observation car to await the superintendent's response.

Yet the petition did not produce O'Neill. After a time, Longcoy—at nineteen years of age little more than a boy—came over in the superintendent's stead. The passengers pounced. "We asked him if he was in authority," Henry White reported, "and he said that he was. We told him we had sent for Mr. O'Neill. He said Mr. O'Neill was not there. We said we want the next in charge. He said it was Mr. Blackburn. We asked him to send [Blackburn] over, and he said that he was there to represent Mr. Blackburn in the matter."

Understandably infuriated but seeing no other choice, White and the other passengers decided to deal with the young man. They first demanded that the railroad furnish them with fifty men—roughly one for each passenger—to take people out over the trail, using whatever ropes or equipment would be necessary. Longcoy regarded this as out of the question. "We have only seven men on the payroll at Wellington!" he insisted. But the passengers had heard about the arrival of the relief train at Scenic the day before. According to White: "We knew that 125 men were working with rotary plows near Scenic and we asked that they be sent to our assistance." When Longcoy again demurred, they asked him to put his refusal in writing. This, too, the young man would not do, claiming that he had no actual authority in the matter. "Well, that is just exactly what we are getting at," White exclaimed. "We want somebody in authority and not you."

Utterly intimidated by now, Longcoy retreated, promising to notify Blackburn of their demands. The trainmaster himself arrived a short time later, visibly angered at being called away from his duties. When given the same request to bring up the men now at Scenic, "Mr. Blackburn sort of went up in the air a little," according to White. Blackburn claimed that there was no way he would redeploy the workers opening the line to come up to Wellington to "take out a lot of able-bodied men." One of the passengers, R. H. Bethel, insisted that Blackburn provide at least enough men to aid the women and children and invalids, but the trainmaster wouldn't hear of it. According to passenger R. M. Laville, "I heard Mr. Blackburn tell [the] committee of passengers that any of them who left the train would do so at their own risk—on their own responsibility—and that as far as the women were concerned, he would not allow them to be taken off. He said that if he caught any of us trying to take the women out of there he would use force, if necessary, to avoid it."

The discussion seems to have cooled off after this heated exchange, with the passengers again returning to the old demand to be moved back to the tunnel. White offered to chop wood himself to provide the required fuel. There was "plenty of wood," he claimed. "The mountains were full of it." The short-tempered salesman even proposed knocking down the Wellington freight house for firewood. This idea was also parried by the trainmaster, but Blackburn did leave that night having made at least one important concession: Though he would not divert any of the men working with the rotary near Scenic, he did agree to provide a handful of men—as many as he could muster at Wellington—to assist the able-bodied male passengers who wished to leave on foot the following morning. He also promised to see about getting some fresh water and taking care of the train's sanitation problems for those who remained behind.

After Blackburn's departure, the gloomy mood dissipated considerably. Somehow the trainmaster's final concessions had put a brighter light on the overall situation, and spirits lifted accordingly. "Nearly everyone on the stalled trains was gay that last night," brakeman Ross Phillips recalled. "Many of the crew, laborers, and the railway clerks played cards, and some of the section hands went down to Bailets' saloon for a few drinks. H. H. White and a group of men and women had quite a hilarious social party in the observation car." George Davis dressed three-year-old Thelma in her fanciest outfit for the occasion, and hotel proprietor Bailets even roasted a chicken (probably one of the last in his larder), which was shared among the passengers and a few of the railroaders who had chosen to sleep in the berths vacated by passengers in the first two groups of hikers.

The party went on for hours. The revelers told stories, gave dramatic recitations, performed tricks for the children, and joined in groups to sing hymns and popular songs. Even Mrs. Covington sang, performing "a sweet little song about the sparrows—something about [how] God took care of the sparrows [so] He would surely take care of us, and it was such a comfort." There was doubtless something a little forced in the celebration—the glow of the festive train like a tiny, somewhat feeble oasis of light and warmth in the tempestuous night—but it served as a welcome distraction from the snowfields disintegrating all around them.

At the same time, final preparations were being made for tomorrow's departure. Nellie Sharp and Libby Latsch, having decided to ignore Blackburn's ban on women walking out, were going around the train cars in search of men's clothing for the trip. They seemed giddy at the thought of exchanging their skirts and starched shirtwaists for straight-cut trousers and shapeless overcoats. Conductor Pettit, for his part, trudged up to the hotel to arrange an early breakfast for the hikers, and Sharp even obtained a meat chopper so that the group might start the day with a nourishing warm hash.

At about 10:30 the passengers and railroaders finally began retiring for the night, though even then the gaiety continued. "When we lay in our berths," brakeman Phillips recalled, "we grabbed the hats off any of the gals who walked down the aisle of the sleeper. Even Mrs. Starrett was boisterous, waving and shouting to the men from the second sleeper." Only one person seemed immune to this outbreak of high spirits: "I don't believe anyone had a premonition of immediate danger except my partner McDonald," Phillips said, referring to brakeman Archie McDonald. "We had all been having such a good time and lots of laughs, but just before Mac went to sleep he said to me from his berth across the aisle, 'We're all happy now. We may be crying before morning.'"

Most others, however, seemed focused on the promise of tomorrow's escape. In his berth, Ned Topping finished the day's entry in the letter to his mother: "I'll have so much to tell you of my experiences when I get home," he wrote, turning again to thoughts of his distant family. "Oh, for a look at little Bill and you all . . . I'll be *so so* happy . . ."

Toward 1:00, when most had already settled into their berths, Pettit came through the train once more. Henry White and Bert Matthews were still in the lounge, talking and smoking after their game of whist, and Pettit stopped to speak with them. White had decided to attempt the hike out, depending on what the weather looked like the next day, so he asked Pettit what he thought of the prospects. The conductor expressed some concern about the wind, which was rising again. "If this wind continues," he said, "we won't get out of here tomorrow." Curious, the men went with him out onto the open vestibule of the car to get a look at the surrounding mountains. This was still, despite everything that had happened over the past six days, an undeniably magnificent setting. "The mountainside was a very beautiful sight," Henry White would later admit. "The snow had fallen so long, and so much of it, that it had covered up all blemishes or disfigurements, and it was just a big, solid mass of pure white snow. It was a sight that you could not pass without being attracted to [it]— you would have to look at it."

The men returned inside after a time and got ready for bed. Soon porter Lucius Anderson was making his final pass through the silent Pullman, cleaning up the empty glasses and extinguishing the lights.

✧

It was probably at about this same moment—at the resort hotel standing a short but incalculably long four miles down the mountain at Scenic Hot Springs—that James H. O'Neill was himself bedding down for the night. After being relieved at the rotary by the arrival of traveling engineer Tegtmeier, the superintendent had climbed down to Scenic to get what was to be his second full night's sleep since the crisis started. There can be little doubt that he needed the rest. The pace he'd been keeping for the past week was brutal, and in the current circumstances, with only one rotary left to assault the endless slides, his task seemed to border on futility. Yet the only alternative to continuing the fight would have been to give up and wait for the storm to end—something that a man of O'Neill's temperament simply could not do.

So O'Neill was going to bed like everyone else. By now, he knew, Berenice would have been feeling his absence keenly. He had doubtless been wiring her whenever he could spare a moment, to let her know that he was safe at least. Each of his telegrams must have come as an enormous relief to her, knowing as she did the constant danger of working out in that fickle terrain. But the news she was most eager to hear—that he was coming home—was something her husband could not yet tell her. With an entire railroad division to get moving again, his job was nowhere near finished. Which is why—early the next morning, after a scant few hours of sleep—he would get up from bed and start all over again. He would organize the relief party at Scenic, make a final check on the X808, and then hike back up the mountain to Wellington. There were still scores of passengers up there relying on him, and as long as a single one of them was trapped in those mountains he would be trapped there too.

12

Avalanche

It was a night of heroism, a night of horror.

—Everett Daily Herald

Tuesday, March 1, 1910
Wellington
1:42 A.M.

After 1:00 A.M. they slept. Rain spattered the windows of the Seattle Express as an edgy quiet filled the train, the darkness relieved only by a dimly flickering gaslight at the end of each car. On the sleeper Winnipeg, Henry White and Bert Matthews had by 1:15 finished their preparations for bed and crawled into their berths—the last of the passengers to retire. Already asleep around them were the other men and women they had come to know so well over the past week—among them Ned Topping, the Gray family, Sarah Jane Covington, George and Thelma Davis, and Ida Starrett, her baby lying quietly on the berth beside her, her son Ray and daughter Lillian in the berths across the aisle. Even porter Lucius Anderson was in bed by now, his long day's duties finally over. He was sleeping soundly in his usual place, on an upper berth at the very end of the Pullman.

On the Fast Mail train right next to the Express, A. B. Hensel and the

other mail clerks had also bedded down. Word of trainmaster Blackburn's approval of the next morning's evacuation attempt had convinced
the postal employees that it was finally time to make their own move.
Eager to end their enforced idleness, the men had locked up all the registered and first-class mail in one of the secure mail cars. Then, at about
11:00 P.M., they'd made up their usual improvised beds, piling empty
mail sacks onto thin pallets at one end of the second-class mail car.

For a time, the mail clerks' rest had been disturbed by a raucous card
game going on next door—in the third-class mail car, at the very end of
the train. Engineer Joe Finn, brakeman Earl Duncan, and conductors
Ira Clary and Homer Purcell had been playing hot rummy for most of
the evening (with conductor M. O. White and others looking on) and
had been making enough noise to compete with the worsening storm
outside. Then the whiskey had run out and they too had settled down
for the night. Finn had apparently left the car at about one and hiked
through the rain back to Wellington, but Clary, Purcell, and Duncan
had instead stretched out on the floor of the mail car, all but played out.
Over the past two days they had been chopping wood to keep the double rotary's engines alive, and they needed to get some rest while they
could. Once Dowling arrived with the X808 and its much-needed supply
of coal, the double would go back in commission, meaning that its
crews would have to start plowing around the clock again.

Even in the town of Wellington itself, few people were now stirring.
With the telegraph wires down, second-trick operator Basil Sherlock
had found himself with "absolutely nothing to do," and so had left the
office early. Feeling rattled by the increasingly unstable snowpack, he'd
returned to his cabin at about 10:00 P.M. and told his wife, Alathea, of
his concerns. Their cabin stood in one of the most slide-prone areas in
Wellington—perched above Haskell Creek at the east end of town—
and Sherlock didn't like the looks of the mountainside behind it. After
some discussion, the two had decided to remain in the cabin only as
long as the snow on their pitched, corrugated-iron roof stayed put. If
the snow slid off anytime before morning (indicating conditions ripe for
a snowslide on the slope behind their cabin), they would gather up their
clothes and "beat it for the tunnel."

That had been several hours ago, and now the couple—like nearly everyone else at Wellington—was asleep in bed. Normally, of course, with trains scheduled to come through the tunnel at all hours of the day and night, the small settlement would be active twenty-four hours a day; any sense of nighttime repose would have been shattered by the regular blasts of steam whistles, the cries of conductors and brakemen, and the clamorous switching of helper locomotives. That night, however—with all traffic stopped and even the telegraph silent—Wellington was uncharacteristically still, lying peacefully under a drenching rain. The town had all but shut down until morning—which was perhaps why almost no one was awake when, sometime in the early hours of March 1, that ever-evolving storm suddenly changed character once again. The prevailing northwestern winds carried in a fierce thunderstorm from the coast. And soon the skies above Stevens Pass were alive with brilliant lightning and the deep, resounding rumble of thunder.

It was a virtually unheard-of phenomenon in the Cascades. Electrical storms were not supposed to happen in the mountains in winter. Even long-term residents of the area had never experienced such a thing. And this disturbance could not have arrived at a worse time. By Monday night, the battered, snow-choked slopes around Wellington had become an enormous trap waiting to be sprung. Already covered with a layer cake of assorted substrata of snow and ice, they were now slathered with a thick icing of dense, wind-packed new snow. The entire mixture, moreover, had been soaked by heavy lubricating rains that had penetrated to its very deepest layers. That beautiful field of white above the trains, in other words, was just a hard, unfathomably heavy slab sitting on top of increasingly unsound layers of highly stressed snow. A single trigger at a single point on that precipitous expanse would be enough to bring down the entire mountainside of snow.

Meanwhile, the noise of the unusual thunderstorm was waking some of the lighter sleepers. On the Fast Mail, Hensel rose from his place among the other clerks. He had been having trouble sleeping even before the thunder started. "My bunk was too hard," he remembered, "so I moved to the other end of the car." Clearing space between some wooden crates of registered mail, he remade his bed there—beyond the side door of the mail car, away from his fellows—in hopes of making himself more comfortable.

In a cabin east of the station, telegrapher William Flannery was also roused by the noise. Curious about the thunder, he padded to the cabin window and pulled aside the curtain. He was just in time to see a bolt of stark white lightning zigzag across the sky, and then another streak in the opposite direction. A clap of thunder followed, and though it was powerful enough to rattle the windowpanes, it did not wake his cabin-mate, conductor Felix Plettl. Amazed but not seriously worried by this bizarre turn in an already bizarre storm, Flannery simply returned to bed and tried to fall back to sleep.

Engineer Charles Andrews was more troubled by the change in the weather. Wakened by the storm, Andrews lay in bed, worried by what the rain and earth-jarring thunder might do to the snow on the slopes above his shack, which stood near the bottom of a narrow gulley. To him the prospect of an imminent snowslide was very real, and so, despite the fact that he'd been working all day at the double rotary, he got up and pulled on his still-damp work clothes. He stepped out into the torrential rain and tried to wake some of the other men in nearby shacks. Shouting to them over the thunder, he warned them of the danger, but they refused to budge and merely told him to go back to bed.

Cold, wet, and uneasy, Andrews then walked down to the unlighted depot. In the distance to the west he could make out the tail end of the passenger train—steam rising invitingly from its rear-vent valve—but he knew that the train was probably full and that he'd find no place to lie down there. So he turned east and headed to the bunkhouse near the tunnel, where he felt he'd be safer. He stepped inside, the damp fug of sleeping workmen heavy in the air, and built up the fire that had been smoldering in the stove. He sat there thoughtfully, warming himself in front of the blaze as the lightning strobed outside, until about ten minutes later, when he heard a sharp explosion of thunder, followed by another sound—deep, resonant, otherworldly, and unlike anything he'd ever heard before.

Some later said it was a lightning strike that started it. Others said it must have been the percussive impact of thunder (though experts deny that sound alone can trigger an avalanche). All that is known for sure is that at 1:42 A.M. something caused a break in the surface integrity of the snowfield on the side of Windy Mountain. A buried weak layer somewhere in the snowpack possibly collapsed with an enormous *whump*, sending a horizontal fracture shooting across the face of the slope about a thousand feet above the trains. And then, with an ominous rumble, the entire slab began slipping inexorably down the mountainside.

John Wentzel, a member of the Wellington section crew, was at Bailets Hotel at the time, fully awake and dressed. Hearing that uncanny rumble, he rushed outside into the storm. What he saw was something that no witness to a large avalanche ever forgets: "It seemed as if the world were coming to an end," Wentzel was later quoted as saying. "I saw the whole side of the mountain coming down, tearing up everything in its way."

Acres of crumbling snow were descending with the magisterial grandeur of a dropping theater curtain. A wet slab avalanche moves slowly—its vast weight causes such intense friction that it can pick up little speed—but its momentum can be tremendous. Scraping up nearly everything in its path, the slide's leading edge can turn into a roiling juggernaut of snow and debris reaching extraordinary heights. According to one estimate, the wall coming down the mountainside would also have been over a half mile wide by the time it reached the tracks. "Trees, stumps, and snow were rolling together in gigantic waves," Wentzel remembered. He realized at once that the slide would just miss the hotel and depot, but the two full railroad trains sat directly below it. "I saw the first rush of snow reach the track [and] swallow the trains," he said. "And then there was neither tracks nor trains . . ."

✧

There were approximately 125 people sleeping aboard the two trains that night. Many probably never even heard the approach of the avalanche, but at least a few were alert enough to recognize what was coming. "I think I was awake when it happened," Henry White would later testify. "I may have been dozing, but I remember very distinctly [the sound] of the snow striking the car." What he heard was, to

White's surprise, not a hard, percussive sound but a "squash"—an enormous splat followed by a shrill implosion of shattering glass. As the car in which he lay began tipping and sliding off the bank, he understood at once that the much-discussed avalanche had come.

"The first impression I had was the shame of it," White would later say, "a feeling of regret and shame." He thought instantly of the children on the train, children he had been playing with that very day— "very beautiful and bright little tots"—and of the other people who had become his friends over the past week. Somehow, despite all of the discussion and argument of the past six days, they had not been able to prevent this disaster from overtaking them, and the sheer waste of it saddened him.

White closed his eyes and held his breath as he felt the train's slide turn into a tumble. Oddly, he felt only a vague, detached curiosity "as to what shape the death blow was coming in, and whether it was to be something run through me . . . like a weapon." But no blow came. "I have no idea of the lapse of time," he continued. "It probably appeared to be much longer than it was in reality."

R. L. Forsyth, in the berth next to White's, was also conscious from the start. "Suddenly our car was lifted bodily from the track," he said, describing the first few seconds after the avalanche struck. For a moment the seventy-five-ton sleeper was held "poised in mid-air," Forsyth claimed. "Then it toppled over the edge and rolled down the steep embankment." As the car fell, other passengers began to shriek in confusion and fear. "It seemed more like a bad dream than anything else—a grinding and roaring and crashing. . . . We went down very rapidly."

At this point, according to several accounts, the plummeting Express seemed to hit an object in its path, veer over sideways, and continue tumbling more erratically, throwing passengers wildly around the car. The sheer violence of the fall must have been awe-inspiring, with the massive locomotives erupting through the passenger cars' wooden walls as they tumbled. Then at least the Winnipeg collided with a larger obstacle and split apart. "Our car popped open like an eggshell," Ross Phillips recalled. "I was thrown through the air and into a pocket of snow."

The men on the Fast Mail were hurled around with even greater force. "Before I was actually awake, the car was tossed up into the air like a football," Ira Clary reported. "The men inside were rattling about the top, bottom, and sides of the car like pebbles in a pan. The car rolled over and over, bouncing, turning, and twisting with incredible swiftness. Then there was a terrific crash and instantly I found myself in the snow. I was completely covered and began to smother."

Impressions vary on how long it took for the trains to reach the bottom of the ravine. Some say it was an instant; another said it seemed like twenty minutes. Once the trains juddered to a stop, though, it's likely that the snow and debris kept coming, burying some cars deeper under the slide, piling ever more weight above them. Finally, after the intense pandemonium of the fall, all movement stopped, and there was silence—an eerie, muffled stillness ruptured only once by the explosion of an acetylene gas tank in the head car of the passenger train. "Everything was still," Henry White remembered. "I expected to hear cries and groans, but I heard nothing. And I knew then that the death roll would be appalling."

"My God, this is an awful death to die," said a voice in the darkness on the last car of the Fast Mail.

Most of those aboard the mail train had indeed perished during the fall, but the vagaries of physics had left a few of them alive—Ira Clary, Homer Purcell, Earl Duncan, and M. O. White among them. These men were sprawled around the shattered third-class mail car, deeply muddled by the fall and now all but buried in snow. At first they managed only to speak a few words to one another in the blackness of the wreck. Then Clary, galvanized by the sensation of smothering, began thrashing like a drowning man, kicking and floundering in the snow. He managed to fight his way to fresh air and soon found himself at the surface, sitting on the wet snow above the ruined mail coach. "I heard Purcell calling and I knew his voice. I asked him, 'Is that Purcell?' and he replied, 'It sure is.'"

In the erratic illumination of lightning, Clary saw a hand sticking out of the snow and began furiously digging around it. It took an agonizingly long time, but he finally freed his fellow conductor and pulled him out of the steep snowbank. Purcell's boots came out of the hole behind him and fell on top of him. It was a small but fortuitous bit of luck. Both men were barefoot, so Purcell gave his socks to Clary and wore the boots himself. Finding themselves only lightly injured, the two began almost at once to search the wreck for other survivors.

"It was raining dismally and the trees all about us were cracking and screeching," Clary reported. "We could hear people calling for help and we began to do what we could." After pulling brakeman Charlie Smart and one or two other men out of the twisted wreckage, they saw one of their friends—fireman J. L. Kerlee, whom they called "Curly"—wedged under some debris. He was trapped near one of the toppled locomotives, its furiously hissing boiler spewing fusillades of hot steam into the air as the intense heat vaporized the snow around it.

Braving the searing white billows, Clary and Purcell ran to assist their friend, but as they approached, the snow collapsed beneath Purcell's feet. "The steam from the engine had melted a big cavern beneath the snow crust," Clary explained, "and [Purcell] fell into this steaming cauldron." Fearing that Purcell would be boiled alive, Clary and Duncan dove to the edge of the molten pit, grasped the rotary conductor's outstretched hands, and pulled him away from the wildly sputtering boiler. Miraculously, Purcell was soaked but not burned. But they knew that the damaged locomotive could explode at any moment. Rushing back to Kerlee, the three men tore at the debris around his body until they could extricate him and drag him to safety.

All of these survivors had come from the third-class mail car, which seemed to have been spared the worst ravages of the slide. Those in the second-class mail car, however, had not fared as well as their neighbors. According to Hensel, his car had split in half at the side doors as the train plummeted down the mountainside. It would later be discovered that the part containing the other mail clerks had been crushed and buried deep, killing them instantly. The half to which Hensel alone had moved lay on its side under a thin covering of snow. The heavy rotary snowplow had landed on top of it, splintering the car's wooden side and penetrating the interior to within inches of Hensel's chest. Fortunately, though, the crates Hensel had moved to make his bed had protected him.

Nearly pinned now by the ruptured timbers, his left collarbone and several ribs broken, Hensel was rapidly slipping into shock. His first thought was that he was doomed to be trapped there until he froze to death, and he wondered if he could somehow write a last message on the hard-packed snow above him. Coming to his senses finally, he instead kicked with his bare feet at the snow. Despite his injuries, he was able to break the surface and push himself feetfirst out of the debris, but when he got outside above the mail car he realized that his watch, keys, and wallet were down there in the wreck. Still not thinking clearly, he crawled back into the ruined car and actually found the items before scrambling to the surface again. Looking up then, he saw lanterns descending as if from the sky and, above them, the lights of Wellington gleaming in the night, far from where they should have been. He called out to the approaching lantern carriers and then, exhausted and disoriented, passed out on the snow.

By now several of the survivors from the passenger train were wandering around the bottom of the canyon, half-naked and in various stages of shock. Shortly after hearing the acetylene tank explode in the distance, Henry White had gotten to his feet and, to his amazement, was able to walk right through a large rent in the side of the Winnipeg, out onto the surface of the slide. The rain was hammering down now, and in the momentary flashes of lightning he glimpsed Lucius Anderson lying on the ground nearby—injured but alive. Apparently in full possession of his senses, White found some blankets in the debris and offered one to Anderson. But the porter, his mind still addled after being knocked cold in the fall, refused the gesture, saying he would instead "turn the steam on in the car."

R. L. Forsyth had come through the ordeal in even better shape than White. Finding himself only shallowly buried after the train had come to rest, he'd managed to dig himself out with little difficulty, but he was wet and shivering. "The first person I saw was Mr. Laville," Forsyth would later testify. "He threw me a curtain and I wrapped up in that." Seeing the others from the Winnipeg, he moved toward them and recognized White, Anderson, and Ross Phillips, who had been dug out of the wreckage—probably by Clary and Purcell—and was now suffering from a badly scalded right leg. Forsyth sank down beside this group, and then, as the electrical storm raked the canyon with bursts of harsh, bone-colored light, the four of them sat there in a row, staring at the phantasmagoric spectacle in front of them, waiting for someone to come down from Wellington to help them.

The first rescuers into the canyon were Charles Andrews and another engineer, Bob Miles. Picking their way down the steep mountainside, whipped by the wind and rain, the two men could see little evidence of the disaster besides a partially buried electric locomotive and the battered rotary snowplow. The only signs of the wooden passenger cars were a dark curtain from a Pullman berth flapping in the wind and a steel pipe jutting ominously from a mound of snow. Then they came upon a more grotesque sight: a man and a woman buried to their necks in snow but still alive. Miles and Andrews sank to their knees to try to dig the couple out by hand (in their haste to reach the trains, the two men had not stopped to pick up any digging tools), but the compacted snow was too hard. Frantic they struggled back up the mountain to Wellington to get shovels. By the time they had found some and returned, the man and the woman were both dead.

Others at Wellington soon followed Andrews and Miles into the ravine. Ed Clark had been asleep in the bunkhouse when the roar of the avalanche awakened him. Grabbing some axes and a few lanterns, he and several other men ran to the edge of the avalanche track and peered over the side. "There was a faint moaning in the gulch," he recalled. "Trees were snapping, and you could hear other slides roaring down. . . . Then the lanterns showed hands beckoning from every little hole in one of the coaches." They scrambled down the face of the avalanche to reach them. "We chopped between the outstretched hands and began to take people out," Clark continued. "Some of the passengers were crying for water. . . . We got some out alive, but some died before we could get at them, although they were alive when we reached the spot."

William Flannery and his cabinmate Felix Plettl had also reached the wreckage by now—and it was instantly clear to both of them that the danger from the slide was not yet past. "When we got down there, I saw a man laying out on the snow," Flannery said. "[I] put him on my back and started up the hill with him, [but] while I was going up the hill, another slide—a portion of the big one that hadn't come down as yet—hit me and knocked me down underneath it, and I lost this man." Buried under the shifting snow, Flannery nonetheless managed to pull himself along the side of a fallen tree until he reached the surface again. But the shock of the impact had utterly disoriented him: "I was in such a dazed condition that I walked down and [had waded] into the river up to my shoulders when I came to and realized what I had done." Desperate to find the man he'd lost, Flannery returned to the wreck and searched for him, "calling and hallooing down through the snow." He never found that man, but he and some other rescuers did locate two more survivors—conductor M. O. White and engineer Duncan Tegtmeier (a cousin of traveling engineer Irving Tegtmeier, now with the rotary above Scenic). They dug their fellow railroaders out of the snow and then helped them climb the steep slope back to town.

Up at Wellington, even W. R. Bailets—at fifty-five, the town's oldest resident—was trying to do his part. Having been awakened shortly after the avalanche by some railroaders from town, he and his wife had quickly gone downstairs to the hotel's dining room and saloon to light the fires in their stoves. Concerned about one of the passengers who had been helping his granddaughter wait tables (probably Catherine O'Reilly or Nellie Sharp), he'd decided to run down to the passing tracks to see if he could find her.

"I had no idea that the train was thrown over," he later testified. "I thought it was just shoved off the track." Only after reaching the place where the trains should have been did he understand the magnitude of the disaster.

Through the gloom, he saw a man ascending from the canyon with a moaning boy in his arms. It was seven-year-old Raymond Starrett, "with a snag, a big splinter stuck right up through his forehead." Bailets told the man to take Starrett up to the hotel and put him in front of the fire. Gripped by the sense of emergency, the hotelkeeper then headed over the edge of the right-of-way—and was almost instantly mired in snow. He floundered around in the deep drifts for a time before recognizing the foolishness of his would-be heroism. "I was played out," he said.

"Sometimes I would be in . . . waist-deep. I would have to draw myself out." Exhausted, he soon concluded that the rescue was best left to younger, fitter men, and so he climbed back up to the hotel to lie down.

By now all of Wellington was awake. Many residents had gathered at the enginemen's bunkhouse at the east end of the settlement—believed to be the safest place left in town—and were trying to figure out how to get word to superintendent O'Neill at Scenic, so that doctors, medical supplies, and extra rescuers could be rushed to the scene. With no other form of communication available, the message would have to be delivered on foot—a dangerous proposition, as the surrounding snowfields were now collapsing with such frequency that the whole mountain seemed to be melting in the rain. Traveling engineer J. J. Mackey volunteered to make the trip himself. After consulting with William Flannery on what supplies would be needed, Mackey dressed himself warmly and set off.

Flannery understood, however, that it would be hours before any help could be expected, even if Mackey got the message through. With trainmaster Blackburn and William Harrington both missing, the telegrapher took it upon himself to start making plans. After a quick discussion with the others present—including Charles Andrews, Bob Miles and his wife, and Basil and Alathea Sherlock—it was decided that the bunkhouse should serve as a temporary hospital. Sherlock, who professed to be the son of a doctor, joined the two women in preparing the place to receive patients. They designated separate men's and women's wards and sent a brakeman over to the hotel to find some linens for bandages. After a few minutes, the brakeman returned, claiming that Bailets (perhaps suffering from the stress of his ordeal in the ravine) was standing on his porch with a gun in his hands, refusing to turn over any merchandise unless it was paid for. Furious, Sherlock ran over to the hotel to confront the man. Although their showdown was undoubtedly exaggerated in Sherlock's later retelling, it seems certain that someone—either Sherlock himself or, more likely, Flannery—was able to persuade the hotelkeeper to see reason. Soon the temporary hospital had its linens for bandages, along with raincoats and other gear and clothing from the hotel's store.

Somewhat later a worried Susan Bailets called Sherlock into the ho-

tel to have a look at Ray Starrett, who was writhing around half conscious on her dining room table with the piece of wood still lodged in
his forehead. Sherlock was shocked by what he saw: "The stick was
about two-and-a-half feet long, an inch wide, and a half-inch thick. . . .
It was an awful sight. From a first glance, one would think the stick ran
right through the boy's head."

Concerned that young Ray could wind up with blood poisoning before a doctor arrived, Sherlock asked Mrs. Bailets to go and find a sharp
razor. She returned a few minutes later with a brand-new blade from
the hotel's shop. Sherlock sterilized it with boiling water and then—
clearly out of his depth—proceeded to perform impromptu surgery on
the boy's head, while Susan Bailets and her husband looked on.

"I cut the stick out," Sherlock explained, "being just as careful as I
could to save the skin and flesh." After bandaging the wound, he bundled Ray up in a blanket and, as the half-conscious boy laughed deliri-
ously in his arms, took him over to the bunkhouse. "While carrying
him, I said to myself, 'If we never find his folks, he is mine.'"

The bunkhouse hospital was in the meantime filling up with the injured. First to appear had been the Snow King himself, wearing nothing
but a bloodied nightshirt. William Harrington had survived after all
and, despite suffering a serious head wound and an injured foot, had
managed to climb up from the wreck unassisted. Homer Purcell had
come next, with a broken arm and other injuries. Taking charge of the
small hospital, Alathea Sherlock quickly saw to their wounds and made
her patients as comfortable as possible near the stove. (She even put Purcell to work rolling bandages—with his good arm—on an improvised
machine that her husband had hammered together.) No one knew for
sure how many people would be carried into the makeshift hospital before the night was over. On the night before there had been about forty-
five passengers remaining on the Seattle Express, along with eight or
nine mail clerks on the Fast Mail. More uncertain was the number of
railroaders on the trains when the avalanche hit. At least a half dozen
men from the plow crews were known to have taken the vacated berths
on the Express, but many other crewmen and laborers had chosen to
sleep elsewhere on the trains that night, thinking the passing tracks a

safer place than the section house and the various shacks making up the town of Wellington itself.

Concerned that the little hospital might soon be overwhelmed, Flannery decided to send a second messenger down to Scenic. Grabbing another man—probably section crewman John Wentzel—the telegrapher wrote out a note to superintendent O'Neill and sent the man down the mountain in traveling engineer Mackey's wake. That left one person fewer at Wellington to aid in the rescue, but Flannery's rationale was clear: If for any reason Mackey didn't reach Scenic, Flannery wanted to be certain that their cry for help still made it to the outside world.

The men of Wellington were meanwhile discovering just how badly they would need that help. Several dozen rescuers had by now descended into the ravaged canyon, and what they were finding down there was appalling. One man reportedly picked up a detached hand lying on the snow; others claimed to have uncovered a severed head in among the wreckage. Some of these stories, of course, were probably apocryphal, but subsequent coroner's records confirm that many corpses pulled from the wreckage were badly mutilated. A few were also severely burned, seared by escaping steam from the damaged engines.

The most devastating discovery was the body of three-year-old Thelma Davis. Only the top half of the pretty toddler was found. It had been lashed to a huge tree trunk, tangled in a web of grotesquely twisted steam pipes.

Toward dawn, one rescuer uncovered the submerged form of a baby. It was eighteen-month-old Varden Gray—unconscious, his nose broken, and his scalp split wide open. The child's parents—John with his healing leg rebroken and Anna injured but still conscious—lay buried deeper in the slide, pinned beneath the wreckage. Judging by modern statistics of avalanche survival, the fact that all three Grays were alive was remarkable. Avalanches generally kill in two ways. Fatal trauma—collision with trees, rocks, or other debris—accounts for about one-third of deaths, but the majority of victims die of suffocation. Densely packed snow asphyxiates some; others die when the pressure of tons of snow on their chests prevents them from breathing; a small minority suffocate when their own breath melts snow around their mouths, which then refreezes as a rigid ice mask. Whatever the situation, though, the chances of survival plummet after just fifteen minutes of burial; only one in ten will normally live longer than a few hours.

In this particular slide, however—where the train wreckage created large air pockets under the snow—some victims had a greater window of opportunity for rescue. Many, like the Grays, lingered on, still able to breathe long after the slide. One man, fireman Samuel A. Bates of the Fast Mail, was buried for hours next to his huge steam locomotive, expecting its boiler to explode at any moment. He tried clawing his way out, digging until his fingers bled, but this only seemed to pack the snow more densely around him. Finally, after six hours, his air supply dwindling and his body near hypothermia, he gave himself up for lost— at which point some rescuers heard his last desperate screams and dug him out.

Once dawn arrived, however, the only casualties being recovered were dead. Solomon Cohen and two electricians who'd been sleeping in a cabin near the motor shed had been among the first of the fatalities pulled out. Now the rescuers were finding others more deeply buried: R. M. Barnhart, the prominent attorney; John Rogers's companion James McNeny; Catherine O'Reilly, the young nurse from Spokane. Their bodies were carried up the rain-lashed slope and placed in the baggage room next to the depot, which had been set aside as the morgue.

By late morning the rescuers worried that no one could be left alive in the wreckage. Even victims who had survived the fall with an ample air pocket around them would probably have run out of oxygen by now. But then Charles Andrews and some other men heard what Andrews later described as "a mewing far off, like a kitten." Scrambling over toward the source of the sound, they heard it more distinctly as a cry for help. Certain that someone was still alive under the snow, they began digging feverishly.

The person calling was Ida Starrett, Raymond's mother. Roused by the initial roar of the slide, she had been fully awake when the train toppled into the canyon. She landed with a jolt when her car hit bottom and was apparently knocked unconscious for a time. After she regained her senses, she understood what had happened. She was lying facedown under the snow, her head in the crook of her elbow and her back pinned painfully by some heavy object; when she tried to move, she found she could do no more than wiggle her fingers.

"I realized," Ida would later say, "that I was not injured so seriously that I would die from that cause, immediately at least." Her thoughts turned immediately to her parents and her children—and she realized that her infant son, Francis, was beneath her, pressed against her abdomen. If she held her breath she could even hear the baby breathing. She wanted to reach down and move him or comfort him or at least touch him, but though she tried desperately to free her arms she could do nothing, and the weight on her back seemed only to press down harder.

For hours she lay there in the frigid darkness, suffering terrible pain but with enough trapped air around her to keep her alive. Probably she was drifting in and out of consciousness, sometimes losing track of where she was and what was happening around her. But she was certain that she knew just when her baby beneath her stopped breathing and died.

Eventually, nearly eleven hours after the slide, she awoke to hear rescuers shouting somewhere above. "I cried out to them, trying to direct them," she said. She listened as the shovelers found and removed several dead bodies from the debris above her, but they couldn't seem to pinpoint the source of her shouts. "I could tell by the sound of their shoveling that they were digging in the wrong place, and [I] told them so. Then they moved nearer and at last I could hear the shovels striking just above my face. I cried a warning."

Someone—probably Charles Andrews—kept calling down to her, making sure of her location, asking if she could see light through the snow. "I kept answering I could not," she said, "until finally . . . a glow of light broke through."

When the rescuers found her, they realized that she was pinned beneath a thick tree trunk they could not hope to move. Andrews called for more tools, and he and the others began to saw away the two-foot-thick piece of timber. The delay was excruciating, but sometime in the early afternoon the pieces of the tree fell away and Ida Starrett was pulled out of the wreckage—nearly frozen and in deep shock. She was the last person from the trains rescued alive.

13

"The Reddened Snow"

This is not an hour for reciting the chapters thrilling, tragic, [or] pathetic of the calamity in the Cascades. The reality of the facts, the pain of suspense, the throbbing of hearts can never be expressed in words. The story is written in the torn mountain, in the reddened snow.

—Reverend W. E. Randall,
from a sermon delivered at
the First Baptist Church of Everett

Tuesday, March 1, 1910
Scenic Hot Springs
Morning

James H. O'Neill first received word of the Wellington snowslide about six hours after it happened. The superintendent had risen early, intending to check on the rotary before organizing a relief party to Wellington. He had slept well. Although some people at Scenic later claimed to have heard the crash of distant thunder overnight, O'Neill had been too deeply asleep to be roused by anything. ("I would not have heard a cannon that night," he would later testify.) But when he and Dowling saw J. J. Mackey approaching them at about 8:00 A.M., looking haggard and grim from his overnight rush down the mountain from Wellington, O'Neill must have known instantly that the traveling engineer was not bringing good news.

The three men stood in the gray, drizzling rain as Mackey explained just how bad it was.

Whatever anguish O'Neill felt at that moment—whatever sorrow or guilt or dread of what was to follow—he pushed it instantly aside. Galvanized by the need for immediate action, he gathered his officers and set to work. The first task, he realized, would have to be rounding up as many men as possible to assist in the rescue. There were scores of men now at Scenic, and many had already been preparing to hike up the mountain to bring food and supplies to the stranded trains. This force would have to be augmented, supplied with extra tools and medical supplies, and sent out as quickly as possible.

Word would also have to be sent to the outside world, but with no working telegraph at Scenic it would have to be done on foot. Only O'Neill himself could take on this latter duty. Only he, as superintendent, had access to the telegraph codebook required for secure communication with headquarters in St. Paul. Only he had the authority to orchestrate the larger rescue effort that would be required—the gathering of medical supplies, the requisitioning of doctors, nurses, and extra workmen, the organization of special relief trains from Everett and Seattle. All of this would require the superintendent's presence at the telegraph key.

So O'Neill put master mechanic Dowling, the second-ranking GN officer present, in charge of the rescue party. Dowling and Mackey would hastily organize their forces and then head up the mountain to Wellington, taking with them J. L. Godby, the attendant from the hotel's hot springs bath, who was the closest thing to a nurse available at Scenic. While this effort was being mobilized, O'Neill himself would hike west down the right-of-way to the first operational telegraph he could find. Assuming the tracks up from the coast were still remotely passable, he figured he should be able to get a well-supplied relief train to within hiking distance of Wellington by nightfall.

O'Neill collected as much additional information as he could from Mackey and set out along the buried tracks toward Skykomish. He may or may not have traveled alone, but the journey would not have been a simple one in either case. Although Scenic marked the western end of the truly extreme mountain terrain, the stretch of track from Scenic to Skykomish was still rugged and slide-prone, and it now had three feet of new wet snow on the tracks. And for a man like O'Neill, whose every instinct drew him *toward* the site of any trouble, it must have been agonizing to head west, away from the catastrophe for which he bore primary responsibility.

At about 11:00 A.M. he reached Nippon, a small station about nine miles east of Skykomish. Here the communication wires were still operational, so he stepped into the small telegraph office, took off his sopping coat, and sat down to compose what must have been the most difficult telegram of his career:

MARCH 1, 1910

AT 4:00 A.M. [*SIC*] LARGE SNOW SLIDE EXTENDING ONE-HALF MILE IN LENGTH CAME DOWN AT WELLINGTON, EXTENDING FROM SNOW SHED NO. 2 WEST OF WELLINGTON TO EAST PASSING TRACK SWITCH, TAKING DOWN WATER TANK, NO. 25 AND 27'S TRAIN, CAR A-16, FOUR MOTORS, MOTOR SHED, ROTARY X-807, ENGINES 702, 1032, AND 1418. ALL PASSENGERS NO. 25'S TRAIN MORE OR LESS INJURED. CANNOT SAY TO WHAT EXTENT UNTIL [WE] CAN GET THEM OUT.

This message, which was translated into code and then forwarded to Great Northern officials throughout the Northwest and eventually countrywide, was as straightforward and matter-of-fact as a telegram could be. But anyone reading it would have instantly recognized its import. A huge avalanche had knocked two packed railroad trains off the side of a mountain into a canyon below. Nothing like it had ever happened in eighty years of American railroading. And the death toll, O'Neill's cautious assessment notwithstanding, was likely to be of historic proportions. Though the superintendent could not know it at the time, the incident he'd just reported was by far the deadliest avalanche in American history. He would be dealing with its consequences for many years to come.

✧

Q: Was the track itself torn away?

A: That could not be determined. . . . The track was not visible at any place west of the station.

Q: Was there any part of the two trains left on the track?

A: Not a particle of either train.

—*J. J. Mackey*

Wellington
Tuesday Afternoon

When Dowling, Mackey, and a force of forty-odd men from Scenic finally reached the avalanche site at about three that afternoon, the small baggage room off the Wellington depot was already filling up with corpses. The rescuers initially on the scene had been pulling bodies out of the wreckage for over twelve hours, and more were being found every hour. The scene was gruesome. "The bodies that are to be taken out are fearfully distorted and mangled," one observer wrote. "The heads of some are smashed and limbs are torn in two and the bowels of some are torn out." Even for men as inured to carnage as these railroaders, the work was all but unendurable. According to engineer Edward Sweeney, when rescuers unearthed a half dozen crushed bodies pinned down by a fallen tree, one of the stricken shovelers approached the engineer and asked if he had authority to supply the men with whiskey to steady their nerves. "I don't have any particular authority," Sweeney replied, "but I'll get you some whiskey."

Appalling as it was on its face, the recovery work was even more daunting because of the constant danger of another slide. Although much of the high-lying snow on Windy Mountain had come down the previous night, there was still enough in place to pose a significant threat to the men crawling over the avalanche site, especially given the weather conditions. Rain continued falling, adding more weight to the snowpack.

Dowling and Mackey immediately had their men unpack their tools and fan out over the avalanche run-out zone, relieving some of those who had been digging all night and all day. The situation was still urgent. Scores of people remained unaccounted for—their colleagues Joe Pettit, Earl Longcoy, and trainmaster Blackburn among them—and while it was unlikely that any of them were still alive, it was not inconceivable. If a single car had come through the slide even partially intact, it could be harboring any number of survivors deep beneath the snow, where the oxygen supply would be diminishing by the minute. Only thirteen hours had passed since the slide, and under extraordinary circumstances avalanche victims can survive far longer than that.*

As Dowling and Mackey looked down over the expanse of the debris field, however, they must have realized that finding a submerged intact car—even if one existed—would be a desperately difficult task. Although darkness had veiled the scene from him the night before, Mackey could now appreciate the sheer vastness of the area over which the two trains had been scattered. The heavy engines had not been carried far down the slope, but the remains of the lighter wooden cars were strewn widely over acres and acres of precipitous terrain. The worst damage seemed to have been caused by the electric locomotives, which had been standing on the track nearest the mountainside. Hit first by the wall of snow and debris, these motors—the largest railroad locomotives in the world at the time—had apparently toppled in succession onto the Seattle Express on Passing Track 1 and then the Fast Mail on Passing Track 2, crushing both beneath them. In fact, Mackey and Dowling soon ascertained that the reason so many of the survivors came from the Winnipeg was that it was standing in the clear of the electrics.

Most of the other cars, though, had been quite literally smashed to bits ("as if an elephant had stepped on a cigar box" one witness reported). And as the men from Scenic began chopping away at the scattered bits of cars—the sound of their hatchets, axes, and shovels

---

* In 1982 a woman in Alpine Meadows, California, would live for five days in a demolished building before being rescued.

echoing down the valley—they began to realize that even the rescue effort was dangerous. The snow was littered with jagged pipes, shards of broken glass, and other potentially hazardous debris. Any opening hacked into the side of a car, moreover, would instantly suck snow, lumber, and sometimes even the rescuers themselves into the wreckage. At times they would find bodies inside and pull them out as if "taking them from a river." More often, the only thing they found was trash—"a car lamp, a sack of mail, a whisk broom, a chunk of coal, a woman's shoe, a drummer's shirt samples," and so on. One rescuer even found a baby carriage on its side near the bottom of the ravine— probably that of Francis Starrett, the infant who had smothered in the wreckage of the Winnipeg. The carriage would still be there days later, as if no one at Wellington could muster the strength of will to move it.

Francis Starrett's mother, meanwhile, was being cared for with two dozen other survivors at the enginemen's bunkhouse. When J. L. Godby arrived there at midafternoon, the Sherlocks and Mrs. Miles had already seen to the immediate needs of nearly everyone. One man had reportedly died from the effects of exposure after being placed in the improvised hospital, but the other patients had been more or less stabilized. Some—such as passengers R. M. Laville and Ray Forsyth— had suffered only minor injuries and were already up and around; others—Lucius Anderson, Ira Clary, Homer Purcell—needed mostly bandaging and rest. Snow King William Harrington had a fairly serious head injury, Ross Phillips was badly burned, and Henry White was battered and heavily bruised around the chest. All of these men sat or lay around the stuffy bunkhouse in various states of disorientation and shock.

The ever-conscientious A. B. Hensel, despite suffering from several cracked ribs, a broken arm, and a broken collarbone, wanted to make sure that all of the registered mail in the trains would be secured once it was found. He had been told the fate of his colleagues and felt dutybound to report the news to the chief mail clerk in Spokane. Ignoring pleas to rest, he insisted on dictating a telegram to one of the hospital volunteers. "I am the only mail clerk to escape alive," it read. "Though badly injured, I am confident of recovery. Alfred B. Hensel." Relayed by foot to the closest working telegraph on the line, this wire turned out to be the first message from Wellington itself to reach the outside world.

In the woman's ward next door, Basil Sherlock was doing his best to assist his wife, Alathea, and Mrs. Miles with the nursing. The toddler Varden Gray, probably the most seriously injured patient, was occupying much of the women's time, especially after the child showed signs of pneumonia. So Sherlock was tending to some of the less grave cases, bringing them hot whiskey slings "to thaw them out from the inside." Anna Gray and Mrs. May (Ida Starrett's mother, who had survived relatively unscathed) smelled the whiskey in the concoction and at first refused to take it, but Sherlock insisted. "[I told them] we were not going to have them coming down with pneumonia and peppering everyone in the hospital," he explained. In the end, the two women relented. "They took their medicine," Sherlock reported, "like a good sport."

Such bullying tactics had no effect on Ida Starrett. Having spent so much time under the snow, she was now severely hypothermic. "I would say she was two-thirds frozen," Sherlock remembered. "I did not take her pulse, but I did put my ear over her heart, which was beating, but it seemed real slow. She was numb all over." The telegrapher and some of the patients—even a few with broken bones—began warming blankets by the stove and wrapping them around her, but she was slow to revive. Still not fully aware that two of her children were dead and that her father was missing, she lay silent and stone-faced in her bunk, clearly in deep shock.

Ida's surviving son, Raymond, his bruised cheek swollen and his cut forehead impressively bandaged, watched her in silence. Finally, feeling desperate, he did whatever he could think of to bring her out of her catalepsy. "I even tried to make her cry," he later admitted. But though he pleaded with her, pulled at her arm, and pinched her, nothing he did could bring her around. The boy could only sit helplessly by her side, more unsettled by her impassivity than by any other part of his ordeal.

✧

AVALANCHE BURIES SPOKANE TRAIN
30 PASSENGERS MAY BE DEAD

—Everett Daily Herald,
banner headline,
March 1, 1910

Seattle
Tuesday Afternoon Through Wednesday

News of the disaster reached the general public sometime later that afternoon. Although the GN would doubtless have preferred to suppress the story until more particulars could be learned, they'd decided to release an announcement shortly after receiving O'Neill's telegram, knowing that the story would soon get out in any case: John Wentzel, the only professed witness to the actual slide, had stumbled into Skykomish that morning, having walked the entire eighteen miles from Wellington. "All wiped out!" he cried before collapsing in exhaustion. It was several hours before anyone could get a coherent story from the man, but they gleaned enough to comprehend the extent of the tragedy. And once Skykomish knew of what would soon be called the Horror at Wellington, it could only be a matter of hours before the rest of the world knew of it too.

The press had been aware for several days that there were GN trains stranded in the mountains, but had known few details. Wary of bad publicity, the Great Northern had been reluctant to share much information, and the resulting newspaper stories had necessarily been vague. With the emergence of Merritt, Rogers, and the other hikers, however, the papers finally had some specifics to work with. The *Seattle Times*, after interviewing George Loveberry upon his arrival in town, had printed an article about the situation on Monday morning, under lurid headlines: "TRAVELERS FACE HUNGER AND DEATH" and "60 PASSENGERS FACE BURIAL IN AVALANCHE." There was also specific mention of the stranded trains in Monday's edition of the *Everett Daily Herald* and several other newspapers.

But when word of the actual avalanche arrived on Tuesday—making such sensationalized scaremongering look more like prophecy—the papers instantly threw themselves into a frenzy. Reporters and photographers, equipped with snowshoes and other climbing equipment, were immediately mobilized and sent out on the road toward Stevens Pass. They were apparently given instructions to start generating copy as soon as possible, for as early as Tuesday evening several of the local dailies already had skeletal accounts of the avalanche on their front pages. And by dawn on Wednesday, the story had made it into papers nationwide.

As the news broke, help of all kinds was hastily dispatched to the mountains. Over the next few days, three different special trains were sent out from Everett and Seattle, transporting scores of doctors, nurses, volunteer rescuers, friends and relatives of victims, and anyone else the Great Northern could muster (including some homeless men from the Seattle city jail) to aid in the rescue and track-clearing efforts. Laden with food, medical supplies, tools, and—in one case—a supply of coffins, the trains were able to travel only as far as Scenic (on the very first day, only as far as Nippon). From there, everything had to be packed in on foot, each man carrying as big a load as he could handle.

By the evening of March 1, dozens of rescuers were making the climb up the steep slope to Windy Point. The rain had all but stopped by now, but the wind at higher elevations was still blowing fiercely, making the ascent particularly treacherous. Andy Pascoe, a GN railroader who had joined a relief train at Skykomish, accompanied one of the doctors up to Wellington on that first night. Dr. E. C. Gleason carried a coal-oil lantern to light the way as Pascoe, a man of some size, followed behind with a shovel, a bundle of splints, seventy-five pounds of food, and the doctor's bag on his back. Above were dozens of other rescuers, their lanterns creating a series of ghostly white halos that meandered shakily up the mountain, throwing erratic shadows on the snow.

Stopping to rest, Pascoe noticed that each lantern seemed to wink out once it reached the top of the slope. He couldn't figure out the reason—until he and the doctor reached the same point, where a strong gust barreling up from the canyon nearly blasted them off their feet. The flame in their own lantern blew out, and in the confusion of trying to relight it in the total darkness, the two men nearly stepped off a precipice above a several-hundred-foot drop.

The first doctor reached the scene almost exactly twenty-four hours after the avalanche. A. W. Stockwell of Monroe arrived at about two A.M. on Wednesday, accompanied by two professional nurses, Leonora Todhunter and Annabelle Lee, who had donned men's clothing and made the hike up the mountain among the earliest rescuers. What the three medical professionals found at the crowded bunkhouse was a surprisingly shipshape hospital. Mrs. Sherlock in particular (she would later be extolled in the press as the "Florence Nightingale of the Cascades") had provided excellent first aid, and by the time the other doctors and surgeons arrived at midmorning, Stockwell realized that he had more medical personnel than he really needed. By the end of the day, he was able to make one of the few positive announcements to come out of those mountains—namely, that all of the injured were now out of danger and would probably recover. Although the more seriously hurt patients could not be moved until the rail line was cleared, they would receive all the care they needed right there at Wellington.

Finally, at about 1:00 P.M. on Wednesday afternoon, James H. O'Neill arrived on the scene. Snowshoeing up the trail from Scenic with a team of undertakers from Butterworth and Sons of Seattle, O'Neill had been astonished at the condition of the right-of-way. So many avalanches had occurred since his last trip down the mountain that the entire four-mile stretch from Windy Point to Wellington was now virtually one continuous slide. And what the superintendent saw once he reached the main avalanche site was sobering.

O'Neill stopped and spent some minutes taking in the scene before him. A thousand feet above the right-of-way, a sharply defined bank of snow ran in almost a straight horizontal across the face of Windy Mountain. This was clearly the line at which the ten-acre slab of snow had broken away. That entire slab had then rumbled downhill, carrying away almost everything on the mountainside. Only a bleak, meager-looking assortment of bent and broken tree trunks remained on the slope above. All the rest—the snow, the rocks, most of the trees, and the underbrush—now lay packed in the canyon below. As hard as limestone in places, the mixture entombed two entire trains, a half dozen engines, a rotary snowplow, several small buildings, and the bodies of roughly a hundred people.

As awful as it may have sounded in Mackey's report, the scene was far worse witnessed firsthand. O'Neill knew that James J. Hill in St. Paul would be anxiously awaiting his assessment of the situation. But how long it would take to recover all that was lost—let alone to repair and re-open the rail line—was something the superintendent could hardly even guess.

✧

March 3rd, 1910

Following from Supt O'Neill at 2:38 P.M.: "Have recovered 29 bodies since accident, 24 injured being cared for here. All equipment total loss except trucks. Have force of sixty men searching but account so much snow and cars being buried it is slow work. Figure have 25 to 30 bodies yet to recover. Weather very bad and we are having some trouble keeping men."

W. C. Watrous,
telegram to L. W. Hill et al.

The First Week of March 1910
Wellington

Over the next several days, dozens more victims were located, removed from the wreckage, and identified, one by one. By Thursday, March 3, the body of R. H. Bethel (a.k.a. "Colonel Cody") had been found, as had that of James McNeny, the friend whom John Rogers could not persuade to hike out with him on Monday. The Lemmans were discovered side by side, their sixteen-year-old daughter now left an orphan with her grandparents in Ritzville. And Nellie Sharp, "the Wild West Girl," was found carrying a diamond ring and $100 in cash—presumably the money she would have lived on while researching her article for *McClure's*.

Many friends and relatives of victims soon began arriving on the scene. Among the first was Edward Boles, who came back from Scenic to search for the brother he'd left behind. A minister from Bellingham arrived on a mission to find the Reverend J. M. Thomson. From Leavenworth (via Seattle and Scenic) came a Miss Katherine Fisher, a "more than ordinarily pretty" woman who had braved the ascent in order to claim the body of her fiancé, a fireman named Earl Bennington.

One associate of Charles Eltinge, T. R. Garrison, had been forced to defy repeated discouragements from railway officials in order to reach the site. After several days of difficult travel—once he even had to climb over two stalled freight trains, "engines and all"—he finally reached Wellington and described the scene: "There was not a sign of anything but a tremendous mass of snow, with here and there a tree trunk sticking out or perhaps a bit of tangled brush. . . . On crawling down the bank, however, I soon saw evidences of the horror beneath. Here were the irons of the passenger coach twisted around the trunk of a tree like a thread of silk. I stumbled against a piece of polished wood with an iron rod piercing it as clean as a knife." Garrison spent the rest of the day looking for Eltinge, but with no success. Continuing his search the next morning, he saw some men climbing out of the canyon with several bodies on stretchers. He stopped them and lifted the sheet from the first one; it was Eltinge himself staring back at him, with only "a dull bruise on his forehead to show the cause of death."

Two sons of Mrs. Covington, Luther and Frank, appeared on Thursday, hoping somehow to find their missing mother still alive. Luther, a prominent Washington clergyman, had traveled with his brother from Seattle to Scenic on Wednesday evening. Hiking up to Wellington the next day, they hurried first to the bunkhouse hospital, but any dim hopes they might have had about their mother's survival were soon dashed. The only older woman in the grim, silent ladies' ward was Mrs. May.

The brothers then moved on to the depot's baggage room and tool-shed, where seven undertakers were already at work, embalming the bodies and preparing them for evacuation. With handkerchiefs held to their noses, the two men paced up and down the long line of bodies, but none even resembled their mother. This, of course, was hardly a relief, since it meant that she could only be somewhere down in the ravine. Bracing themselves, they descended into the debris field, where there were now 150 people crawling over the wreckage. But although they searched all that day, they could find no trace of her.

Frustrated and exhausted, overwhelmed by the sheer ghastliness of the scene and finding no place to sleep at Wellington, they returned to Scenic that night—only to be told that their mother had been discovered in the wreckage of the Winnipeg shortly after their departure. It would have been her fifty-first wedding anniversary. "My heart is well-nigh broken," their sister Mrs. George P. Anderson wrote to another sister when she heard. "We cannot as yet realize or understand how or why it should happen to one who has lived so noble and glorious a life."

Most aggrieved was Melmoth Covington Sr., who had held out hope for his wife's rescue to the very end. "It has come hardest on poor Father," Mrs. Anderson continued. "The worst pang of intense pain [is] past, yet he will always miss her so intensely; it is very, very sad."

For other families, however, the suspense was to go on much longer. Among those still missing by the end of the week were George Davis, Ned Topping, and William May. Some of these men may have been among the unidentified bodies already lined up in the baggage room. Since almost all of the victims had been dressed in nothing but night-clothes, with no documentation on their persons, they had to be identified by appearance alone—a particularly difficult task in cases where mutilation was extreme. Eventually, the unclaimed bodies became too numerous for the shed and had to be stored in the station building, where they were lined up so tightly that, according to one report, "survivors, diggers, and newspapermen have accidentally stepped on a discolored hand or foot in getting in and out of the telegraph office."

✦

Through it all, superintendent O'Neill went on without relief, stoic but clearly devastated. He was receiving accolades from many on the site for his perseverance and determination. King County coroner James C. Snyder, who had come up to Wellington on Thursday with a number of detectives and postal officials, had returned to Seattle the next day with all kinds of praise for the man in charge. "Superintendent O'Neill has handled the railroad end of the affair in a masterly manner," Snyder said to reporters. "No one could have done more than he did, and I never saw a man show such generalship. . . . He seems to have an utter disregard for his own personal safety or health."

No matter how solacing in theory, these encomiums probably did little to ease O'Neill's torment. Especially hard for him had been the discovery of his business car at 1:00 P.M. on Friday. The A-16 had barely been budged from the tracks by the avalanche. Instead, the slide had sliced off the top of the car and crammed it full of snow and debris. Suffocated inside were steward Lewis Walker, stenographer Earl Longcoy, and trainmaster Arthur Blackburn, found "in an attitude as if he had been sleeping peacefully, his face in his hands." These had been O'Neill's friends, men he worked with every day. Blackburn had been a guest at his wedding. When at home with Berenice, O'Neill sat in the fine Morris chair the trainmaster had given them as a gift.

Then the body of conductor Joseph Pettit turned up. This was another difficult death for O'Neill, and not just because Pettit was a friend. The conductor had left a widow and five children back in Everett. In an age before widespread life insurance, they would likely be left with no means of support whatever.

"Last night, when he dropped to rest on the floor, he had aged years," one reporter wrote of the superintendent on March 4. "His rather boyish face was scarred with lines that will never leave."

Adding to O'Neill's woes was the fact that the rescue effort itself was plagued by difficulties and unpleasantness. In the first few days after the avalanche, several of the foreign track workers were caught in possession of clothing from the wreck. Early reports that the men had actually been looting corpses later proved false, but the rumors caused such a xenophobic uproar that O'Neill finally had to send all foreigners from the avalanche site to work elsewhere on the mountain. At least one temporary laborer, a man who gave his name as Robert Roberts, actually had to be arrested—for stealing a gold watch that belonged to victim Solomon Cohen.

Soon the weather, too, was creating problems again. After several days of rain that had done much to melt away the snow covering the wreckage (for a time, the water draining through the debris field had created bloody trails that rescuers could follow backward to their sources), another blizzard had set in on Friday night, forcing a halt to all rescue activity for nearly a full day. Still other crises arose. Three telegraphers were reportedly stranded at the small station at Berne without food. An unidentified body had been seen in a creek somewhere on the east slope. A watchman at Drury had been killed when an avalanche crushed the small cabin in which he had taken refuge.

And always the threat of another slide hung over the rescuers. On the night of March 3, the rain and warm temperatures caused the snow on the roof of the Bailets Hotel to slide off with a loud din, bringing everyone in town out of their beds. Bailets was so anxious about the possibility of a second slide that he took his family to sleep in one of the outfit cars on the spur tracks east of town. In the succeeding days, many workers began walking through the tunnel every night to sleep at Cascade Tunnel Station on the other side. Even O'Neill hiked the three dark miles every night, alone with whatever grim thoughts he might have been thinking.

The press, meanwhile, was churning out as much prose as possible about what was now one of the biggest disaster stories in Pacific Northwest history. The first actual journalist didn't reach Wellington until the evening of March 2, but the lack of on-site reporting hadn't prevented some papers from concocting stories of their own imagining, and the wilder the better. The *Seattle Post-Intelligencer* had been especially creative. According to the March 3 edition, for instance, engineer Charles Andrews had been sleeping on one of the trains on the night of the slide but, "moved by a power which appeared to Andrews to come from a source other than the physical," he had arisen and gotten off minutes before the train was hit—a story that Andrews later vehemently denied. Over the next few days, the *Post-Intelligencer* and other papers printed more absurdities: that packs of mountain lions and wolves were patrolling the disaster site; that a burbling baby had survived the slide unharmed while both of its parents had perished; that one stranded train crew was forced to kill and eat a cat; and—perhaps most egregious of all—that a buried coach was uncovered by rescuers several days after the slide with ten people still alive inside (a patently implausible story that was nonetheless picked up by newspapers as far away as France).

The *Seattle Times,* somewhat more measured in its reporting, had the advantage of having the first man on the scene to provide eyewitness testimony. J. J. Underwood had snowshoed up from Scenic on the evening of March 2 and wanted to file his first story the next day, once the telegraph wires were restored between Wellington and Scenic. He went to the office at the depot and asked first-trick operator William Avery to wire the story to the *Times* offices in Seattle. O'Neill was present and at first tried to stop him. "We're not going to let you send that stuff out from here," the superintendent said, all too familiar with the type of embellished misinformation that often passed for news in that age of yellow journalism.

Underwood, however, would not be put off. He told O'Neill that he would hike down to Scenic if necessary to file his reports. When this threat seemed to have no effect, he changed his tack, assuring the superintendent that he was above the tawdry sensationalism practiced by the *Times's* competitors. This latter claim is perhaps debatable, given that his first dispatch contained gaudy verbal fugues like "Death everywhere, suffering and sorrow most poignant, the wailing of women, the subdued sobs of the few children saved from the grip of the avalanche," and so on.

Some of Underwood's subsequent reporting, however, did have a definite evocative power. His descriptions of the rescue scene were especially vivid: "The task of digging for the dead, especially at night, is inexpressively eerie. Surrounded by rugged, snow-capped mountains, with the haunting fear of new slides never absent from the minds of rescuers, scores of men ply diligent shovels in efforts to bring forth the bodies of victims. Twinkling lanterns gleam over the tangled masses of snow, mere specks in the widespread desolation." Although Underwood did get some of his facts precisely wrong—he claimed, for instance, that the women on the Seattle Express had begged that the train be kept *out* of the tunnel—his sometimes purple reporting was at least far more reliable than that of the irresponsible journalists who followed him.

Yet another specter hanging over O'Neill's head was the judgment of his superiors in St. Paul. James J. Hill (probably on the advice of GN lawyers) was making no public comments on the disaster, but O'Neill knew that the old man was probably more wounded by it than he had let on. The perceived freakishness of the accident was generating worldwide publicity. "I was greatly distressed to read of the extraordinary misfortune which has overtaken one of your trains," an associate from J. P. Morgan wrote Hill on March 3. "I do not think I ever heard of such a thing as an avalanche sweeping [a] train off the track. I trust that the damage will not be anything like as serious as reported in the papers."

But Hill knew that the damage was much worse. Early public statements about the death toll had been conservative, but the office diaries of the GN general manager reveal that Hill and his corporate staff knew as early as the day of the avalanche that some eighty-five lives had been lost. And although the precise number killed was perhaps not important from a practical standpoint, there was a psychologically critical threshold that would matter a great deal to Hill. If the death toll at Wellington exceeded 116—the number of people who had died in a 1904 train accident in Pueblo, Colorado—the Wellington Disaster would come to be known as the deadliest rail accident in American history. This was clearly a distinction that the chairman was eager to avoid.

Unfortunately, O'Neill simply could not tell Hill or anyone else how many people were dead, since he had no idea how many had been sleeping on the trains on the night of the slide. During the week of the trains' entrapment, a group of thirty foreign laborers had reportedly been bedding down in a day-coach smoker on the passenger train, but many of these men were probably among those who had walked off the job over the weekend. Until that coach was found, then, O'Neill would have no accurate sense of what the final tally would be.

So rescuers kept digging, turning up a few new bodies every day. Hair-accessories entrepreneur Libby Latsch was found by the end of the week, as was customs official H. D. Chantrell, but no one could find any trace of the missing smoking car. Now that the rescuers were getting deeper into the slide, they were finding the snow even denser and harder to work through. "The snow was packed so hard about the bodies we took out," one digger reported, "that an impression like an alabaster cast remains in the frozen whiteness."

By Monday O'Neill was convinced that it would be a full month before all of the victims were found and accounted for. He was even considering running steam hoses over the snow to melt it faster—an idea that seems highly impractical if not desperate. But the superintendent was apparently ready to try anything. With so many people still missing, it was beginning to look as if it might even be well into the spring before the cleanup work was done and O'Neill could finally go back home.

✧

> How puny is man in the face of angered nature! And yet how indomitably and hopefully persistent. He is swept from the earth like the wheat before the sickle or the chaff before the wind. His toilsome labors are made nothing of; the greatest achievements are crumbled to dust. Yet, driven by that impulse within him, he buries his dead, clears up the debris, and returns to his task, even while he can yet feel the wings of Death hovering over him.
>
> —Seattle Star *editorial*

On the Line Between Skykomish and Leavenworth

For many in the Great Northern Railway company—particularly for those at corporate headquarters in St. Paul—the recovery of the dead at

Wellington was not the most urgent task to be accomplished in those first two weeks after the avalanche. As general manager J. M. Gruber would later remark, what the Great Northern was facing in its Cascade Division was nothing less than "the greatest blockade of a railway system ever witnessed." Although some GN traffic was being successfully routed through the Cascades via the Northern Pacific lines, all too much of it—particularly freight, the bread and butter of any railway system—was piling up at rail yards both east and west of the mountains. The backup was already starting to hurt the company's profit picture: The Great Northern, which had been losing significant revenue ever since the line had become blocked on February 23, would continue to lose money every hour until the line was cleared and open to traffic once again.

Unfortunately, that task was proving to be enormous, even with rotaries working from both directions and supported by hundreds of shovelers. On the east slope, assistant superintendent J. C. Devery had been working west with the borrowed Kalispell rotary since the day before the disaster but had made only moderate progress. One mile-long slide at Merritt had required thirty-six hours of nonstop work to clear; another half-mile slide at Gaynor (the slide that had foiled Snow King Harrington's rotary on Saturday night) had eaten up more time still. Even after the special relief train from the east had caught up with them, bringing J. M. Gruber and G. H. Emerson and pulling no fewer than ten coal cars, a carload of dynamite, a complete wrecking outfit, and a healthy supply of 250 well-rested laborers, progress had been remarkably slow. Then, on March 6, they encountered a tremendous slide at Berne—"one of the largest I have ever seen," according to one GN veteran—which had left snow one hundred feet deep on the tracks. Despite having all of that dynamite at their disposal, it was almost four days before they could clear the slide and move on.

Work on the western slope was being plagued by similar delays. The arrival of an extra rotary from the Northern Pacific fleet on Thursday, March 3, helped matters considerably. The subsequent appearance on Saturday of general superintendent E. L. Brown and scores of extra men took even more of the pressure off Dowling and his exhausted

crew. But the west-slope effort was soon being hampered by a resur-
gence of labor difficulties among the temporary snow shovelers. "Have
had considerable trouble holding men," Brown reported to headquarters on Saturday night. "They are quitting as fast as we can get them out
here, fearing trouble from slides."

Even so, by Sunday night, helped by clearing weather and the arrival of a shipment of dynamite and black blasting powder, the west-
slope crews had made enough progress to get within hiking distance of
the stranded X800-X802 between Windy Point and Wellington. Coal
was packed in to the double by three hundred laborers, and once it was
revived and ready for work, the railroad had a full contingent of three
double rotaries working simultaneously on the line. By Tuesday,
March 8—one week after the slide—it was beginning to look as if the
Cascade Division might be back in operation within days.

One unavoidable cause of delay was the evacuation of the dead
and wounded from Wellington. Blasting and plowing had to be
stopped whenever these processions came through, and since some
of Brown's black-powder charges had destroyed parts of the main
trail, new routes had to be blazed around the gaps. The first of the injured passengers to be evacuated—Ray Forsyth and R. M. Laville—
came down the mountain on March 2 with three of the doctors
whose presence at Wellington was no longer needed. Later that same
day, a half dozen injured trainmen descended, including conductors
Ira Clary and Homer Purcell and fireman Samuel Bates. The largest
group came out on Sunday—a "pathetic procession," according to
the *Seattle Star,* consisting of passenger Henry White, William Harrington, Pullman porters Lucius Anderson and Adolph Smith, and
three other trainmen. "As the little party reached the point on the
trail where they looked down 1,000 feet of sheer descent," the *Star*
reported, "guides and survivors alike bared heads and gave silent
thanks for their salvation."

Henry White, still sore and somewhat unsteady from the battering
he'd taken in the slide, seemed particularly impatient to be getting off the
mountain. "I'd rather take a chance on dying [on the trail] than to stay at
Wellington any longer," he told a reporter when asked why he hadn't

waited for the track-clearing to finish before making his escape. When prompted for a comment by another newsman, the ever-loquacious White obliged. "You can tell the people for me," he responded blithely, "that I am glad to be out of this place and will welcome the sight of the City of Seattle as a long-lost relative. By the way, I wish you would send me a set of pictures of the gentlemen with me. They are the finest, bravest, jolliest, best-hearted lot of fellows I have ever had the honor of meeting." Given the role White was to play in the court cases to follow, this bit of hearty bonhomie seems decidedly odd, if not disingenuous. White was already harboring some heavy resentments against the railroad and its employees, and it wouldn't be long before he would be airing them in public—to the detriment of Snow King Harrington in particular.

As the group made its way down the trail, though, their feeling of camaraderie was apparently genuine enough. Much hilarity ensued when the disheveled survivors proceeded to slide down the slope to Scenic (though at a somewhat less precipitous place than that used by the Merritt and Rogers groups). "It's not half-bad coming down that hill," fireman George Nelson told another reporter at the bottom. "If my leg was all right, I could get a lot of fun out of it."

Evacuating the dead proved to be a somewhat more somber procedure. In the first few days after the slide, O'Neill had ordered a dozen or so Alaskan sleds for the transport of bodies to Scenic, and they were getting plenty of use. As a test case, the superintendent had sent a party with only two bodies (those of Solomon Cohen and R. H. Bethel) on Friday, March 4. When that trip proved successful, he sent a full contingent of thirteen sleds the next day, the bodies wrapped tightly in distinctive brown-and-white-checked GN blankets and strapped securely to the sleds. John Polson, an undertaker from Butterworth and Sons, described the scene:

> We left Wellington at noon, with six men to the first Alaskan sled, and four to each of the other twelve sleds, each carrying its body. Two feet of snow had fallen overnight, and the trail was most difficult. We were two hours and a half reaching the summit above Scenic, and then the hardest part of the work faced the party.

It was here, at the slope nicknamed Old Glory, that a lifeline had been tied to a sturdy tree, with the other end secured at the bottom of the thousand-foot drop. Taking each wrapped body from its sled, the workers would tie a rope around its feet. Then they would carefully lower it down the slope, one man below, holding the lifeline and guiding the body headfirst, while the man above controlled the descent with the rope looped around his waist. Once at the bottom, the bodies were held at Scenic until they could be loaded onto a waiting train and transported to the coast.

Among those performing this grim task was Bill J. Moore, the young brakeman who would later help unearth the very last avalanche victim in July. He had been up at Wellington for several days, digging for bodies, and was now manning the sled that carried the remains of Catherine O'Reilly, the Irish-born nurse. He was finding the job unsettling—he seemed particularly rattled by the fact that O'Reilly had lost a hand in the disaster—but the scene at the bottom was what stuck with him for many years afterward. "I seen 90 bodies at Scenic depot," he would later recall (probably exaggerating the number), "and I was only 19 years and 8 months [old]." Like many of those at work in the rescue effort, this "hardened railroad man" was scarcely more than a boy.

There were many more bodies to come. On March 6 and 7 the crushed mail cars from train No. 27 were finally unearthed, containing the remains of A. B. Hensel's eight colleagues. William May and George Davis were soon found, and then, at last, Ned Topping, his ongoing letter to his mother lying in the wreckage beside him. But even as late as March 10 there were still well over two dozen of the missing and unidentified to be accounted for. And although part of the long-lost smoking car was finally found on the evening of March 7, it was still uncertain days later how many bodies it actually contained.

As all of this was going on, the nine more seriously injured survivors remained in the bunkhouse hospital, too frail to be moved until a train arrived. A. B. Hensel was still entirely bed-ridden with his injuries, but the two railroaders—engineer Duncan Tegtmeier and brakeman Ross Phillips—were both recuperating well, the latter no doubt helped by the presence of his wife, Carrie, who had made the climb up from Scenic in the first days after the avalanche. Both adult Grays were also doing better now, and even little Varden had regained much of his strength.

Only Ida Starrett remained in grave condition. Physically she was making progress, but her mental state was of some concern to Dr. Stockwell and the other caregivers. She knew now that her daughter and baby son were dead, but she seemed determined not to give up on her father. "Confined to the hospital and unable to comprehend real conditions in the gully beyond the depot," the *Seattle Star* reported, "she and her mother clung to the hope that her father would be saved, that he had escaped somehow."

The news could not be kept from her forever. When told that the remains of William May had finally been recovered, the last of Ida's will seemed to dissolve away. "Let me die," she allegedly whispered, and for a time even the comfort of Raymond by her side could do little to ease her suffering.

◆

The next day Basil Sherlock was visiting the hospital when a nurse came up to him carrying little Ray in her arms. "Here is a young man that has been asking to see you for some time," she said. The boy had been eager to meet the "doctor" who had cut the long piece of wood from his forehead. "I got up and looked at him," Sherlock later remembered. "He smiled and I smiled back, then we shook hands. [But] I could not talk, for I had seen his two sisters and grandfather lying dead on top of the snow."

Sherlock was apparently suffering some psychological wounds of his own after the experience he'd been through. The day after being relieved at the hospital by Dr. Stockwell, the telegrapher had decided to quit his job effective immediately and put as much distance between himself and Wellington as he could. With this in mind, he had approached O'Neill on the slope above the avalanche site on March 3, while the latter was looking over the rescue work. When Sherlock appeared, O'Neill spoke to him about his stenographer, Earl Longcoy, whose body at that point had not yet been found. The boy, O'Neill said somberly, had been only nineteen years old. He had just moved to the West Coast a few months earlier, and now his sister and widowed mother were at that very moment following him west to take up residence in Everett. As far as anyone knew, they had not yet heard of young Earl's death.

Oblivious to his chief's reflective mood, Sherlock chose this moment to hand the superintendent his resignation letter. O'Neill read it with apparent disbelief and handed it back. "You do not want to quit," O'Neill said simply. "Take a vacation for a while and go back east. Then, when you return, you will want to stay on." But Sherlock was determined. Though he promised to remain on the job until properly relieved, he told O'Neill the he was going "to some place where the water would not run, let alone the snow."

Others at Wellington were showing greater resilience. When a reporter asked Duncan Tegtmeier what he planned to do when he recovered from his wounds, the barely ambulatory engineer replied gamely, "Why, get them to give me another engine, of course. Do you think I am going to waste five years I spent learning this trade just because I got this one bad shakeup?"

It was Tegtmeier who, late on March 10, heard the approach of the first engine to reach Wellington after the avalanche. After spending days blasting through the enormous slide at Berne, J. M. Gruber's convoy of rotaries and relief train had finally reached Cascade Tunnel Station that morning and was now coming through the tunnel. Tegtmeier, whose trained ear had been listening for this very thing, reportedly grabbed some crutches and pushed aside a frightened nurse in his rush to get outside. The engineer's eagerness, though, was probably shared by everyone at Wellington. The arrival of Gruber's train, after all, meant that the town was once again connected to the outside world—after sixteen full days of total isolation.

General manager Gruber, looking as weather-beaten as any of his laborers, hopped off the rotary and headed straight for the bunkhouse hospital. He immediately offered to make up a special train with his own private car to carry the injured eastward to Spokane, where they could be properly hospitalized. Of the nine people remaining at the bunkhouse, though, only Hensel wanted to go to Spokane; the rest, hoping to get to the coast, debated over whether they should wait for the west slope to be cleared, so that they might be taken down to Everett and Seattle directly. Their eagerness to get off the mountain, however, carried the day. Despite the fact that many of them— particularly the Starretts—dreaded the idea of getting back on any train, all nine decided to go east.

Gruber had the special backed up to the bunkhouse. Anna Gray and Mrs. May were able to walk onto the train without assistance, but the other seven were carried on. (Hensel would later remember being lifted through the car window on a stretcher.) Then everyone at Wellington stopped work to see the injured on their way, waving and shouting farewells as the train pulled eastward out of the bruised and battered town.

It was two days later, at 7:00 A.M. on Saturday, March 12, just as the sun was rising over the Cascade peaks, that the rotaries on the western slope finally broke through the last remaining feet of blockage and met on the flanks of Windy Mountain. Word was quickly wired out to all Great Northern stations and the world: "The siege of snows is ended." After nearly three weeks of punishing labor, the Cascade Division was once again open for business. Time, which had come to a dead stop at Stevens Pass sometime on the morning of February 23, was finally moving once again.

James J. Hill, following the situation from St. Paul, was profoundly relieved. "You have all done well," he cabled to Gruber when the job was nearing completion. "When you get through, the Company should not forget the men who have worked so constantly and so long. I wish you would thank them for me." Hill being Hill, he also made sure that no one rested on any laurels: "[I] think it important," he added, "to get the mail train on a regular run as early as you can without delaying other work."

Saturday's victory over the snows unfortunately proved to be short-lived. A few trains did make it successfully over the hump on that day (crowded, according to one report, with an unusually high number of rubbernecking passengers), but the snow-covered Cascade slopes were still not entirely quiet. Sometime after midnight early Sunday morning, a westbound Oriental Limited train ran into some heavy snow that had sloughed onto the tracks near Windy Point. One or two of the cars derailed slightly, so the train was stopped, the wheels were rerailed, and then the entire train was pulled back to the safety of a nearby snowshed to wait for a rotary to clear the heavy snow ahead.

Just as the plow was about to eat through the last of the obstruction, however, a large avalanche came screaming down the slope above it. Twenty gangmen working ahead of the rotary saw it coming and ran for their lives, but the plow itself could not be reversed in time. Hit broadside by the charging mass of snow and debris, the plow, its pusher engine, and five flatcars of coal were sent hurtling five hundred feet down the mountain, smashing one steel bridge and two spans of another. Almost the entire plow crew had been able to escape in time, but one engineer and one Italian laborer were caught by the edge of the slide and sucked into the plunging tumult. The engineer lived, but the laborer was lost, not to be found for many weeks.

For O'Neill, this must have seemed like the reprise of a nightmare—another train full of passengers trapped on the mountain amid faltering snowfields. Fearing any replay of the recent debacle, the superintendent hurriedly conferred with Gruber and Brown, and they decided to immediately evacuate all passengers and send the train itself back to Spokane. The rattled travelers were taken to the top of the much-used slope of Old Glory (now being called "Dead Man's Slide" by the newspapers) and gently guided down to Scenic.

This latest slide incident, though unsettling, turned out to be a minor setback. By Tuesday, March 15, the line had been cleared again and normal traffic could resume. To the relief of everyone in the division, the stranding of the Oriental Limited would turn out to be the last major problem of the snow season on the Stevens Pass line.

On that same day—March 15—James H. O'Neill was finally able to leave the mountain and return home to Everett. Berenice, who had been awaiting his return for over three weeks, would be there to meet him with baby Peggy in her arms, feeling as relieved as a woman could possibly be. But although the immediate crisis was now past, O'Neill's own ordeal was hardly over. His work on the mountain might have been finished (even the majority of the mail had been recovered by now), but he would soon be faced with tasks that were in some ways even more difficult. For one, he would have to personally find Earl Longcoy's mother and sister and inform them of the young man's death. He would also have to pay his respects to the widow of Lewis Walker, his steward on the A-16. Hardest of all, he would have to explain to them—and later to the world at large—why and how the whole terrible incident had happened in the first place.

14

Inquest

That thousands of tons of snow, rock, and mud came down is quite evident; that the timber was all destroyed by fire; that many lives were lost, caught like a rat in a trap, is equally true. But what does it matter if all the officials have to do is to say, "Well, it is the will of Divine Providence," and the county authorities accept that as a sufficient explanation? Would it not be proper at this time to suggest that there are some very good reasons why these accidents occurred other than the will of God?

—Seattle Union Record

March 1910
Seattle

The initial reaction of the public to the tragedy at Wellington, as might be expected, had been highly sympathetic to all involved. Passengers, rescuers, and train crews had all been showered with the kind of indiscriminate praise that victims of major disasters often receive. Paeans to the energy and courage of Jim O'Neill were particularly numerous, culminating in an adoring profile by J. J. Underwood in the March 6 *Seattle Times* under the headline "O'NEILL HAILED NOW AS KING OF SNOW FIGHT-ERS." The piece was so adulatory in tone—"He always is cool, deliberate, calculating, methodical, but on the alert, grasping difficult situations like a flash"—that its author may in truth have been trying to flatter the superintendent in order to get greater access to the avalanche site.

As the rescue effort wore on, however, a current of reproach began to surface in much of the press coverage. The stories being told by survivors John Rogers, Henry White, and Edward Boles started raising questions about whether the crisis had really been handled as wisely or as conscientiously as it could have been. Specifically, criticism began to focus on the refusal of O'Neill and trainmaster Blackburn to grant the passengers' requests to move the trains back from their precarious position on the mountainside. According to Boles, for instance, the trains at Wellington had been left in "what proved to be the most dangerous position possible to find."

Once the front of unqualified support had thus been breached, other criticisms began to emerge. On March 5 a story appeared in the *Seattle Star* censuring the Great Northern for allowing forest fires to burn away the tree cover on the slopes around Wellington. Under the execrable headline "DOLLAR-A-DAY JAP COULD HAVE PREVENTED SLIDE," the story claimed that the GN had failed even to try to stop a fire that had raged the previous summer—a blaze that, if addressed early enough, could have been extinguished by a small force of laborers. Although the railroad later claimed that the forest cover had burned off not the previous summer but rather many years earlier, the *Star*'s basic point was harder to contradict: "Had the slope been wooded, as it was before the fire, the slide could never have occurred, as the trees would have held the snow and would not have allowed it to start."

The same day's Seattle *Argus* carried a similarly unsympathetic piece called "The Trouble with the GN," blaming the railroad for not building enough snowsheds on the line between Scenic and Wellington. Two years earlier, the writer had watched as a snowslide came dangerously close to hitting a moving passenger train on the high line above the Scenic hotel. In the author's opinion, the incident should have been a clear warning of the potential danger there and elsewhere on that stretch of track. "[I] could not help wondering why a more elaborate system of snowsheds had not been provided. Even to an inexperienced eye, it was obvious that they were necessary."

But it was the labor issue that was proving to be most troublesome for the Great Northern. A letter to the editor of the *Seattle Star*—given prominent display in the March 5 edition—complained about the rail-road's ingrained practice of hiring the cheapest labor it could find. Here again, the headline was designed for maximum provocation: "DID PENNY SQUEEZING COST 100 LIVES AT WELLINGTON?" And the body of the piece was overtly incendiary: "The Great Northern railroad will never hire able men for its mountains or any of its work," letter writer W. M. Wilson maintained. "They are the ones that imported Japanese labor because it was cheaper. They could get them for $1.25 a day. When this trouble came, they brought Italians up there to fight the snow. What do the Italians know about snow anyway? Why did they send Italians? Only because they were cheaper."

The Great Northern was allegedly even skimping on the job of re-covering the dead. Another letter published in the Spokane *Spokesman-Review*—this one from George W. Towslee—complained that the railroad was devoting the bulk of its available manpower to the task of opening up the rail line, and that even those assigned to search the ava-lanche site were primarily interested in finding lost baggage and express materials. "Relatives and friends of the dead men were obliged to hire men to dig among the wreckage," Towslee wrote. "I could not afford to hire anyone to dig for my brother's body and had to wait until the very last. As a result, it was 10 days before he was taken out."

For its part, the union of the still-striking switchmen was doing everything possible to encourage such expressions of anti-railroad senti-ment. Displaying its own brand of cynical disrespect for the victims, the union's Press Committee was blatantly using the tragedy to score points against GN management, focusing on the issue of the coal shortage. "It was positively known for weeks prior to the Wellington disaster that great danger was imminent in the mountain region, on account of the scarcity of coal," the committee maintained in the March 12 Seattle *Union Record*. "Officials were warned of the facts, and contrary to all common sense and reason they would not heed the warning. At differ-ent times and for several days in succession, the rotaries, or snow ma-chines, were absolutely useless, because they had no coal on the engines to run them."

The Press Committee went on to attribute this problem directly to the GN's refusal to settle the switchmen's strike: "If the Great Northern had the men who went on strike November 30th doing the switching, the accident, or at least the lives of the people, would not have been sacrificed to greed." Lest anyone be left in doubt about who exactly was responsible for the tragedy, the committee added, "Mr. Hill thought he was going to crush the manhood out of a few thousand switchmen by starvation, but he has failed utterly, and instead has slaughtered innumerable innocent lives."

As self-serving as these accusations may seem, they were not entirely without validity. The missed delivery of coal from Leavenworth in the days before the storm suggests that the Great Northern may indeed have been operating at less than peak efficiency during the strike. Accurate or not, the accusations of the switchmen must have been especially galling to Hill. The Empire Builder was on the verge of publishing his magnum opus—*Highways of Progress,* a distillation of his half century of experience in business and economic development—and he was not about to let a few two-bit labor agitators accuse him of something close to manslaughter. His philosophy of efficient business practices (which John F. Stevens was later to describe as "penny-wise, pound-wise") could not be held responsible for what was clearly an uncontrollable natural event. The whole notion that labor issues had anything at all to do with the disaster, therefore, was to be pointedly ignored by everyone in the company.

Despite the railroad's attempts to write off the switchmen's muckraking efforts, the union did succeed in rousing the ire of the general public. Before long, the uproar became so intense that coroner James C. Snyder saw no alternative but to hold a formal inquest into the Wellington matter, in order to determine officially whether any human fault had played a role in the tragedy. It goes without saying that Hill and the rest of the Great Northern management were not pleased.

Before any inquest could be held, however, Snyder wanted all of the missing persons accounted for, and this was going to take some time. Recovery efforts at Wellington were moving slowly, and even many of the bodies that *had* been found were not yet successfully identified. About ten days after the avalanche, Ned Topping's father and brother finally arrived in Seattle from Ohio, delayed by the traffic mayhem that had not totally subsided. William V. B. Topping and his son Roger proceeded immediately to Butterworth and Sons to claim Ned's body, but when the attendant in the morgue pulled back a shroud covering the badly mutilated corpse, neither father nor brother could identify him. Another corpse— also mutilated and of approximately the same height and weight—had been found nearby in the wreckage of the Winnipeg, and the Toppings wondered whether this might actually be Ned. Overcome by uncertainty, the old man and his surviving son could only stand by helplessly while Lucius Anderson, the Winnipeg's porter, was called in to help. Anderson made the definitive IDs: One corpse he recognized as Ned's and the other was that of Bert Matthews, who had been sleeping in an adjacent berth. Having no choice but to accept the porter's judgment, the Toppings claimed the body and made arrangements to carry it back to Ohio to bury alongside Ned's wife and daughter.

Another case of mistaken identity involved Joseph Benier, a timber cruiser who was supposed to have been a passenger on the Seattle Express. He showed up at Butterworth and Sons a few days later and told undertaker F. R. Lewis that there had been some slight confusion. "My friends say that you have me downstairs dead," Benier allegedly remarked. "I want to say that I am the livest man in town." Despite being positively identified as one of the corpses by more than twenty friends and coworkers, Benier had actually been incommunicado in the woods during the storm and had missed his scheduled return train. Now back in Seattle, he wanted to set the record straight. So the overworked undertaker obliged, quietly removing the tag on the body in question and replacing it with one that read: "No. 83, unknown."

Perhaps the single most farcical ordeal was that suffered posthumously by the rancher John Brockman. After word spread that Brockman's estate was worth upwards of $60,000 (a prodigious sum in 1910 dollars), several fake relatives showed up to claim the rancher's body. Apparently none could provide definitive proof of kinship until the arrival of Brockman's actual brother (who, as a result of some parental whim, bore a name identical to that of his sibling). This second John Brockman proceeded to inform the undertakers that the body they had labeled as his brother was actually someone else. The real Brockman was eventually found (his body had been misidentified as that of J. Liberti, an Italian laborer) and the matter was finally settled, but not before notarized affidavits from several Washington towns had been gathered to close any possible legal loopholes.

By now, many of the other victims were being laid to rest in the places they had come from. Nellie Sharp was buried by her parents in Bloomington, Indiana. In Spokane, George Davis's widow saw her husband and three-year-old Thelma interred with all due ceremony by the Iroquois tribe of which he was a member. The bodies of all five Becks, meanwhile, were laid into a single grave in Livermore, California, near the home they were returning to after two years in Washington. And in Everett, where twelve hundred people attended a memorial service for the victims at the Everett Theater on Sunday, March 13, Mrs. Joseph Pettit, surrounded by her five children, saw her husband buried in the Evergreen Cemetery at the southern end of town.

At the First Methodist Episcopal Church in Olympia, Sarah Jane Covington was given a large, elaborate funeral, during which she was eulogized for her charitable works, her enduring interest in the reform movement and progressive thought, and her efforts in rearing and educating no fewer than seven children and twenty-two grandchildren. It was a cathartic ceremony for the Covington clan, but perhaps an even more comforting tribute came a few days afterward, in a letter that her son Luther received from his mother's fellow passenger Anna Gray. "Dear Friend," the letter began, "Mr. Gray, myself, and Baby are home at last, and while we are all marked for life, we are thankful that God has saved us without the loss of one."

Mrs. Gray proceeded to tell Luther all about the week she had spent with his mother—about the comfort Mrs. Covington had offered herself and Mrs. Lemman during the crisis, about the stories of her grandchildren she had told to divert them, about the little underskirt they had made together for baby Varden. "Now Mr. Covington," she continued, getting to the main point, "about the only thing of mine that was saved [from the wreck] was that little skirt. It was her last work and it was a work of love for another. Would you like to have it?"

The letter was signed simply: "Your true friends, Mr. and Mrs. John Gray and Baby."

✧

As all of this was going on, the Legal Department of the Great Northern Railway was busily preparing its case for the inquest. After failing in their efforts to prevent the investigation in the first place (this would be the first train accident in Washington history to merit such a proceeding), the railroad's lawyers were doing everything in their power to influence it in their favor. Acknowledging that "nothing in the company's affairs is of greater importance," the GN's assistant general solicitor in St. Paul, J. D. Armstrong, exhorted the Spokane-based legal team that "neither time nor expense should be spared" in ensuring that the best possible face was put on the company's performance in the crisis. In a March 16 telegram, Armstrong even insisted that "effort should be made to secure jury of representative businessmen," though exactly what kind of effort was tactfully not specified.

It was clearly understood in all of these communications that the findings of the coroner's inquest could potentially provide a basis for future negligence claims against the company. An actual negative verdict, finding the railroad directly responsible for the deaths, would obviously be disastrous for the company, setting the stage for numerous suits from passengers and employees alike. But even a positive outcome could create difficulties if the evidence raised during the inquest showed the railroad or its officers as lacking in any way. To prevent such an occurrence, Frederick Dorety, the extremely capable litigator who would represent the company, had been preparing a thorough defense, collecting detailed affidavits from many of those present at Wellington in the week before the avalanche. With what little time he had available to him, he tried to immunize the company against every possible issue that could be raised, including the forest fires, the coal shortage, the strike of snow shovelers, and the decision to keep the trains on the passing tracks. "We are making every effort to block the possibility of any litigant ever securing any adverse testimony on any of these points," Dorety wrote to Armstrong on March 11. He was encouraged, moreover, by an article that appeared in the *Seattle Times* citing the opinion of several local lawyers that, based on the facts as reported in the newspaper, the railroad was in all likelihood not liable. "On the whole," Dorety concluded, "we have every reason to believe that the verdict of the Coroner's jury will be extremely favorable."

The inquest convened at 11:00 A.M. on Friday, March 18, at Foresters Hall in downtown Seattle. Earlier that morning, superintendent O'Neill had taken the train down from Everett with a party of his colleagues, including master mechanic Dowling, traveling engineers Mackey and Tegtmeier, and assistant trainmaster Harrington. Since emerging from the mountains on Tuesday, O'Neill had barely had a few days to rest and collect himself, and he was still showing the strain. According to one report, "Deep furrows are plowed in the face of Superintendent O'Neill"— and as chief witness in the investigation, he was not to get much respite anytime soon.

"The Inquiry into the cause of the death of John Brockman and eighty-seven or more others, Deceased," was to be conducted by a young assistant prosecuting attorney named A. H. Lundin. As prosecutor, he would be investigating the case before coroner Snyder and a jury of six "average" citizens, including two mine operators, two real estate developers, a contractor, and (perhaps as a sop to the working classes) a man identified as "a dyer and cleaner." Given the unusual circumstances, the proceedings would also be observed by the state railroad inspector and by three members of the Washington State Railroad Commission. Created three years earlier in response to increasing demands for regulation of the industry, the railroad commission was now required to examine every train accident that occurred on Washington lines, and here it was combining its own investigation with that of the coroner. Based on what they heard at the inquest, the committee members would make recommendations on how the Great Northern and other railroads could prevent such disasters in the future.

The general public, of course, would be making its own decisions, and as the hearing approached, sentiments seemed not to be going the railroad's way. "All kinds of rumors are in circulation," one newspaper reported a few days before the inquest. "The people demand to know the truth. . . . If the officials of the company, in their zeal to open the road, refused to take time to care for the safety of their passengers, the facts should be made known."

The source of at least some of those rumors was now sitting in Foresters Hall, eager to be called as a witness. Henry White, the only surviving member of the passenger committee that had repeatedly called for a meeting with O'Neill during the crisis, had been making no secret of his dissatisfaction with the superintendent's performance. In the days after the avalanche, moreover, he had called on the GN's claim agent in Seattle to see about compensation for property he had lost in the wreck. Referred to the legal department, the salesman was told that the company wouldn't pay him a cent—"[not] even for the shirt on his back." This refusal had naturally only piqued his indignation, and he was now spoiling for a fight.

Shortly after 11:00, O'Neill was called to testify as the first witness. Looking uncharacteristically formal in his suit and narrow bow tie, the superintendent was sworn in and seated before Lundin began the questioning. At first, the prosecuting attorney was as courteous and straightforward as could be, seeking only to establish the particulars of the events leading up to the disaster. O'Neill cooperated willingly. Without any trace of defensiveness or evasion, the superintendent explained the rationale behind each of his decisions, taking time to describe the terrain at Stevens Pass, the day-by-day progress of the storm, and the time and location of every important snowslide that had affected operations over the week. He even obliged the jury by giving them a short but cogent summary of how rotary snowplows work.

When it came to fixing responsibility for the orders that put the trains in the path of the avalanche, O'Neill was unequivocal. "I gave them orders," he stated, a bit of his old Dakota diction slipping into his sentence. In other words, he absolved conductor Pettit of any culpability in the matter, refusing to scapegoat a man who was no longer alive to defend himself. And though the day's testimony went on for hours more—with Harrington, Mackey, and J. C. Wright all supporting O'Neill's actions—the papers already had their lead: "O'NEILL ASSUMES ALL BLAME FOR MOVING TRAINS," ran the *Seattle Times* headline that evening. The implication was clear: Whether or not O'Neill had made mistakes in his handling of the situation, he at least had the integrity to take the blame on himself.

On Saturday morning, the second day of the inquest, several of the surviving passengers testified, and the jury got a somewhat different perspective on events. One of the first witnesses of the day was R. M. Laville, the electrician from Montana who had walked away from the wreck uninjured, and his testimony proved distinctly hostile to the railroad. "Fear was in every heart for several days before the catastrophe," Laville said, adding that everyone aboard was "terrified" by the prospect of a slide. According to Laville, the railway had been putting them in jeopardy "by struggling along with an inferior snow-fighting force, which was small because wages high enough to satisfy workmen were not offered." He also claimed that had men been made available to help them, "every passenger on the train . . . would have reached Scenic without difficulty."

Struck by this new light on the situation, the jury members—who were allowed to participate in the interrogation—started peppering Laville with questions. They listened with deep interest as the young man described the mood of increasing desperation among the passengers in the days leading up to the avalanche. Laville took pains to describe their frustration over O'Neill's refusal even to meet with them, let alone grant their wish to have the train moved back to the tunnel. In perhaps the most arresting testimony of the day, he recounted the February 28 meeting between the passenger committee and Arthur Blackburn, during which the trainmaster had refused to provide sufficient manpower to evacuate all passengers off the mountain on foot. "He said that if he caught any of us trying to take the women out of there," Laville said, "he would use force, if necessary, to prevent it."

Dorety did what he could to blunt the impact of these revelations, which hardly cast the railroad in a sympathetic light. And much of the rest of the day's testimony did go the railroad's way. Once Laville had stepped down, several other passengers—among them John Rogers, George Loveberry, and the lawyers Jesseph and Merritt—presented testimony that was highly sympathetic to the Great Northern in general and to O'Neill in particular. ("I never met nicer gentlemen in my life than Mr. O'Neill, Mr. Pettit, and Mr. Vogel," Merritt claimed at one point. "They were working all the time, day and night.") And perhaps the most convincing witness was the state railroad inspector himself, E. W. Perley, who stated categorically that O'Neill's every decision was strictly in line with standard operating procedure, and that no other acceptable course of action would have altered the outcome:

> Q: From the evidence which you have heard here, would you say that [any other course] would have averted this catastrophe?
> A: No sir; I do not see that anything could have been done more than has been done.
> Q: You consider it was something beyond human ability to cope with?
> A: I do.

At this point in the proceedings it was decided that the jury should be taken up to Wellington to see the disaster site in person. The inquest was therefore adjourned until Monday, when the participants were transported by train into the mountains. As the six jury members disembarked at the Wellington depot, they could finally appreciate the full extent of the devastation that had been wrought by the disaster. Enough of the snow had melted by now to reveal the torn and twisted remnants of the trains in the ravine below. Men were crawling over the gleaming wet wreckage like scavengers, preparing the equipment for salvage and searching for the last few victims still to be accounted for. Above it all brooded the high Cascade peaks, still heavy with snow, still looking ominously dangerous against a clear and sunny sky.

O'Neill led the group east from the depot to the spur tracks near the tunnel, where a railway coach had been prepared to receive them. Here more witnesses were called, many of them Wellington residents who had been unable to come to the proceedings in Seattle. W. R. Bailets, the hotelkeeper, got a particularly close questioning. Asked if he thought the spur tracks would have been a safer place to put the trains, he said he did and that he had even encouraged some passengers to make a fuss about it:

A: I asked them, I says, "Why don't you insist on them moving you up here?"

Q: You thought this was a safer place then?

A: Well, I really did, and [now] I *know* that it was.

Dorety and O'Neill felt that this could not go unanswered. Recalled as a witness, the superintendent described how impractical such a move would have been during the storm. "These three tracks here contained about six outfit cars," he said, pointing through the train car windows. "From the switch to the end of the spurs there were six to ten feet of snow. . . . We had made no attempt to use these tracks at any time during the winter season."

But the jury and the railroad commissioners (perhaps influenced by the absence of snow in the area three weeks after the disaster) were apparently not ready to let go of the idea of the spur tracks.

"Suppose similar conditions would occur next winter," one juror asked the superintendent. "Where would you place [the trains] for safety?"

"Could you have pulled back on this track if you had wished to on the 26th?" asked another.

"How many men would it have required to shovel [the spur track] out in one day?"

O'Neill responded convincingly to all of these questions. He also made certain to stress the fact that he and dozens of other veteran mountain railroaders had preferred to sleep in the trains on the passing tracks—a choice that, as the Seattle *Argus* put it, the men had backed "with their lives—and lost."

✧

The worst days for the railroad's case, however, came on Tuesday and Wednesday, when proceedings returned to Foresters Hall in Seattle. The first witness to be called was Henry White, and the four days he'd waited to testify had done nothing to temper the salesman's vengeful mood. Articulate, vivid in his descriptions, and full of righteous anger against the company that had mistreated him, he turned out to be a railroad attorney's worst nightmare—an obviously wronged man with the intelligence to match his sense of grievance.

After outlining the various impromptu meetings among the passengers over the course of their week of entrapment (culminating in the creation of the typed petition that O'Neill never saw), White rehearsed the litany of excuses given for not moving the trains: the unpleasantness and impracticality of being in the tunnel, the lack of coal and manpower to clear the track, the inability of a single engine to move the train upgrade, and so on. Unlike most of the other terse and sometimes incoherent witnesses, White was extremely thorough in his answers, giving jury members a much more visceral sense of what it was like to be trapped on that mountain for six long days. And after a particularly extended account of the final meeting with trainmaster Blackburn, the salesman uttered the single pungent sentence that probably did more to hurt the railroad's case than any other: "So," White concluded his long speech, "through lack of coal and lack of help, we were forced to remain in that position, right at the base of a thousand-foot mountain."

This was an extremely damaging comment, the more so for being succinct and eminently quotable. But for O'Neill, who had doubtless been sitting in Foresters Hall in a state of ever greater distress, White's testimony only became worse:

Q: Was there any demand or request made to be moved back to the tunnel, or near the tunnel, prior to the 28th, Mr. White?

A: No, not of anyone in authority, because we could not get anyone in authority. That was the request we were going to make of Mr. O'Neill, but he was too sleepy to come around and see us. That little sleepy spell cost ninety-five lives.

It was a sentence that would play through James O'Neill's mind for many years to come. Dorety tried his best to defuse White's criticism of the superintendent ("Don't you know that, as a matter of fact, he was working day and night . . . ? Didn't you feel that he and the men who were working with him had sufficient experience, so that what you would tell him or suggest would not be [of] much assistance?"). The harm, however, could not be entirely undone. And it was only exacerbated when Sarah Jane Covington's daughter Mrs. George Anderson was called to present some of the more poignant entries in her mother's diary. "No one can tell anything about when we will get out," she read to the jury. "Some are in deadly fear that another landslide will come down on us. . . ."

O'Neill's discomfort through all of this must have been acute. But to his relief, it didn't go on much longer. The inquest ended shortly thereafter with testimony from three officials working for other railroads, all of whom supported the superintendent's actions, and then the jury went into deliberations.

Awaiting the verdict, the GN lawyers were hopeful but wary. "For the present," F. V. Brown wrote to Armstrong on March 22, "I can only say that, in the judgment of Mr. Dorety and myself, there has been no evidence introduced that would in any way tend to show negligence on the part of the Company or its employees. Of course, it is impossible to anticipate what the Coroner's Jury will do. There seem to be some members of the jury intent upon finding some cause for blame, while other members of the jury seem to be outspoken in their opinion that everything was done by the employees of the Company according to the dictates of good judgment, and that nothing was left undone which could reasonably be required in the exercise of due care." The Great Northern was also encouraged by the findings of the Chelan County coroner with regard to the east-slope deaths. After looking into the beanery slide that had killed Harry Elerker and John Bjerenson and the slide at Drury that had killed watchman Fred Johnson, coroner Saunders exonerated the railroad of any negligence in either instance.

The opinion of the press as to the strength of the GN's case was somewhat different. According to a writer for the *Argus,* the testimony of O'Neill's fellow railroaders had been all but useless, given their own self-interest in the case. "If I was the manager of a railroad," the writer observed, "I would [have no trouble] finding men to testify that I had done just as they would have done." The jury, he insisted, should instead focus on the simple facts of the case, which made the strongest argument of all: "In the Wellington disaster the trains were destroyed, many lives were lost, and there were ways in which those lives could have been saved. In fact, the course adopted [by the railroad] appears to have been the only one by which they could have been lost. The men who came out were saved. There was a spur track at Wellington which was safe. And all the expert testimony in the world won't change the facts."

On Wednesday, March 23, the coroner's jury returned with their verdict. "John Brockman and eighty-eight [*sic*] or more others," they announced, "came to their deaths on the 1st day of March, A.D. 1910, by reason of a snowslide at Wellington, King County, Washington, the cause of which was beyond human control."

That last phrase—"beyond human control"—was the one the Great Northern officials had been hoping to hear. Unfortunately, it wasn't the end of what the jury had to say:

> We find that the trains were not placed in the safest place to avert a possible accident, as the Company had other sidings east of said depot on which the trains should have been placed, that are safe from any snowslides. The evidence shows that the Great Northern Railway Company did not have sufficient coal at Wellington to cope with all possible emergencies. The evidence also shows that by reason of small wages of only fifteen (15) cents an hour for shoveling snow, out of which wages the laborers have to pay $4.50 per week for board, about thirty-five (35) laborers left Wellington who should have been retained regardless of wages, for the purpose of providing for the safety and welfare of the passengers.

For O'Neill, this addition to the verdict must have seemed like a personal attack. All three points of criticism in it concerned issues over which he'd had direct control. By faulting his judgment on these issues, the jury had all but condemned O'Neill's entire performance as leader of the campaign against the storm.

For the company as a whole, however, it was—as one GN official would later put it—a "hermaphrodite verdict, one-half in exoneration and one-half censure." Brown fired off a telegram to Armstrong: "WE FEEL POSITIVE NO FOUNDATION IN TESTIMONY FOR CRITICISMS CONTAINED IN VERDICT. ALSO NO LIABILITY IN ANY WAY FOR ACCIDENT." Later, in a sharply worded comment to the newspapers, Brown took issue with the jury's judgments, claiming that the entire notion that the trains should have been moved back to the spur tracks "seems to have been an idea originated by the jury after visiting the ground three weeks after the slide and after the snow had disappeared." He also insisted that the criticisms regarding the coal supply and the shovelers' job action were "matters of management" that were not within the province of the jury. "If ever a railroad was entitled to a clean bill of health, the Great Northern was in this matter. In justice to Superintendent J. H. O'Neill and other officials whose efforts to relieve the blockade showed more than ordinary devotion to duty, the criticism of the jury should not have been made."

Such attempts at damage control aside, Armstrong was understandably vexed. "The verdict itself," he wrote back to Brown, "seems to be thoroughly unsatisfactory." Specifically, the jury's statements pertaining to the greater safety of the spur tracks, the insufficiency of coal, and the failure to retain the snow shovelers could all be toeholds for future civil actions against the Great Northern. As Armstrong had pointed out in an earlier letter to Dorety: "If the evidence at the Coroner's Inquest does not make a fairly clear showing on our part, the company will unquestionably be deluged with suits." That "clear showing" had obviously not been made, and so now the matter of the Wellington avalanche would be headed to the courts.

15

Act of God

WELLINGTON SLIDE LAWSUIT ON TRIAL

Boy Sues for Father's Death
—Other Cases Contingent
on Outcome of Trial

—Wenatchee Daily World

Tuesday, October 21, 1913
Seattle

To locals it was known as the "Cruel Castle." An enormous neoclassical Victorian pile, it stood high on First Hill overlooking downtown Seattle, a symbol of the city's brash and always outsized ambitions. When first built in 1890, the King County Courthouse had been something of an absurdity—a too grandiose monument for a raw young metropolis still struggling to be noticed by the world. A quarter century later, it seemed somewhat more appropriate to its surroundings. Standing in the shadow of its heavy, two-hundred-foot tower, one could now look west over a dense jumble of commercial office buildings, warehouses, and rail yards, backed by the brisk maritime traffic of Elliott Bay. Thanks largely to those rail yards and shipping wharves, Seattle had outstripped rivals like Tacoma, Olympia, and Everett to become the economic powerhouse of the region. The city, in other words, had grown into its courthouse, the way an adolescent grows into one of its older siblings' suits.

It was in this ponderous edifice that Superior Court Trial No. 94,511—a.k.a. *Topping vs. The Great Northern Railway Company*—was scheduled to begin on a rainy afternoon in October 1913. In the three and a half years that had passed since March 1, 1910, other matters had displaced the Wellington Disaster at the forefront of the city's collective consciousness. Halley's Comet had come and gone, a new mayor had been elected, revolutions had transformed Mexico and China, and Theodore Roosevelt had become the first (former) president to fly in an airplane. But for those individuals who had lived through the avalanche—and for the families of those who had not—the disaster was a vivid and perpetual presence in their lives, a source of continued pain, bitterness, and unappeased anger.

There were some who, in the intervening years, had tried their best to move on from the tragedy. Ida Starrett, now living in British Columbia with her mother and son, apparently felt no lingering rancor against the Great Northern. After she and Raymond had recovered from their wounds, the railroad had been—in her words—"most kind" to them, arranging for nurse Annabelle Lee and injured brakeman Ross Phillips to accompany them back to Canada. (Ray remembered Phillips doing a clog dance for him on the train.) After quickly burying their dead and making an out-of-court settlement with the railroad, the family had simply attempted to put the incident behind them as quickly as possible.

Other survivors had been less forgiving. It had taken mail clerk A. B. Hensel more than sixteen months to recover from his injuries, and long afterward he still experienced occasional paralysis on one side of his body. Now back at work, he was traveling regularly over the trans-Cascade line, passing the scene of the disaster several times a week. Seeking redress for his suffering, he had in May 1910 filed a $30,000 suit against the Great Northern (a suit that actually named James H. O'Neill individually as a codefendant, citing his and the railroad's "many instances of faulty action"). But the case had been so encumbered by pretrial motions from the GN defense team that Hensel had finally been forced to settle out of court, and for a figure that had done little to assuage his resentment.

Now Hensel would get another chance to air his grievances against the railroad, for he was to be the initial witness for the plaintiff in the Topping trial, the first Wellington-related case to reach a jury. Lawyers for both sides in the suit had together subpoenaed over two hundred witnesses for the long-awaited showdown. With several similar trials pending and a host of other potential actions hinging on the outcome, it was to be an unusually hard-fought case, particularly on the part of the railroad. For almost four years, the Great Northern had been forced to live with the criticisms explicit in the verdict of the coroner's inquest jury, and this was the company's chance to finally answer them. At stake was not just an enormous amount of money but also the reputation of James J. Hill's entire Great Northern Railway as one of the safest and best-run railroads in the country.

The GN, of course, had been anticipating this moment ever since the inquest. Even before the coroner's jury had handed down its verdict in 1910, the company had already been working behind the scenes to limit the damage to its public image and win back the confidence of shippers and the public. Two days before the end of the inquest, Samuel Hill (a prominent Northwest industrialist who was also the Empire Builder's son-in-law) had invited Governor Marion Hay and state railroad commissioner J. C. Lawrence to a conference at his home. Writing about it afterward to his father-in-law, the younger Hill had reported with relief that the commissioner was inclined to view the Wellington matter as, "all things considered," an unforeseen disaster. But Lawrence did want the Great Northern to articulate its plans to prevent a recurrence, so that the commission could include such plans in its own final report.

Responding by return mail, James J. Hill had declared that he himself would be traveling out to the Cascade Division to personally assess the situation. "You can say to Governor Hay and Commissioner Lawrence," he wrote, "that the Company will put the line permanently in shape to avoid any future trouble. . . . There is only one course to take, and that is the one that will avoid future delays no matter from what source they come." Since this letter was later released to the newspapers, the Empire Builder might more prudently have referred to avoiding "future deaths" rather than "future delays," but the effect of the letter on the Washington State Railroad Commission was the desired one. By the end of the month, the commission had completely exonerated the railroad.

That still left the small matter of actually fixing the problem at Stevens Pass. On April 22, 1910 (the day after the death of Mark Twain), the last of the major wreckage at Wellington was recovered, the damaged rotary and one final engine being hoisted out of the ravine and loaded onto a flatcar to be carried off the mountain. A week later, both James and Louis Hill, along with GN chief engineer Hogeland and a contingent of other engineering experts, came west as promised to discuss plans for securing the Cascade crossing. Their subsequent report to the railroad commission was well received, and on July 25, in a press conference in Olympia, commissioner Lawrence made the second public announcement that the GN had been hoping for. Praising Hill and his railroad for their cooperation, the obliging Lawrence outlined the company's plans. Beginning with a massive excavation at Wellington itself, the railroad would erect an enormous snowshed over the tracks, constructed of concrete rather than the usual wood. The Great Northern would also build additional sheds all along the line to Scenic to serve as "shelter stations" for trains in the event of future blockades. "The work will run into hundreds of thousands of dollars," Lawrence announced, "[but] the public may rest assured [that] the road over the mountain will be as safe as it is possible to make it."

For Hill and the Great Northern, it was an important, if expensive, step in winning back the confidence of passengers and shippers that had been lost as a result of the avalanche. And to further erase any lingering unease among the public, in October 1910 the railroad quietly changed the name of the station at the west portal of the tunnel from Wellington to Tye. All GN literature and timetables were altered accordingly, allowing inattentive customers to believe that the Great Northern Railway's transcontinental line somehow no longer went through Wellington, site of the famous disaster.

Even as these changes were being put into effect, the seemingly endless switchmen's strike was also brought to a resolution. After doing
their best to sabotage the Great Northern and its witnesses during the
coroner's inquest ("Those chumps," the union's dyspeptic Press Committee had written, "would slander their parents if the company told
them to do so"), the switchmen on April 12 finally agreed to call off the
strike. Although they had not achieved many of their desired changes in
working conditions, they did get almost all of the pay increase under
dispute—five cents an hour as opposed to the asked-for six. It was, in
other words, another split decision in the ongoing war between the
Hills and their railroad's labor, but one whose ill effects—at least in the
form of the criticisms that had been raised at the Wellington inquest—
would linger far longer than most.

What all of these various concessions to labor, popular perception,
and governmental oversight cost Hill psychologically is easy to imag-
ine. Apology and accommodation did not come easy to the old Gilded
Age warrior, and pandering to what he perceived as outsiders, no matter how necessary, must have infuriated him. Even so, he could bite his
tongue for only so long, and soon Hill was again letting his famous
temper show. Before the memories of Wellington had even begun to
fade, he was back to his old habit of fulminating in the press about all
of his favorite subjects, including the wastrel ways of the American
public ("The people are living at a tremendous rate, taking money for
living expenses that should be returned to productive industrial chan-
nels"), the high wages demanded by American labor ("The rise in the
wage rate is the biggest factor in the rise in the cost of living"), and the
continuing abomination of progressive-style meddling in corporate affairs ("There is a popular idea that a railroad may be compelled to do
just as may be pleasing to some people. By unwarranted interference
with railroad operations, the people will be hurt. They will see this
eventually").

The seventy-five-year-old Hill was still waging those same battles in
October 1913. If anything, the temper of the times had grown even
more distasteful to him. The onslaught of progressivism had intensified

over the last three years, culminating in the hard-fought presidential election campaign of 1912, a campaign in which, as Robert Wiebe has observed, all three major parties "claimed the privilege of completing the national progressive movement." One of the most left-leaning elections in American history, it had occasioned not only the return to politics of Hill's nemesis Theodore Roosevelt (now running under the banner of the newly formed Progressive, or Bull Moose, Party) but also a surprisingly strong showing for Socialist candidate Eugene Debs, who captured almost 6 percent of the vote. And the ultimate victory of Democrat Woodrow Wilson promised much more in the way of crowd-pleasing, big-government, anti-business regulation. All in all, for a railroad man like Hill, the future seemed ominous enough, and the Wellington trial was not likely to be one of its bright spots.

Fortunately, the Great Northern's legal team, still spearheaded by F. V. Brown and the seemingly indefatigable Frederick Dorety, had been diligently preparing its case for over three years, determined to make it impervious to challenge. In consultation with J. D. Armstrong at company headquarters in St. Paul, they had been commissioning detailed contour maps of the Stevens Pass area and collecting every relevant document they could find. (According to Basil Sherlock, GN attorneys had come through Wellington even before the lifting of the snow blockade in 1910, collecting "every record and every bit of paper that had any writing on it.") As expected, the inquest verdict had triggered a flood of legal claims, not only from relatives of victims but also from freight customers seeking compensation for lost or damaged shipments. The GN's initial strategy for these claims had been simple: Since the company had technically been found not liable for the disaster, all claims stemming from it were categorically denied. However, realizing that they would need the goodwill of their surviving employees in the inevitable trials to come, they had arranged to make special payments to the families of men who had died in the avalanche—specifically, $1,000 for the dependent families of married trainmen and $500 for the dependent families of unmarried trainmen. These monies were offered as "gratuities or donations," and to receive them, the families had to sign away their right to seek any other compensation from the company.

For someone like the widow of conductor Joseph Pettit, of course, this offered settlement was woefully inadequate. The man whom passenger John Rogers had called "a hero" of the Wellington Disaster had left five children to be taken care of, and $1,000 was simply not going to suffice. Fearing destitution, Mrs. Pettit had made a special petition to the Great Northern for $2,500. But although the company's lawyers were sympathetic to the widow's "hard case," GN managers decided that making an exception for her would set a dangerous precedent. Although records of the final settlement with Mrs. Pettit are no longer extant, the amount ultimately granted by the company was low enough to cause bitterness among the conductor's descendants for many years to come.

Even with the prospect of employee suits neutralized by such payments, however, the Great Northern still had to face numerous legal claims from passengers and from mail employees, track laborers, and snow shovelers (whose families were also left out of the company's compensation plans). These cases the lawyers attempted to dispense with as cheaply as possible, and with some success. A $100,000 suit in the name of R. M. Barnhart, the forty-year-old attorney from Spokane, was quickly made to disappear. (One of the lawyers representing Barnhart's estate was none other than John Merritt, the passenger whose sympathetic testimony in the inquest had been so helpful to the company.) Another suit—a $40,000 claim brought by the widow of Charles Eltinge, the Spokane banker—was settled for just $6,500.

Eventually, though, Armstrong, Brown, and Dorety found the one suit they wished to bring to trial as a test case for all the remaining actions hanging over them. Why they chose the Topping case in particular—a $40,000 claim brought on behalf of the late salesman's minor son by the boy's grandfather—is unclear; the resulting trial was not likely to generate much goodwill toward the railroad, pitting the giant corporation against a five-year-old orphan. But something about the case (perhaps, as we'll see, the plaintiff's choice of attorney) had appealed to the GN's lawyers, and so they had gone forward with it—though again they tried to delay it as long as possible with various pretrial hemmings and hawings.

By October 1913, with the trial finally set to come before a jury, Brown and Dorety were fairly confident of their case. With only one exception, the dozens of railroaders they had interviewed had backed up every single one of O'Neill's decisions, and as Dorety had professed convincingly in a letter to Armstrong, "I believe that no employee made a single statement that he did not honestly believe." The one dissenter—a former employee named McFadgen—had made several worrisome declarations, telling the GN lawyers that O'Neill had made major mistakes in his handling of the situation. McFadgen, however, was determined not to testify and had successfully eluded all attempts by the court to locate him. The Great Northern's lawyers could also reassure themselves that the burden of proof in the case was squarely on the plaintiff. In order to find the defendant negligent, the plaintiff would have to show that the railroad had failed to exercise the degree of care that a "reasonable and prudent person" would have exercised in the same situation. Given this high threshold of proof, Brown and Dorety were convinced that the law was on their side.

✧

The trial began on Tuesday afternoon, October 21. Many casual spectators had gathered at the courthouse on First Hill (nicknamed "Profanity Hill" for the expletives uttered by those who had to climb it), but the seats in the fine wood-paneled courtroom also held more than a few of those who had lived through the terrifying events of the Wellington Disaster. Testifying for the railroad would be John Rogers and George Loveberry (the only two passengers on the railroad's list of witnesses), as well as James O'Neill, William Harrington, Ira Clary, and numerous other Cascade Division employees. For the plaintiff there were, besides Hensel: John and Anna Gray, Susan Bailets, and (doubtless to O'Neill's dismay) Henry H. White, who no longer lived in Seattle but who had returned from his native Minnesota to testify. Also present was William V. B. Topping, Ned's aging father, acting in the name of his grandson, Bill, the child whom Ned had mentioned so often in the letter he'd been writing on the train.

All present rose for the entrance of the Honorable John E. Humphries. A somewhat gruff, plainspoken man, Humphries had probably been less than eager to take on this controversial trial. With a highly indignant public on one side and an extremely powerful corporation on the other, the judge ran the risk of making some influential enemies, especially if he ended up dismissing the case or taking some other presumptive action. Humphries was therefore determined to put the facts before the jury of twelve with as little interference as possible. If doing that required a full month of testimony (the amount of time he had set aside on the schedule for this trial), he was fully prepared to let it be so.

After various preliminaries, Judge Humphries allowed Fred Williams, the lead attorney for the plaintiff, to introduce his first witness. He called A. B. Hensel to the stand, and from the very first moments of his interrogation of the witness, it was clear that Williams intended to launch the broadest of attacks on O'Neill and the railroad. Not only would he attempt to impugn the decisions O'Neill had made once the trains reached Wellington, but he would question the wisdom of bringing them up the mountain in the first place. Hensel had apparently revealed to him that train No. 27, the Fast Mail, had been warned against attempting Stevens Pass even before leaving Leavenworth early on the morning of February 23. A "government official" on train No. 2—one of the last eastbound trains over the mountains—had allegedly told the Fast Mail's chief clerk that it would be foolhardy to attempt a crossing that night, with the storm raging as it was. Naturally, Williams wanted to get this fact on the record. He tried several times to allow Hensel to tell the story, but the vigilant Frederick Dorety would simply not let that happen.

WILLIAMS: Mr. Hensel, do you know whether or not the statement made by the government officials was communicated to the officials on Train No. 27?

DORETY: I object as immaterial whether it was communicated
to any of the officials of Train No. 27. I object to that.

JUDGE HUMPHRIES (to Williams): This [trial is about] Train
No. 25.

WILLIAMS: I understand that, but that question is just prelimi-
nary.

DORETY: I think it is immaterial whether it was communicated
to the officials on Train No. 27, or not.

JUDGE HUMPHRIES: I will sustain the objection to that.

In other words, Dorety argued that any such statement, aside from being inadmissible as hearsay, would be irrelevant to this case, which concerned a death on train No. 25, the Seattle Express, not one on train No.
27, the Fast Mail.

It proved to be a successful parry on Dorety's part, and only the first
of many subsequent instances in which the GN lawyer blatantly outma-
neuvered his ineffectual opponent. Fred M. Williams, Esq., may have
had other lawyerly virtues, but his performance in the courtroom over
the next few days suggests that litigation was perhaps not his strong
point. Irritable, even nasty at times, he frequently got his facts wrong,
mixed up dates, directions, and numbers, and asked confused and con-
fusing questions of witnesses. ("I presume these questions are all
proper," Dorety quipped after a few of Williams's more muddled in-
quiries. "I don't know what any of them mean!") Though backed by an
experienced former railroad lawyer named L. F. Chester, Williams often
seemed unfamiliar with the basics of railroad operation. He bickered
testily with the judge and with his opposing counsel, and at one point
even made fun of a witness's poor grammar—tactics not widely regarded as conducive to winning a jury's sympathy.

Williams's case for the plaintiff, moreover, turned out to be relatively thin, relying too heavily on the three points of criticism in the
inquest verdict: the greater safety of the tunnel or the spur tracks, the
loss of the striking snow shovelers, and the shortage of coal—the very
issues the Great Northern had spent three years preparing to neutral-
ize. After finishing with Hensel, Williams called only nine other wit-

nesses to testify, and one of them, Susan Bailets, actually did his case more harm than good by pointing out that the slope above the spur tracks was both steeper and more slide-prone than the one above the passing tracks.

Even when questioning a witness as smart and motivated as Henry White, Williams failed to get much prosecutorial traction. He elicited none of the personal ire against O'Neill that White had displayed at the coroner's inquest, and he even let pass an opportunity for White to convey to the jury the sheer horror of the slide.

WILLIAMS: Were you conscious when the coach went over?
WHITE: As far as I know, I was conscious during the whole period.
WILLIAMS: That train and the passengers were swept into the ravine below?
WHITE: Yes sir.
WILLIAMS: And then you were brought up after the wreck?
WHITE: Yes sir, about four hours after.

That was the extent of the description Williams asked for. The attorney merely moved on to other matters, squandering a chance to inspire even a modicum of visceral outrage in the jury.

When, after only three days of testimony, the plaintiff rested, Dorety and Brown immediately made a motion to dismiss the case on the grounds of insufficient evidence. Judge Humphries was inclined to grant the motion—Williams had hardly made a convincing case—but he was simply feeling too much pressure from public sentiment to do so. In a moment of startling candor (later reported in the newspapers), he told the GN lawyers, "Were I permitted, I'd like to unravel the case for you, but I have been bombarded and ridiculed and told to let this case alone, so I am really afraid to do what you ask." The motion for dismissal was therefore denied. The Great Northern would have to present its defense in court.

Unlike their opponent, however, Dorety and Brown had prepared a powerful case. On the same day that the plaintiff rested, Dorety set his well-choreographed, exhaustively researched effort in motion. He began by establishing the topographical and meteorological background against which the events of February 22 to March 1 had taken place. Producing a parade of expert witnesses—including surveyors, civil engineers, the district weather observer from Merritt, and a series of veteran GN railroaders—Dorety attempted to establish that the spur tracks, far from being a safer place than the passing tracks, were actually far more dangerous. Witness after witness echoed the GN's major points: that the Wellington avalanche had been a snowslide unprecedented both in character and in location, that it had resulted from a snowfall of unprecedented length and intensity, and that it had seemingly been triggered by the violence of an unprecedented wintertime thunderstorm. The intent of this litany of unprecedenteds was to create an indelible impression among the jurors that the slide was an unforeseeable event. "It will be conceded by everyone, of course," Dorety had noted shortly after the inquest, "that we cannot be held responsible for the results of the snowslide if the same could not possibly have been anticipated." Insofar as he had established this conditional, his case had arguably already been made.

But Dorety knew that the best way to prove the railroad's conscientiousness would be to produce the "reasonable and prudent person" who had actually been in charge of the situation at Wellington: superintendent O'Neill himself. In a letter written after the inquest in 1910, Dorety had made special mention of O'Neill's value as a witness: "I will say, in justice to Superintendent O'Neill, that his personality probably prevented an even harsher criticism by the jury, as he made a very favorable impression, and the jury were evidently in sympathy with him personally." So now, after the abstract wrangling over slope grades and snow conditions that had characterized the first half of the company's case, Dorety would use O'Neill to put a human face on the railroad's struggle against the storm—by letting him tell the story of his weeklong fight in simple, unadorned language that the jury could easily understand.

On the fair and breezy afternoon of Monday, October 27—nearly a week into the proceedings—Dorety called to the stand the most anticipated witness of the trial. Now forty-one years old, O'Neill was no longer the relatively youthful man he'd appeared in February 1910. He had since turned the corner into early middle age, and now his hair was a little grayer at the temples, his finely cut features a little fuller and more careworn. He and Berenice had also had the second child they'd conceived shortly before the Wellington ordeal. James Jr. had been born the summer following the avalanche, at a time when James Sr.— true to form—had been absent, solving an operations problem up at Stevens Pass.

He was, however, no longer the superintendent of the Cascade Division. Just the previous July, O'Neill had been promoted to assistant general superintendent for all GN lines west of Troy, Montana, and was currently based in Spokane with Berenice and the children. The warm sentiments expressed in Hill's congratulatory telegrams in 1910 had apparently been sincere, and far from using O'Neill as a convenient scapegoat, the company had actually rewarded him for his efforts. In fact, several weeks earlier, he had been invited to St. Paul for a grand celebration of James J. Hill's seventy-fifth birthday. Obviously, despite the taint of the Wellington Disaster, O'Neill was still a company favorite, valued for his talents and his devotion to duty.

Dorety began the questioning at 2:00 P.M., after the lunch recess. Proceeding with impeccable logic, the GN attorney first established O'Neill's credentials as a railroad man, eliciting details about his long ascent from fourteen-year-old track laborer through the ranks to his current position of responsibility. Dorety also demonstrated the superintendent's expertise as a snow fighter, helping him calculate on the stand the approximately 1,350 trains per year that he had successfully run over the mountain during snowstorms in the course of his tenure as division head—without any passenger deaths until the time in question.

With this background in place, Dorety went on to guide his witness through as straightforward a narrative of the week's events as Williams's frequent and often wrongheaded objections would allow. Absurdly, the plaintiff's attorney attempted to exclude nearly everything O'Neill said as irrelevant, speculative, or inadmissible hearsay. The court overruled nearly all of these objections (How could O'Neill explain himself if he couldn't cite the information he based his decisions on?), but Williams continued making them—until, after an especially annoying objection, an exasperated Dorety exclaimed, "I submit the motion is frivolous and ridiculous, and counsel should be restrained from making interruptions of that character." Even those sympathetic to the plaintiff's cause may at this point have been tempted to cry, "Amen!"

Despite such harassments, O'Neill was eventually able to put most of his version of events before the jury.

> DORETY: Why were [the trains] put on the passing track?
> O'NEILL: [It was] the handiest place to get in and get out, and the safest place on the hill. . . .
> DORETY: Why were the trains not placed on the tunnel spurs at that time?
> O'NEILL: The tunnel spurs were blocked with snow and there were cars on the spurs. . . .
> DORETY: Under existing conditions as they were on the night of February 24th, how long do you think it would have taken to clean the tunnel spurs and place the trains on them?
> O'NEILL: I do not think we could have cleaned them at all; the snow was blowing so bad that it would be impossible to shovel them out.

Dorety concluded the examination by again eliciting the most compelling piece of evidence in support of the prudence of O'Neill's decisions: the fact that at least thirty to forty trainmen were, of their own volition, sleeping on the trains when they could have slept anywhere else at Wellington, and that O'Neill himself, if he had been present on the night of the avalanche, would have been in his business car right there beside them.

Williams's cross-examination of O'Neill was, from the very beginning, as hostile (and as ineffectual) as might be expected. The attorney appeared unprepared at times and frequently grew frustrated with his own inability to frame a comprehensible line of questioning. For the rest of that afternoon and the following morning, he tried his best to demonstrate that O'Neill should have put the trains anywhere else but where they were—in the tunnel, on the spur tracks, even under the snowsheds immediately west of town. Each time he did so, O'Neill would patiently explain why such a step would have been inadvisable, infeasible, or just plain impossible. Becoming ever more desperate, Williams began to harp on the tunnel option, trying to undermine all of O'Neill's reasons for not putting the trains there, coming up with increasingly convoluted and impractical "solutions" to the problem.

"Now, Mr. O'Neill," he said at one point, "to meet such a condition in another way, couldn't you have detached the two cars and put them on the spurs there and then backed that engine and heated the train by its connection, moving the express and the baggage car away and the engine up to the head vestibule car in the train?"

But O'Neill had an answer for even this tortuous hypothetical: An avalanche coming down the slide-prone slope above the tunnel portal could then have trapped the train inside. "It would have buried them in," he said simply.

In utter frustration, Williams took one last wild shot.

WILLIAMS: Wouldn't it have been better to have buried them in the tunnel with a snowslide than to have buried them in a gully below where the train stood?
O'NEILL: No.

Then the lawyer simply gave up.

WILLIAMS: No. All right. That is all.
(Witness excused.)

Clearly, his cross-examination of O'Neill had not been a conspicuous success, but Williams had at least one surprise in store. After O'Neill stepped down, Dorety proceeded to bolster the superintendent's testimony with that of other important players in the snow-fighting efforts.

Railroaders M. O. White, Walter Vogel, Edward Sweeney, Homer Purcell, Irving Tegtmeier, Bob Meath, Ira Clary, and William Courtenay (some of whom had been injured in the slide) all supported their superior's claims, drawing a clear picture of a valiant but ultimately futile battle against a storm unlike any ever experienced in the Cascades.

Then former Snow King William Harrington was called to testify. Stepping up to the stand, the man whom the *Seattle Times* had compared to a "Roman gladiator" may have cut an impressive figure, but he was clearly uncomfortable in the formal setting of a courtroom. As long as he had Dorety's shrewd and sympathetic questioning to help him along, Harrington was fine, and he actually gave the jury some of the most forthright accounts of how difficult and exhausting the fight against the storm had been.

> DORETY: Had you tried any shoveling out by hand yourself during this snowstorm?
>
> HARRINGTON: I didn't do anything much but shovel for about six days.
>
> DORETY: How did you succeed in your attempt?
>
> HARRINGTON: There was times when we could not gain a point with shoveling, on account of the wind; the wind was blowing [the snow] faster than we could move it by shovel.

However, once under cross-examination by Williams, Harrington proved to be a less than ideal witness for the Great Northern cause. More than once during his testimony, he contradicted himself, and when Williams read some of his inquest answers back to him, Harrington hurt his own credibility by claiming not to remember making the statements in question.

The truly decisive moment came when Harrington resumed the stand the next morning after an overnight recess. Williams had apparently learned something new and important during that interval, and he immediately pounced on the railroader once the opportunity for recross-examination arrived. Establishing first that Harrington had hiked down the mountain several days after the disaster with Henry

White and some of the other injured survivors, Williams dropped his bombshell.

> WILLIAMS: On that trip down and while you and Mr. White were resting, did you not have a conversation about this slide, and in that conversation did you not say to Mr. White, "That train ought to have been put in a safe place. That was a hell of a place to leave it"?

This was a sensational revelation, one that seemed suddenly to electrify a courtroom lulled by days of ineffectual cross-examination. Harrington, of course, immediately denied having made the statement, but Williams hastily recalled White to the stand in rebuttal. When he asked the salesman whether Harrington had made the comment attributed to him, White was emphatic: "Yes sir," he said—with a certainty that brooked no contradiction.

Clearly rattled, Dorety immediately attempted to discredit the story by establishing that no one else present at the time had heard the alleged comment. He also brought out that during a subsequent three-hour conversation between himself and White—as the two rode together on a train from Scenic—White had never even mentioned it. But there was only so much the GN lawyer could do to vitiate the effect of this surprise testimony. If such an incriminating statement had indeed been made by a veteran railroader—by the Snow King, no less—it would naturally cast doubt on all previous testimony about the relative safety of the passing tracks (much of which, admittedly, had seemed suspiciously unanimous and well rehearsed). As at the coroner's inquest, then, Henry White, with a few short but devastating words, had arguably done the Great Northern and James H. O'Neill more harm than all the strident newspaper editorialists and anti-railroad activists in the country.

It's impossible to say how much impact all of this had on the jury's assessment of the case. Certainly Harrington's alleged remark caused enough excitement among the spectators to prompt a scolding from Judge Humphries—after the next recess, the judge gave a long lecture to the courtroom on the subject of not talking loudly about the case in the hallways within hearing of the jury. Dorety also went on to bolster his already strong case with further exculpatory evidence, eliciting support for O'Neill both from other railroaders, including J. J. Dowling, and from the passengers John Rogers and George Loveberry. But the "hell of a place" comment had cast a pall over the entire Great Northern case. Whether or not it had actually been uttered, the statement was likely to linger in the memory of the jurors, coloring their view of the credibility of every GN witness who had testified.

When the evidence in the case was complete, the GN lawyers made another attempt to get a dismissal or at least a directed verdict on the basis of insufficient evidence. Here again, Judge Humphries felt he simply could not comply. Whatever his own opinion about the strength of the plaintiff's case, his goal was to let the jury have its say. So he simply gave his instructions to the panel of twelve and then—over the further objections of the GN lawyers, who had their own version of the instructions they wanted the judge to give—allowed them to retire.

The jury's deliberation was short and apparently uncontentious. The very next day, on November 1, the jurors filed back into the courtroom with their verdict. It was in favor of the plaintiff, William Topping.

O'Neill, when he heard this verdict, must have been crushed: All of the efforts he and his men had made—the days and days of unrelenting, backbreaking work, with few pauses for food or sleep—had suddenly been nullified at a single stroke. According to the jury, Edward Topping and every other victim of the avalanche had died through the negligence of the Great Northern Railway and its officers. And even though the $20,000 award granted by the jury was only half of what was originally sought, the amount was still, by 1910 standards, significant—large enough to dispel any notion that the jury regarded O'Neill's extraordinary efforts as any kind of mitigating factor.

The GN lawyers immediately appealed. Money aside, this case was simply too important to lose. Over the next few weeks, they regrouped and focused their energies on the appeal. And although it took many months of further legal wrangling, their labors ultimately paid off. In August 1914 the Washington State Supreme Court issued its decision, and it was firmly in the company's favor: "It is plain, from the evidence in the case and from the undisputed facts," the court ruled, "that this avalanche was what is known in law as *vis major,* or an Act of God, which, unless some intervening negligence of the railway company is shown to have cooperated in it, was the sole cause of the accident, and for which the railway company is not liable." Noting that the Great Northern "was using every energy, almost superhuman efforts, to raise the blockade," and that avalanche predictions "are clearly beyond the knowledge of men," the court determined that it was "too plain for argument that no negligence of the appellant was shown. . . . It was the duty of the trial court, therefore, to have granted a nonsuit, or to have instructed the jury to return a verdict in favor of the appellant." The original jury's verdict, in other words, was reversed, with the plaintiff obliged to pay back the $20,000 award, plus 6 percent interest and $264 in court costs.

This ruling was naturally a relief to James J. Hill and to every other railroad owner in the country. Letting the original decision stand would have been a precedent ominous for big corporations of every kind. In some ways, however, the quick reversal of the jury's decision denied real justice to just about everyone else connected to the Wellington Disaster. For many of the victims—the family of Ned Topping, the parents of Nellie Sharp, the mother of Thelma Davis, even survivors such as A. B. Hensel and Henry White—the decision meant that their moral victory had been short-lived. They now came away from the tragedy with little except bitterness and (for those who would settle their cases) a financial reward that could hardly compensate adequately for their suffering. And for the Great Northern railroaders, the decision provided little in the way of vindication for their monumental efforts. The public, after all, had given its opinion through the jury. The stigma that O'Neill must have felt when he returned to his family in Spokane on that early November night in 1913, after the original trial verdict, would not have been lessened much by a technical legal ruling made by a few aging judges in Olympia.

The supreme court's decision did in fact prove to be controversial, with some anti-railroad observers accusing the justices of being in the

pocket of Jim Hill and his powerful friends. However, such inflam-
matory claims aside—and considering the thrust of the case as it was
actually tried—the supreme court probably did come to the right decision. Reading the trial transcript almost a century later, most objective
observers would find the jury's verdict clearly unsupported by the evidence as presented, especially with the high standard of proof required
to establish negligence. True, in light of the antipathy felt by much of
the public toward the railroads at this time, the original verdict was
perhaps foreseeable. In the eyes of many people, the railroads had been
abusing the public trust for years, and whether or not the Great Northern was guilty of such abuse in this particular case was irrelevant to
many. As one outraged correspondent had written to the GN's general
solicitor after being denied a Wellington claim, "The people are rising
up in arms against the injustice that is practiced by concerns such as
yours, and the day is not far distant when you and I will see, if you are
as young a man as I am, that different tactics will be pursued by the
people over whom the railroads are ever prone to take advantage."

Fortunately or unfortunately, those different tactics—litigation, regulation, governmental oversight—were at this time already making in-
roads against the power of the great American railroad conglomerates.
As James J. Hill was sensing with greater indignation every day, the era
of railroad hegemony—that long half century when railroads could do
more or less as they pleased, especially in the American West—was
rapidly coming to a close. Admittedly, in this one case the Great Northern did win its ultimate day in court, but the tide of history was clearly
moving against the Victorian laissez-faire attitudes that had allowed the
railroads and other trusts to gain such great influence and authority
without any corresponding answerability. A new, more modern con-
ception of the balance of power between Big Business and the people
was already surfacing, ushering in a time when labor, government, and
the public would all have a say in how the railroads did their business.
As Theodore Roosevelt had said back in 1904, "Corporate cunning has
developed faster than the laws of nation and State. . . . There must
come, in the proper growth of this nation, a readjustment." By 1913,

thanks in large part to Roosevelt himself, that readjustment was well under way.

But there was another force, even more formidable than unions and government regulators, that was now working against the supremacy of the railroad industry: competition. The automobile—in the guise of Henry Ford's revolutionary Model T, the first affordable car for the masses—would soon offer personal mobility of a kind that passenger trains could never hope to match. Trucks would shortly be able to transport goods directly from producer to customer without costly transfers or huge minimum tonnage requirements. As for speed, the airplane, which in 1910 was rapidly becoming feasible as a mode of commercial transportation, would eventually make Fast Mail trains seem as archaic as the Pony Express.

Railroads, of course, would never actually fade away from the American scene. Even now, at the beginning of the twenty-first century, they remain the most useful form of transportation for many kinds of heavy, high-volume freight. But trains would eventually lose their centrality to the culture of modernity that they themselves had helped create. Total railroad track mileage, after peaking in 1916 at an all-time high of 254,037 miles, would begin to shrink every year thereafter, soon bringing to an end the golden age of American railroading. This slow atrophy was already becoming apparent to perceptive observers in the first decade of the twentieth century—James J. Hill among them. "By the time you're forty," he told his son Louis in 1905, "be out of the railroad business." It proved to be good advice. By the 1920s, the passenger rail industry had entered an era of decline that, except for a brief revival during World War II, would continue for the rest of the century.

Viewed against the background of the great transition in the structure of industry and government that was occurring in the Progressive Era, the Wellington avalanche can not really be regarded as a major impetus of change. Granted, some significant modifications in railway operations did come about as a direct consequence of the tragedy. Shortly after the destruction of the Fast Mail at Stevens Pass, for instance, the

U.S. Post Office Department began requiring that all Railway Mail Service cars nationwide be constructed of steel rather than wood. The events of 1910 also forced many changes in the local operations of the Great Northern itself, including an acceleration of the move toward wireless communications and a massive snowshed-building effort in the Cascades that eventually put 95 percent of the track from Wellington (now Tye) to Scenic under snowshed or tunnel protection. However, the Wellington Disaster was not—to cite a much overused bit of current-day parlance—the "Avalanche That Changed America." It was instead more a symptom than a cause of the great transformations then occurring throughout the country. The decades right around the turn of the twentieth century, after all, were plagued by industrial and transportation disasters of the Wellington type. The newspapers of 1910 were full of such horrors—sinking steamships, exploding factories, devastating fires—culminating in that most famous of all such disasters, the 1912 sinking of the *Titanic*.

It was, in short, a time when mankind's technological reach had profoundly exceeded its grasp, when safety regulations and innovations in fail-safe communication and operations technologies had not yet caught up with the ambitious new standards of speed and efficiency required by American Big Business. As telegrapher Basil Sherlock would write some fifty years afterward, the events at Wellington would have played out much differently in a more advanced technological age. "Such places would have radio and we would be able to contact the outside world. Helicopters would come to [the] rescue, with tools to work with and help."

In 1910, unfortunately, there were no radios at Wellington and no helicopters to come to the rescue of the Seattle Express and the Fast Mail. James H. O'Neill and his men were forced to work with the resources they did have available to them—temperamental snowplows, fragile telegraph and telephone connections, and countless man-hours of hard physical labor. Given the limits of these resources, the fact that these men fell short in this one extreme situation was perhaps excusable. As John Rogers pointed out afterward, the railroaders "could not battle the clouds away." But the failure of their efforts at Wellington, no matter how courageous those efforts may have been, was what history would ultimately remember about the disaster, and it was something that all of them—Jim O'Neill in particular—would be forced to live with for the rest of their lives.

EPILOGUE

A Memory Erased

The mailed fist of progress will be thrust forward through a mighty mountain barrier on its westward drive when America's largest tunnel—the Great Northern bore through the Cascades—is formally opened.

—Seattle Times

On the cold, clear evening of January 12, 1929, a select group of railroad officials, politicians, journalists, and other assorted dignitaries gathered in the snow-blanketed Cascade Mountains for the dedication of the Great Northern Railway's New Cascade Tunnel. The ceremony, which would be broadcast live to some thirty-eight radio stations and an estimated audience of fifteen million Americans nationwide, was to be an elaborate, heavily orchestrated affair, designed to mark the beginning of a new chapter in the railroad history of this country. With the opening of the much-anticipated tunnel—at 7.79 miles, the longest in the Western Hemisphere—the Great Northern's main line through the Cascades would achieve a new standard of safety and reliability. Those miles and miles of steep, twisting track between Berne in the east and Scenic in the west were to be entirely bypassed—the rails pulled up, the stations closed, the old tunnel boarded up and abandoned. Instead, the new mountain crossing would run deep under that slide-prone territory, shortening the route by nine miles and eliminating the need for some forty thousand feet of snowsheds. As GN vice president L. C. Gilman would later remark, "The weakest link in our transportation chain has been replaced by one of the strongest, and we can now regard our rail-road as complete." The line through Stevens Pass—perhaps the last truly untamed section of the American railway system—was to become a thing of the past.

It had not been an easy decision for the Great Northern to make. The new tunnel had been fabulously expensive to build, costing $25 mil-lion in all, including the necessary line electrification and route reloca-tions. Despite the fact that it had been constructed at a record pace of one mile every 4.8 months, it had required almost four years of frantic and disruptive work to complete. But the company had judged the proj-ect a wise investment. The Stevens Pass crossing had in recent times be-come an embarrassing anachronism for any railroad that trumpeted itself as modern. In the years since the Wellington avalanche, a fortune had been spent annually on the construction, maintenance, and repair of snowsheds, and even that effort had not really secured the line. Snowslides had continued to plague the railroad every winter. In one season alone—the legendary winter of 1915–16—slides had hit a pas-senger train near Corea (eight killed, twenty-two injured), buried a sec-tion crew near Leavenworth (four killed), hit another train at Alvin (three killed), and destroyed a bridge near Scenic, closing the line for an entire month. Even the Empire Builder himself had eventually recog-nized the need for some alternative. "Some of you," he had said to asso-ciates on his very last train trip through this territory in 1914, "will live to see this mountain grade eliminated."

Hill himself, alas, had not. After retiring as GN chairman in 1912 (having never drawn a salary in his entire career with the company), he had continued working as feverishly as ever for four more years. Then, in the spring of 1916, he'd been laid low by the ailment that had tor-mented him on and off for years—an acute case of hemorrhoids. Al-though a bevy of physicians had been brought in on the case—including even the Mayo brothers from their eponymous clinic in Rochester, mak-ing their first house call ever—the patient's condition had only worsened as infection and gangrene set in. Ultimately, there had been little the as-sembled doctors could do but stand by and watch his decline, lamenting the hardheadedness of a man who had conquered a continent but had proved too stubborn (or too squeamish) to undergo the simple surgery that would have cured his chronic condition long ago.

By May 28 Hill had lapsed into a coma. Family members were hastily summoned; friends and associates were notified. And at 10:00 A.M. the next day—on a gloriously sunny spring morning, surrounded by his wife and all but one of his children—the man whom Yale University had once named "the last of the wilderness conquerors" was dead. "Greatness became him," an editorialist in the *New York Times* wrote of Hill the next day. "Whatever he had done, it had been greatly done. We salute the memory of a great American." His wife of nearly forty-nine years offered a far more personal tribute to her husband. "How desolately lonely the house seems," Mary Hill wrote in her diary a few days after his death, "and must for time to come."

On Wednesday, May 31, at 2:00 P.M.—the exact hour of Hill's funeral—every train operating on the Great Northern Railway stopped for five minutes, no matter where it was or what its schedule. Considering Hill's lifelong obsession with punctuality, it was perhaps a misguided if well-intended gesture.

Some thirteen years after his death, Hill was now receiving yet another tribute at the opening of the New Cascade Tunnel. As millions tuned in their radios, the ceremony began promptly at 6:00 P.M. Pacific time, with "the dean of American broadcasters," Graham McNamee, introducing GN president Ralph Budd at the tunnel's eastern portal. Standing aboard a special inauguration train filled with dignitaries, a flu-stricken Budd gave the opening speech and formally dedicated the tunnel in the name of James J. Hill. The locomotive was then christened by Leona Watson, that year's Apple Blossom Queen of Wenatchee, after which the train was supposed to proceed into the flag-draped portal and through the tunnel toward Scenic, where it would crash dramatically through a paper cover stretched over the western portal. Technical difficulties put the train fifteen minutes behind schedule (forcing the NBC engineers to hastily switch over to an unscheduled second musical number), but it finally did burst through the covered portal, to the cheers of hundreds on the other side.

More high-tech radio switching followed—to Washington, D.C., for an address by Interstate Commerce commissioner J. B. Campbell, to San Francisco for a solo by contralto Ernestine Schumann-Heink, to Philadelphia for a few words from Pennsylvania Railroad president W. W. Atterbury. Then the broadcast veered back to Washington, D.C., where President-elect Herbert Hoover gave the keynote address from his S Street home. "Never have we witnessed a more perfect coordination of the forces of American industry than in this great job," the future president intoned. "It gives every American the satisfaction of confidence in the virility of our civilization."

Within months, of course, Hoover would preside over a significant affront to that virility when the stock market crashed in October, plunging the country into a long period of economic impotence. But for the moment, the lions of American politics and industry could roar as loudly as they wanted to. It wasn't as if they hadn't earned their bragging rights. Thanks to the combined efforts of these titans, the Last Mountains had been conquered—yet again.

When the radio broadcast ended at 7:00 P.M., about six hundred guests assembled for a banquet at the dining hall of the Scenic construction camp. The guest of honor was none other than John F. Stevens, now much celebrated as the man who'd rescued the Panama Canal project from disaster. After the main course, Stevens addressed the audience, which included such notables as Washington's Governor Roland H. Hartley, Louis W. Hill Jr. (grandson of the Empire Builder), Arthur Curtiss James (a GN director and one of the world's richest men), and the presidents of the Seattle, Tacoma, Spokane, and Washington State chambers of commerce. Standing beside a twenty-five-cubic-foot cake depicting the Cascade Range in full relief, the engineer spoke at length about the discovery of the pass that bore his name, the building of the original line, and the new tunnel, for which he had served as consultant. "And so the new tunnel is put in operation," the seventy-six-year-old engineer concluded, "and I am very, very pleased. A long tunnel was a dream for years, and I am so glad to have lived to see it an accomplished fact. But I can't help feeling a regret to know that the old line is a thing of the past, and that I probably will never see it again, for I put in some of my best days on it."

Seated not far from Stevens at the speakers' table was a man who knew the ins and outs of that old line as well as anyone on earth. James H. O'Neill, at fifty-six looking heavier but still remarkably hale and energetic, was marking his forty-third year with the Great Northern Railway. Nine years earlier, in 1920, he had been promoted to general manager of the GN's operating department, in charge of all lines west of Williston, North Dakota. But although he had now reached the heights of upper management, his work habits hadn't changed much in the past two decades. Despite increasing trouble with rheumatism in recent years, he was still a compulsive workaholic, still more comfortable out on the line than in his office, and still writing apologetic notes and telegrams to Berenice and his three children for his frequent absences. ("Peggy dear," ran an all too typical note to his daughter. "Account receiving a telegram about 10 o'clock could not wait until morning. You were asleep and of course did not want to awaken you, so left for the station promptly. Hope Boy and everybody else are well when I return Saturday, so you can all take a trip with me to Montana next week. Love to all, Dad.")

For as hard as it may be to believe, in 1929 James H. O'Neill was still being called away to fight the Cascade snows. Great Northern corporate archives contain telegrams written by O'Neill as late as 1936 that seem virtually identical to those he had written a quarter century before—reporting slides near Leavenworth, an iced-up engine at Skykomish, a disabled rotary plow somewhere east of Berne. Someone else may have been directly responsible for cleaning up those messes nowadays, but they were still, on one level or another, Jim O'Neill's problems. And each one of them, no matter how minor, must have carried with it an echo of those he had faced—and been blamed for—decades earlier at Wellington.

He was not, however, a broken man. Judging from family archives and stories, the events he'd endured in 1910, while they may have permanently scarred him, had not ruined Jim O'Neill's life. His humor and playfulness seem to have survived the tragedy intact. One anniversary, for instance, he had a ring for Berenice secretly baked into a loaf of bread, which he then asked her to slice at the dinner table, while his three delighted children looked on. (The ring was henceforth known invariably as "Sunshine," just as a favorite candelabrum was always referred to as "George," though for reasons that have been lost to family memory.) O'Neill seems to have gone on to lead an ordinary life of ordinary happiness, hunting ducks and fishing for steelhead in his always scarce free time.

But he had never strayed far from the train whistles that had ensnared him as a child. O'Neill, who had been a young trainmaster at Great Falls when Butch Cassidy's Wild Bunch held up their last train, still lived and breathed the railroad in the modern times of the late 1920s. And though he would never advance beyond his current position of western general manager, there would be many more highlights in his career, including a stint as a rail tester for the special train of Franklin Delano Roosevelt in 1934, during which he was once or twice mistaken for the president himself.

Appropriately enough, he would never retire, working right up to the day he died of a sudden heart attack at home in Seattle on January 11, 1937. He was sixty-four years old and had worked for the Great Northern for exactly fifty years. "Our love was the proudest thing in my life," Berenice would afterward write to their daughter Jean. "Even the memory of a love like that is richer treasure than most lives ever know." Berenice herself, though so much younger, would die on May 17, just four months later.

In his apparent ability to rebound from the effects of the Wellington Disaster, O'Neill had been more fortunate than many other veterans of the avalanche. Ida Starrett, who lived to be an old woman, refused even to talk about the episode for decades. She eventually remarried, operated a grocery store outside Seattle, and then moved to a chicken ranch near Mukilteo, Washington. And while her mother ended up suffering no permanent physical effects from the avalanche (Mrs. May "danced till she was 80," according to her grandson), Ida spent her last years in a wheelchair as a result of her Wellington injuries.

Ray Starrett grew up to become a tall, handsome man, the longtime safety supervisor for Puget Sound Power and Light Company in Olympia. Though he would retain few memories of the avalanche in later life, he would forever bear a scar on his forehead from the makeshift surgery he'd undergone on the dining room table of the Bailets Hotel. In 1960, a half century after the avalanche, he received a surprise letter from the maker of that scar, retired telegrapher Basil Sherlock, who asked him—significantly—to send along "a picture of yourself taken recently with your hat off." Still feeling uneasy about this decision to cut the stick out of Raymond's head—"nobody ever told me if I did right or wrong"—Sherlock had never forgotten the boy or the episode that had convinced him to leave the Pacific Northwest for good. "Last March first our newspaper came out with a story in the way of a 50-year anniversary of the avalanche at Wellington," he wrote from Willmar, Minnesota, where he and Alathea now lived, "and since then [I] cannot get you out of my mind. Perhaps you will not remember me now."

Starrett did remember him, and the two exchanged several letters. Ida was also still alive at this point, living in a nursing home in Everett, but she chose not to participate in the correspondence. "We do not blame her," Sherlock responded. "For a good many years we were like soldiers coming back from war, we did not wish to talk about it."

A. B. Hensel also refrained from discussing the avalanche for much of his life. A risk-averse, safety-minded man in subsequent years, he never learned to drive a car and kept all of his money in jars around the house, refusing to trust banks. He eventually married, had two daughters, and continued to work for the Railway Mail Service until his retirement in 1950 (after a career of forty-seven years and two months). Only upon leaving the mail service did he begin to talk and write about his experiences at Wellington.

Many of the railroaders involved continued to work for the Great Northern for the rest of their careers. Ira Clary, the diminutive rotary conductor who went down in the slide, eventually rose to the position of Cascade Division superintendent (he was known as the "Little Giant" among his men). The career of Snow King William Harrington, on the other hand, seems to have peaked sometime before his ill-fated superior court appearance. Having replaced Arthur Blackburn as trainmaster for a time after the latter's death, he was by 1913 working as a conductor again. In a strange coincidence, he was the skipper in charge of the train

(No. 25, again) that was hit by a snowslide near Corea in January 1916. Though nowhere near as large as the Wellington avalanche, the slide hurled a dining car and a passenger coach 250 feet down the mountain, killing eight passengers and injuring twenty-two others. Harrington himself was apparently unhurt. However, after this second narrow escape, it's not surprising that he soon opted for a safer job, finishing his career as first a yardmaster and later a dispatcher—positions that would allow him to go home to his family every night.

The widow of conductor Joseph Pettit lived to see three of her sons go on to railroad careers. One of them, Paul, died in an accident while on duty, yet another victim of this most dangerous profession. Another son, Joe Jr., lost his job as a GN switchman for violating Rule G—the liquor rule—but was reinstated after the local business agent of the Brotherhood of Railway Trainmen intervened on his behalf. The agent was none other than Bill J. Moore, much older now, paying a last favor to the dead conductor who had been his good friend.

Other participants in the Wellington story seem simply to have disappeared into the oblivion of ordinary existence. About the later lives of many—Henry White, John Rogers, the lawyers Merritt and Jesseph, R. M. Laville—little or nothing is known. Interestingly, at least one survivor, the baby Varden Gray, would live to capitalize on his avalanche experience; as an adult, he became a traveling evangelist and dubbed himself the "Duke of Wellington." Most of those who'd lived through it, though, were forever sobered by the event. As Basil Sherlock wrote in 1960 to Ray Starrett, "Perhaps you wish to forget it. For over fifty years, I have. Twenty-five of those years were spent working on the graveyard shift, 12M to 8 A.M. And when the hands of the clock would point to 1:10 A.M. on March first, I would shut my eyes and see it all over again."

But now, on January 12, 1929, as the Great Northern Railway feted itself at Scenic for introducing a new era of safe, reliable travel through the wilds of the Last Mountains, only one man present truly understood the full price that had been paid for breaching that wilderness with a railroad line. James H. O'Neill listened as the addresses went on and on into the night, full of high-blown rhetoric about progress, technology, and the end of the threat of nature: "The switchback has become tradition," one speaker opined. "Snow troubles in the Cascades [are] only a memory and the snowsheds antiques." About the victims of the Wellington avalanche—the unacknowledged impetus behind the engineering marvel currently being celebrated—nothing at all was said. The town itself would soon be abandoned, turned over to the elk, the bears, and the coyotes "howling in the doorways of deserted dwellings." After thirty-five years of life, it would stand empty and silent and remote once more, four miles above the bustle at Scenic, a now useless concrete snowshed the only monument to its dead.

A Final Note on the Wellington Avalanche

Whether the Wellington avalanche was a tragedy that could reasonably have been anticipated by those in charge of the situation was—and still is—a debatable question. Avalanche science was barely in its infancy in 1910, and as the Washington State Supreme Court noted, avalanche predictions at that time were "clearly beyond the knowledge of men." Several reports published in the wake of that year's snowslide season, however, indicate that perhaps more was known than the Great Northern cared to admit. An article in the June 1910 edition of the *Monthly Weather Review* and a report published by the U.S. Forest Service in November 1911 suggest that a basic grasp of what was occurring at Stevens Pass was not beyond the knowledge of the day, and that a slide above the trains should not have been regarded as such an improbability.

Admittedly, the reports do support many of the railroad's contentions about the unusual nature of conditions in late February 1910. Edward A. Beals, author of the *Monthly Weather Review* article, confirmed that it had been an unprecedented avalanche season both in the Cascades and in the northern Rockies. "Avalanches in these mountains are of common occurrence every year," he wrote, "but this year there were more than ever before known." The period in question actually saw thousands of slides across the Northwest, including large ones in Idaho and British Columbia (such as the Rogers Pass slide, Canada's deadliest) that resulted in particularly high numbers of casualties. Beals's report also verified the unusual length of the late-February storm, revealing that it was actually not a single storm but three separate disturbances that passed through the area in close succession.

The type of slide that occurred at Wellington, moreover, was regarded as relatively rare in the area. Witnesses at both the inquest and the trial claimed that the vast majority of slides in the Cascades were what are now called loose-snow avalanches. They were perceived as more or less predictable, coming down in draws and canyons where they had come down in past years. (Thornton T. Munger, author of the Forest Service report, even used the term "canyon slide" for this type of avalanche, as opposed to "slope slide" for what is now called a slab avalanche.) Loose-snow avalanches tend to start at a single point and fan out in the form of an inverted V, and they can start quite literally at the drop of a hat. As the trapper Robert Schwartz testified at the inquest, by shaking a bit of snow off a single tree branch, "a bird or an icicle or a puff of wind can start a snowslide."

However, the absence of a draw or canyon above the passing tracks certainly did not make that slope immune to the slab-type of avalanche. Weather patterns in the days and weeks before March 1 had in fact created ideal conditions for this type of slide. At roughly thirty-two degrees, the slope of the mountainside at that point was also right within the optimum range for sliding. Even the covering of burned trees that the GN regarded as a factor working against avalanche formation actually had the opposite effect. Thick forest may discourage slides from forming, but sparse tree cover provides weak points in the snowpack where avalanches can start more easily.

It would be unfair to assert that O'Neill and Blackburn should have foreseen the imminent danger of a slide and diverted all of their limited resources to either moving the trains or evacuating those who slept on them. But certainly the particular risk created by a hard freeze followed by a thawing trend was not unknown to the men of the Cascade Division. Even the lowly trackwalker Thomas O'Malley testified as much at the inquest. "Heavy wet snow on the hills will do it," he said in answer to a question from state railroad commissioner Lawrence on how slides start. "Sometimes the snow is frozen underneath, and [if we] get a couple nights' fall of snow, it will slide right off the hard crust."

In retrospect, it's clear that the situation at Wellington should have been handled differently. As conductor Walter Vogel admitted in his court testimony, other locations around Wellington, "as shown by conditions afterwards," would have been safer places to put the trains. But "conditions afterwards" are unknowable beforehand. In a crisis of this type, the gaps between foresight and hindsight are invariably great, and the parallax they create is one that historians and other latter-day observers cannot afford to ignore.

APPENDIX

A Wellington Roster

The exact number of people who died in the Wellington Disaster will probably never be known for sure. No official passenger lists were kept by railroads at this time, and even employee records were imprecise and error-ridden (often because many employees worked under a series of false names to escape less than ideal employment histories). The composition of the temporary work gangs was especially fluid, with transient laborers leaving and arriving without notice, often identified in railroad documents solely by number. In a remote place like the Cascade Division, it was all too easy for the death of a foreign laborer with no local ties to go unreported.

The official death toll as compiled by the Great Northern Railway was ninety-six, including a number of unidentified laborers. This total rises to one hundred if it includes the two men who died in the beanery slide on February 25, the watchman who died in the avalanche at Drury on March 1, and the laborer who died in the March 13 slide that reclosed the line once it had been cleared. But mysteries remain. The *Seattle Times* of March 15, for instance, reported the arrival in Seattle of the body of "Joseph Furlin of Everett," an alleged passenger whose name did not appear on the official Great Northern list or in the coroner's death record (though a later newspaper story hints that this may merely have been an alias for John Brockman).

The following is a list of the known dead, the injured, and a few of those who were spared.

Ahern, Lee D.	mail weigher	killed
Anderson, Lucius	porter	injured
Andrews, Charles	engineer	at Wellington, unharmed
Annan, John	rotary engineer	injured in March 13 slide
Avery, W. V. ("Mississippi")	telegrapher	at Wellington, unharmed
Bailets, Susan	postmistress	at Wellington, unharmed
Bailets, W. R.	hotelkeeper	at Wellington, unharmed
Barnhart, Richard M.	passenger	killed
Bates, Samuel A.	fireman	injured
Beck, Emma	passenger (child)	killed
Beck, G. L.	passenger	killed
Beck, Mrs. G. L.	passenger	killed
Beck, Marion	passenger (child)	killed
Beck, (unknown)	passenger (child)	killed
Begle, Grover W.	express messenger	killed
Bennington, Earl Edgar	fireman	killed
Bethel, R. H.	passenger	killed
Bjart, John	laborer	killed
Bjerenson, John	waiter	killed in beanery slide
Blackburn, Arthur Reed	trainmaster	killed
Blomeke, Antony	engineer	at Wellington, unharmed
Bogart, Richard Clarence	mail clerk	killed
Bohn, Fred	mail weigher	killed
Boles, Albert	passenger	killed
Boles, Edward W.	passenger	hiked out on Monday
Bovee, William	brakeman	killed
Brockman, John	passenger	killed
Bruno, Peter	laborer	killed
Campbell, Alex C. (Ed)	rotary conductor	killed
Carroll, J. O.	engineer	killed

Chantrell (or Cantrell), H. D.	passenger	killed
Chisholm, Alex	passenger	killed
Christy, G.	laborer	killed
Clark, Ed	railroader	at Wellington, unharmed
Clary, Ira	rotary conductor	injured
Cohen, Solomon	passenger	killed
Corcoran, William	engine watchman	killed
Covington, Sarah Jane	passenger	killed
Davis, George F.	passenger	killed
Davis, Thelma S.	passenger (child)	killed
Devery, J. C.	asst. superintendent	with the rotary on the east slope; unharmed
Dinatale, Guiseppe	laborer	hiked out on Monday
Dorety, William	brakeman	killed
Dougherty, Anthony John	brakeman	killed
Dowling, J. J.	master mechanic	at Scenic, unharmed
Drehl, H. J.	express messenger	killed
Duncan, Earl S.	brakeman	injured
Duncan, William A.	porter	killed
Dupy, Archie R.	brakeman	killed
Elerker, Harry	cook	killed in beanery slide
Eltinge, Charles S.	passenger	killed
Field, Samuel	passenger	hiked out on Monday
Finn, Joe	engineer	at Wellington, unharmed
Fisher, Earl	fireman	killed
Flannery, William	telegrapher	at Wellington, unharmed
Forsyth, Raymond	passenger	injured
Fox, John D.	mail clerk	killed
Giammarusti, Inigi	laborer	killed
Gilman, Donald Cameron	electrician	killed
Gilmore, M. E.	brakeman	lightly injured
Gray, Anna	passenger	injured
Gray, John	passenger	injured
Gray, Varden	passenger (child)	injured
Guglielmo, Mike	laborer	killed
Harrington, William	asst. trainmaster	injured
Hensel, Alfred B.	mail clerk	injured
Heron, George A.	passenger	killed

Hicks, Milton	brakeman/painter	killed
Hoefer, George	mail clerk	killed
Horn, Milton	passenger	hiked out on Sunday
Jarnagan, Benjamin	engineer	killed
Jenks, G. R.	fireman	killed
Jennison, Charles William	brakeman	killed
Jesseph, Lewis C.	passenger	hiked out on Sunday
Johnson, Fred	watchman	killed in Drury slide
Jones, Sidney H.	fireman	killed
Kelly, John Edward	brakeman	killed
Kenzal, William	brakeman	killed
Kerlee, James L.	fireman	injured
La Du, Charles F.	mail clerk	killed
Latsch, Libby	passenger	killed
Laville, R. M.	passenger	injured
Lee, Sam	passenger	killed
Leibert, Gus	laborer	killed
Lemman, Ada	passenger	killed
Lemman, Edgar	passenger	killed
Liberati, J.	laborer	killed
Lindsay, Steven E. (Ed)	rotary conductor	killed
Longcoy, Earl Rumsey	stenographer	killed
Loveberry, George	passenger	hiked out on Sunday
Mackey, J. J.	traveling engineer	at Wellington, unharmed
Mackie, John	passenger	killed
Mahler, Albert G.	passenger	killed
Martin, Francis S.	engineer	killed
Matthews, Bert	passenger	killed
May, William M.	passenger	killed
May, Mrs. William M.	passenger	injured
McDonald, Archibald (John)	brakeman	killed; body found in July
McGirl, Nellie G. (a.k.a. Nellie Sharp)	passenger	killed
McKnight, R.	passenger	hiked out on Monday
McNeny, James	passenger	killed
Meath, John Robert	rotary engineer	at Wellington, unharmed
Merritt, John W.	passenger	hiked out on Sunday
Mertz, H. L.	laborer?	hiked out on Monday

Miles, Robert	engineer	at Wellington, unharmed
Miles, Mrs. Robert	wife of engineer	at Wellington, unharmed
Monroe, James	passenger	killed
Morris, C. H.	trainman	lightly injured
Nelson, George (Bat)	fireman	injured
Nino, Peter	engine watcher	killed
O'Neill, James H.	superintendent	at Scenic, unharmed
O'Reilly, Catherine	passenger	killed
Osborne, T. L.	engineer	killed
Partridge, Harry Otto	fireman	killed
Parzybok, John K.	rotary conductor	killed
Pettit, Joseph L.	passenger conductor	killed
Phillips, Ross	brakeman	injured
Porlowlino, Antonio	laborer	killed
Purcell, Homer E.	rotary conductor	injured
Quarante, Donato	laborer	killed in March 13 slide
Raycroft, William E.	brakeman	killed
Rea, Edward R.	passenger	hiked out on Sunday
Ritter, Frank	passenger	hiked out on Monday
Rogers, John	passenger	hiked out on Monday
Ross, L.	fireman	killed
Schwartz, Robert	trapper	at Wellington, unharmed
Sherlock, Alathea	wife of telegrapher	at Wellington, unharmed
Sherlock, Basil J.	telegrapher	at Wellington, unharmed
Smart, Charles	brakeman	injured
Smith, Adolph	porter	injured
Smith, Carl	laborer	killed
Sperber, E. A.	passenger	hiked out on Monday
Starrett, Francis	passenger (child)	killed
Starrett, Ida	passenger	injured
Starrett, Lillian	passenger (child)	killed
Starrett, Raymond	passenger (child)	injured
Stohmier, Andrew	brakeman	killed
Suterin, Vasily	laborer	killed
Tegtmeier, Duncan	traveling engineer	injured
Tegtmeier, Irving	traveling engineer	with the rotary near Corea; unharmed
Thompson, Benjamin G.	passenger	killed

Thomson, Rev. James M.	passenger	killed
Topping, Edward W. (Ned)	passenger	killed
Tosti, Giovanni	laborer	killed
Towslee, Hiram	mail clerk	killed
Tucker, John C.	mail clerk	killed
Vail, J. R.	passenger	killed
Van Larke, Angus	railroader	hiked out on Monday
Vogel, Walter	Fast Mail conductor	with the rotary near Corea; unharmed
Walker, Lewis George	steward	killed
Ward, J. S.	trainman	lightly injured
Wells, Julian E.	brakeman	killed
Wentzel, John	laborer	at Wellington, unharmed
Wertz, H. L.	passenger	hiked out on Monday
White, Henry H.	passenger	injured
White, M. O.	rotary conductor	injured
Wickham, "Big Jerry"	brakeman	at Scenic, injured in fall
Yerks, G. R.	fireman	killed
Young, Charles	passenger	hiked out on Monday
Unidentified	laborer	killed
Unidentified	laborer	killed
Unidentified	laborer	killed
Unidentified	laborer	killed
Unidentified	laborer	killed
Unidentified	laborer	killed

NOTES

NB: *The dates of all newspaper stories, letters, telegrams, and other primary sources, unless otherwise specified, are from 1910.*

Abbreviations Used in Notes

CIT	Coroner's Inquest Testimony
EDH	*Everett Daily Herald*
GN	Great Northern
NP	Northern Pacific
NYT	*New York Times*
SCT	Superior Court Transcript
SDC	*Spokane Daily Chronicle*
SEC	*Spokane Evening Chronicle*
SIH	Spokane *Inland Herald*
SPI	*Seattle Post-Intelligencer*
SS	*Seattle Star*
SSR	Spokane *Spokesman-Review*
ST	*Seattle Times*
SUR	Seattle *Union Record*
TDL	*Tacoma Daily Ledger*
WDW	*Wenatchee Daily World*

The book's opening quotation—"The difference between civilization and barbarism . . ."—is cited in Albro Martin, *James J. Hill and the Opening of the Northwest* (New York: Oxford University Press, 1976), p. 403.

Prologue: A Late Thaw

The recovery and identification of Archibald McDonald's body was described in newspaper accounts of the time, including articles in the *Seattle Times, Seattle Post-Intelligencer, Everett Daily Herald,* and *Wenatchee Daily World* (July 27–30). Details about the life and experiences of William J. Moore (including the quote about "cordwood") come from an August 2004 interview with his son Barney Moore and an unpublished letter from the elder Moore to Ruby El Hult, dated June 7, [1960] (Ruby El Hult Papers, Washington State University Manuscripts, Archives and Special Collections, Pullman, WA).

On the postavalanche salvage and recovery efforts, see newspaper accounts, especially *ST,* March 6–14; *WDW,* April 22. Also: "Great Northern's Cascade Division Snowsheds: 1910 to 1929" by Stuart Vesper (Great Northern Railway Historical Society Reference Sheets Nos. 179 and 183, June and December 1991). Unsalvaged items left in the canyon as observed on-site by the author and as photographed (eighty-seven years later) by Martin Burwash, *Cascade Division* (Arvada, CO: Fox Publications, 1997).

On the character of working life at "the end of the world" (as the Cascade Division was known), see "The Wellington Disaster—March 1, 1910: Reminiscences of Basil J. Sherlock" (Washington State Historical Society, Tacoma, WA). "I will never forget this" is from the margin notes in Bill J. Moore's annotated copy of Ruby El Hult's *Northwest Disaster* (Portland, OR: Binford & Mort, 1960), kindly lent to the author by Barney Moore.

Details of the beanery slide come mainly from contemporary newspaper accounts (especially the *EDH* of February 25) and from recollections of telegrapher Warren Tanguy as recounted in the *ST* of November 15, 1959, pp. 2–3. "Howling, cantankerous blizzard" is a quotation from the *SPI* of February 24. Particulars of the Mace, Burke, and Rogers Pass slides, as well as those involving the horse barn and the bobsledding cabin, are from reports in *ST* and *WDW* from February 28 to March 10.

"So fierce is the storm" is from the *ST* of February 24. "Passengers by Sunday were in a frantic state" is a quotation from John Rogers cited in the *ST* of March 2. Details about the three families come from Hult, p. 4, from a front-page article on the Starretts in the Spokane *Inland Herald* of March 3, and from other newspaper accounts. "We knew we were in a death trap" is from a March 18 letter from Anna Gray to Luther Covington (Covington/Brokaw family collection).

"To hike out is to take your life in your hands" was said by J. J. Mackey (Coroner's Inquest Transcript, p. 92.) "He had scarcely gone a step" was quoted in the Spokane *Spokesman-Review* of March 3. "The final victory of man's machinery" is a quotation from Simon Patten, as cited in George E. Mowry's *The Era of Theodore Roosevelt and the Birth of Modern America, 1900–1912* (New York: Harper & Brothers, 1958).

Second-guessing about culpability for the disaster as reported in contemporary newspaper accounts, particularly in the Seattle *Union Record,* and in the following court documents: Coroner's Inquest Transcript (hereafter CIT), "In the matter of the inquiry into the cause of the death of John Brockman and eighty-seven, or more, others, Deceased" (Testimony taken before King County Coroner J. C. Snyder, commencing March 18, 1910); and the Superior Court Transcript (hereafter SCT), "Statement of Facts: *Topping vs. Great Northern Railway*" (Superior Court of the State of Washington, in and for King County: Case No. 11,949).

1: A Railroad Through the Mountains

The opening quotation—"This winter is hell of a time"—is from a court affidavit by Nyke Homonylo in the archives of the Wenatchee Valley Museum, Wenatchee, WA.

"Cold Wave Is Hieing Hither" was perpetrated in the February 21 edition of the *EDH*. Other specifics about weather and the resulting railroad difficulties come from surviving GN telegrams (unless otherwise attributed, all telegrams cited are from the private collection of Robert Kelly, Renton, WA) and from regional newspapers. The quote by James E. Vance is from his book *The North American Railroad: Its Origin, Evolution, and Geography* (Baltimore: Johns Hopkins University Press, 1995), p. 214. The high Cascades as "snowiest region" derives from snowfall data available from the U.S. National Climatic Data Center (www.ncdc.noaa.gov).

The early career of James H. O'Neill is outlined in a magazine profile by Walter E. Mair, "O'Neill of the Great Northern," which appeared in the May 1932 issue of *Railroad Stories*. Other personal history is from newspaper features ("I never saw more pluck": *ST*, March 6) and obituaries, as well as 1910 U.S. Census records. Quotations from O'Neill's telegrams and letters, as well as personal information about Berenice, their courtship, and their marriage, come from family scrapbooks in the possession of Jeanne Patricia May, their granddaughter.

The "call of the railroad" as quoted in *The Story of American Railroads* by Stewart H. Holbrook (New York: Crown, 1947), p. 3. The description of the division superintendent's job is from a *Scribner's* article, "The Freight-Car Service," by Theodore Vorhees, later collected in *The American Railway: Its Construction, Development, Management, and Appliances* (New York: Scribner's, 1889), pp. 274–75. The average annual snowfall at Stevens Pass (over fifty feet) as reported in "The Pacific Extension and Cascade Switchbacks: 1889–1892" by W. C. Hartranft (Great Northern Railway Historical Society Reference Sheet No. 172, December 1990).

The literature on early Everett is unexpectedly rich and often delightful. Louis Tucker registered his dislike of the place ("a city with none of the social graces," "as a terrior yaps at a great Dane," etc.) in his *Clerical Errors* (New York: Harper and Bros., 1943). A more sympathetic view is presented in three highly enjoyable if often repetitive memoirs by journalist Max Miller, particularly *The Beginning of a Mortal* (New York: Dutton, 1933) and *Shinny on Your Own Side* (New York: Doubleday, 1958), which provide an atmospheric portrait of the city from a child's perspective. The city is also blessed with an intelligent and elegantly written history: *Mill Town: A Social History of Everett, Washington,* by Norman H. Clark (Seattle: University of Washington Press, 1970). Other information from the 1910 *Polk's City Directory* and from *Everett: Past and Present* by Lawrence E. O'Donnell (Everett: Cascade Savings Bank, 1993).

The railroads' transformation of the West is a subject dear to the hearts of many American historians, covered in works ranging in scholarliness from Robert H. Wiebe's opaque but brilliant *The Search for Order: 1877–1920* (New York: Hill and Wang, 1967) to Dee Brown's highly readable *Hear That Lonesome Whistle Blow* (New York: Holt, Rinehart and Winston, 1977). "All of that land wasn't worth ten cents" as quoted in Holbrook, *Story*, p. 5. The rhetorical flourish from Miles C. Moore ("the true alchemy of the age") was cited in D. W. Meinig, *The Shaping of America*, vol. 3, *Transcontinental America, 1850–1915* (New Haven: Yale University Press, 1998), p. 6. But the most directly pertinent single work on the topic is Sarah Gordon's excellent *Passage to Union: How the Railroad Changed American Life, 1829–1929* (Chicago: Ivan Dee, 1996).

Washington's late connection to the railway network is most vividly illustrated in the maps reproduced in John Stover's *Routledge Historical Atlas of American Railroads* (New York: Routledge, 1999). Population growth statistics for Seattle and other Washington cities come from a variety of sources, including O'Donnell, p. 30; "The Promotion of Emigration to Washington, 1854–1909" by Arthur J. Brown (*Pacific Northwest Quarterly* 36, [1945]), pp. 3–17; the *WDW* of February 11; and Works Project Administration, *Washington: A Guide to the Evergreen State* (Portland, OR: Binford & Mort, 1941), pp. 217–20. Ray Stannard Baker's comment, "Everything seems to have happened within the last ten years," was made in his article "The Great Northwest," published in the *Century Magazine* of March 1903 (vol. 65, no. 5), p. 653.

The term "instant civilization" is from James Bryce, as quoted in Carlos Schwantes, *Railroad Signatures Across the Pacific Northwest* (Seattle: University of Washington Press, 1993), p. 182. Mark Sullivan's characterization of still-raw Western settlements— "towns with a marble Carnegie Library at 2nd Street"—is from his always evocative *Our Times: America at the Birth of the Twentieth Century*, originally printed in 1926, modern edition by Dan Rather (New York: Scribner, 1996), p. 39.

The GN's plans for line improvements in 1910 were announced in all of the local papers, including the *EDH* of February 21. In this chapter, as in subsequent chapters, train movements and other operational details are culled from a variety of sources: Great Northern telegrams; a court document, "Movement of Trains and Rotaries on the Hill from February 22d on to Slide"; excerpts from the Operations Diary of J. C. Devery—all from the Robert Kelly collection—as well as court testimony from CIT and SCT.

2: The Long Straw

The opening quotation and other details about doings in Spokane on that Washington's Birthday Tuesday are from the *SIH* of February 22.

Lewis C. Jesseph's story is told in a memoir, "We Escaped the Wellington Disaster," printed in *Confluence*, vol. 5, no. 1 (North Central Washington Museum, Wenatchee, 1988). My description of the two Pullman cars relies on "Early Great Northern Sleeping Cars, Part II" by Kenneth R. Middleton (Great Northern Railway Historical Society Reference Sheet No. 252, June 1997). No. 25's H-class Pacific engine as cited in Charles and Dorothy Wood's indispensible *The Great Northern Railway: A Pictorial Study* (Edmonds, WA: Pacific Fast Mail, 1979). Details about Spokane history and geography come principally from the Works Project Administration's *Washington: A Guide to the*

Evergreen State and *This Town of Ours . . . Spokane* by Jay J. Kalez (Spokane: Lawton Printing, 1973), as well the 1910 *Polk's City Directory*. The GN's Havermale Island depot was described in an article published in the *SSR* of February 25, 1902.

For the makeup of the passenger list of train No. 25, and for background about much of the story to follow, I am indebted to *Northwest Disaster* by Ruby El Hult, an account of the avalanche that is still highly readable and remarkably accurate after nearly fifty years. The GN's official list of people on the trains was published in the *ST* of March 10.

The issue of the name of train No. 25 is not without controversy. Other sources list the train variously as the Seattle Local, Spokane Local, Spokane Express, and Seattle Flyer. The reason for this is clear: At this time, all GN trains had official numbers but most did not have official names, so a train near its point of origin would naturally be referred to by its destination, while a train near its destination would be called by the name of the city of its origin. For the sake of clarity, however, I have chosen to refer to the train throughout as the Seattle Express, which is how it was listed in the Spokane newspaper timetables.

Sarah Covington's letter to her daughter and excerpts from her short diary are preserved in the archives of the Washington State Historical Society (Tacoma, WA). Some information also comes from Covington family archives, in particular a March 4 letter to Sadie Gregg from her brother Luther Covington. A transcript of Ned Topping's day-by-day letter (which was found in the wreckage after the avalanche) was kindly provided by his grandson John Topping and is now in the Robert Kelly collection. The story behind Nellie Sharp's presence on the train was printed in *ST*, March 12. "The American poetry of vivid purpose" is from William Dean Howells's underappreciated novel *The Rise of Silas Lapham* (1885; reprint: New York: Signet, 1980), p. 75.

Details about Henry White come mainly from his inquest and court testimony, and from articles in the *SS* of March 3 and the *SPI* of March 6. That White was "not of a disposition to anticipate trouble" is from CIT, p. 436. "We knew that the Great Northern Railway" is from Jesseph, p. 176.

Excerpts from J. C. Devery's Operations Diary, here and elsewhere, are from the collection of Robert Kelly.

The average duration of storms in the Cascades was gleaned from much of the testimony in CIT and SCT. The incident of the stalled freight at Scenic as detailed in a GN telegram from O'Neill dated February 22, 1:00 P.M., and from the court affidavit of Dowling, Mackey, and Tegtmeier. (NB: Unless otherwise stated, all court affidavits cited hereafter are from the Wenatchee Valley Museum.)

Information about the Fast Mail train comes from "Great Northern Railway Mail Services" by Stuart Holmquist (Great Northern Railway Historical Society Reference Sheet No. 177, June 1991); Jeff Wilson's *The Great Northern Railway in the Pacific Northwest* (Waukesha, WI: Kalbach Books, 2001), p. 114ff; and from Don Moody's *America's Worst Rail Disaster: The 1910 Wellington Tragedy* (Plano, TX: Abique, 1998), pp. 17–23. Performance statistics for the Fast Mail during its first months are from the President's Subject Files (GNR Corporate Records, the Minnesota Historical Society, file 132.E.16.4F). That the Fast Mail normally preceded Train No. 25 across Washington is mentioned in O'Neill's inquest testimony, CIT, p. 22. "The Fastest Long-Distance Train in the World" is from the *Brooklyn Standard Union*, November 30, 1909.

O'Neill's conversation with J. C. Wright, the engineer of the Oriental Limited, as testified in CIT, p. 110ff.

The quotation from Alfred B. Hensel is from SCT, p. 8. Pettit's character as attested to by several witnesses in the same transcript, and from contemporary newspaper accounts. The release of train No. 25 from "Movement of Rotaries," p. 2. The story of Mrs. Blanche Painter's narrow escape is related in the *EDH* of March 4 and in the *Leavenworth Echo* of March 11.

3: Last Mountains

Hamlin Garland's "Western Landscapes" appeared in the *Atlantic Monthly* of December 1893.

For the discussion of the early history of efforts to cross and survey the "Last Mountains," I am principally indebted to several books: Kurt Armbruster's authoritative and impressively thorough *Orphan Road: The Railroad Comes to Seattle, 1853–1911* (Seattle: University of Washington Press, 1999); *The Cascades: Mountains of the Pacific Northwest,* edited by Roderick Peattie (New York: Vanguard Press, 1949); James E. Vance's *The North American Railroad*; JoAnn Roe's careful, useful *Stevens Pass: The Story of Railroading and Recreation in the North Cascades* (Caldwell, ID: Caxton Press, 2002); and Carlos Schwantes's fascinating and elegantly written (if oddly titled) *Railroad Signatures Across the Pacific Northwest.*

"The crossing of the Rocky Mountains" and "restless with the restlessness of youth" are from Peattie, p. 54 (in the chapter entitled "The Last Frontier" by Margaret Bundy Callahan). The geology of the Cascades is described in the same work's "The Cascade Range" by Grant McConnell. The quotation from Isaac Stevens ("The amount of work in the Cascade Range") is cited in Armbruster, p. 7, as is George McClellan's thorough "disgust" (p. 11). The NP's subsequent confirmation of that disgust ("There is no place to cross the mountains") is from Roe, p. 53. "The entering wedge" comes from the always inventively metaphorical *Seattle Times,* as quoted in Armbruster, p. 49.

The characteristic Hill quotation about "Swedes and whiskey" is cited in Schwantes, p. 133. (NB: The quotation is rendered in some sources as "Give me snuff, Swedes, and whiskey . . .")

The second part of this chapter draws on the four main biographies of James J. Hill. The earliest—Joseph Gilpin Pyle's two-volume *The Life of James J. Hill* (Garden City, NY: Doubleday, Page, 1917)—was written by a Hill employee, most of it while the old man was still alive, and is thus about as unbiased as a corporate press release, which it sometimes resembles. Stuart Holbrook's *James J. Hill: A Great Life in Brief* (New York: Knopf, 1955) is highly enjoyable to read, but it relies heavily on the substantial body of Hill apocrypha and is not entirely authoritative. By far the most detailed and exhaustive modern biography is *James J. Hill and the Opening of the Northwest* by Albro Martin (New York: Oxford University Press, 1976), although its revisionist disdain for the old "robber baron" view of megacapitalists like Hill may carry the pendulum a bit too far in the opposite direction. Finally, Michael Malone's more recent *James J. Hill: Empire Builder of the Northwest* (Norman, OK: University of Oklahoma, 1996) is brief but extremely useful, and probably the most objective of them all.

"The shaggy-bearded, barb-wired" description of Hill is by Holbrook, though in his *The Story of American Railroads,* p. 173, not his biography. (NB: About Hill's genius, Grover Cleveland once said, "I am perfectly sure that I have never known a man who was at once familiar with so many big things and who also had the gift of carrying about and remembering what most men in his position would deem too small for their attention," quoted by George F. Parker in *McClure's,* April 1909, p. 577.)

An important source for information about the plotting and building of the GN's Pacific extension is *The Great Northern Railway: A Pictorial Study* by Charles and Dorothy Wood.

"What we want is the best possible line" is cited ubiquitously in the Hill literature, but for the record can be found on p. 366 of Albro Martin. The claim of Marias Pass as the lowest Rockies crossing of any transcontinental comes from "How Great Northern Conquered the Cascades" by D.W. McLaughlin (Great Northern Railway Historical Society Reference Sheet No. 213, March 1994, p. 2). When evaluating Stevens's claim as "rediscoverer" of the Marias Pass (which had allegedly been "lost" for decades after its original discovery in 1840), it's worth taking note of a letter in the Stevens Papers, addressed to Stevens from the GN's chief engineer, E. H. Beckler, that all but tells the younger man where to find it (E. H. Beckler to John F. Stevens, November 23, 1889, John F. Stevens Papers, Georgetown University Library, Washington, DC).

"The process of reconnaissance for a railway line" is from John F. Stevens's address given at the dedication ceremonies for the opening of the second Cascade Tunnel (*Dedication and Opening of the New Cascade Tunnel: A Monument to James J. Hill* [Great Northern Railway Company, 1929]). (It's interesting to note that Stevens Pass was so named despite the fact that the actual legwork involved in finding it had been done by the engineer's assistant, Charles Haskell.)

NB: The route selection of a railroad is critical since an increase in grade of just 1 percent—i.e., a rise of roughly fifty feet to the mile—nearly triples the amount of pulling power required to move a cargo.

Thomas Burke's oratory on how Hill changed the Northwest is cited in Armbruster, p. 180. Schwantes's somewhat ironic offering about the "twin ribbons of iron or steel" is from p. 96 of his *Railway Signatures.* The rather stunningly honest admission about "the weakest link in our transportation chain" was made by GN vice president G. L. Gilman in his banquet address at the New Cascade Tunnel ceremony (*Dedication,* p. 9). And Stevens's claim about the virgin quality of his eponymous pass ("There was no evidence whatever") comes from *On Reconnaissance for the Great Northern: Letters of C. F. B. Haskell, 1889–91,* edited by Daniel C. Haskell (New York: New York Public Library, 1948), p. 29.

4: A Temporary Delay

The excerpt at the head of the chapter—"Dear Mother & all of you"—is from the Topping letter, p. 1.

Details, quotation ("I was born"), and dialogue ("Good morning, Porter," etc.) concerning Lewis Jesseph's activities on February 23 are from his memoir, p. 176. Henry White's movements on Wednesday morning from his court testimony (CIT, pp. 94 and 127ff). The description of Cascade Tunnel Station and the beanery draws principally from Ruby El Hult, pp. 11–14, and from recollections of telegrapher Warren Tanguy as recounted in the *ST* of November 15, 1959, pp. 2–3. (NB: Hult and other sources have the names of the cook and his waiter reversed and slightly different as "Henry Elliker" and

"John Olson"; however, the names used here come from an official coroner's document as reported in *WDW* of March 22.) "It was a dirty hole" from the Topping letter, p. 4.

Excerpt from Sarah Jane Covington's diary. Information about Alfred B. Hensel from "Alfred B. Hensel, Wellington Survivor" in the Seattle Genealogical Society Bulletin, vol. 48, no. 3 (Spring 1999), and from his superior court testimony (SCT, pp. 5–40 and 67–93). The anecdote about his rehearsal of mail-sorting skills comes from a 2004 interview with his daughter Dolores Hensel Yates by the author.

For information about the Railway Mail Service I am principally indebted to *Mail by Rail: The Story of the Postal Transportation Service* by Bryant Alden Long with William Jefferson Dennis (New York: Simmons-Boardman, 1951) as well as Moody, pp. 17–23, and Holmquist.

O'Neill's telegram to E. L. Brown dated February 23 is from the Robert Kelly collection.

Particulars about the difficulties encountered by rotary snowplow X807 come from the superior court testimony of Homer Purcell (SCT, pp. 665–78), various telegrams from the Kelly collection, and "The Movement of Rotaries," p. 3. "Will not run any trains" is from O'Neill's telegram of 9:30 A.M., February 23.

"SIX TRAINS STALLED" is from the *ST*, February 23.

"It's 1:00 P.M." is from the Topping letter, p. 5. Details about Ida Starrett and her family come mainly from the *ST* of March 3, Ruby El Hult, p. 4, and from a front-page article on the Starretts in the *SIH* of March 3. The $500 settlement of the Starrett case is outlined in a letter from D. H. Kimball to J. D. Armstrong dated March 29 (GN Legal Department Files, George Fischer Collection of the Museum of History and Industry, Seattle). Loveberry's comment about the tunnel ("It was draughty and dirty") was made in his superior court testimony (SCT, p. 780), while Wright's ("the dirtiest, blackest hole") is from his coroner's inquest testimony (CIT, p. 114).

For the history of the Cascade switchbacks and the first Cascade Tunnel, see Charles and Dorothy Wood, pp. 132–34, and "The Pacific Extension and Cascade Switchbacks" by W. C. Hartranft. "A miracle of engineering" from Hartranft, p. 5. "Every railroad man's nightmare" from Malone, p. 147. According to a published GN guide to the switchbacks, the safety of the switchbacks was a result of the railroad's much-heralded devotion to detail: "It will be noticed that most careful examination is made of every part of the train before the ascent is commenced. Every wheel and truck, all air brake mechanisms, signals, etc., are thoroughly inspected so as to guard against the possibility of accident" (as quoted in Hartranft, p. 7).

On the building and early operations difficulties of the Cascade Tunnel, see another Hartranft work, "The First Cascade Tunnel" (Great Northern Railway Historical Society Reference Sheet No. 175, March 1991), as well as McLaughlin (p. 6ff) and Ralph Hidy et al., *The Great Northern Railway: A History* (Boston: Harvard Business School Press, 1988), pp. 168–71. The quote about workers "standing at the bar" is from Sherlock, p. 5. "The wickedest town on earth" is cited in Hult, p. 13. (NB: The opening of the tunnel eliminated 8.5 miles of track distance, almost 1,400 feet of elevation [700 up and 700 down], and 2,332 degrees of curvature—the equivalent of six and a half complete circles. It also cut scheduled running times for most trains through the pass by about two hours.)

The reference to the longer tunnel in Switzerland is from Hartranft, "The First Cascade Tunnel," p. 5, as is the quotation "If Mr. Hill still [refuses]" (p. 10). "You couldn't see for the smoke" is from the Tanguy interview in the *ST* of November 15, 1959, pp. 2–3. "Many a hobo stole his last ride" is from Sherlock, p. 4. (NB: The GN tried to address the smoke situation by fitting out engines with curved smokestack extensions, using a special grade of clean-burning coal, and supplying gas masks for all engine crews.)

The best source for the electrification of the tunnel is *When the Steam Railroads Electrified,* revised second edition, by William D. Middleton (Bloomington: Indiana University Press, 2001), pp. 155–65. "You can put your hand on the wall" is from O'Neill's testimony in SCT, p. 597.

The creation of a double rotary at Cascade Tunnel station is corroborated in "Movement of Rotaries," p. 2. And Topping's envoi—"It's now nine"—is from the Topping letter, p. 6.

5: Over the Hump

M. O. White's testimony at the head of the chapter is from SCT, p. 625.

Information about telegraphers Flannery and Avery are from their court affidavits (Wenatchee Valley Museum); Sherlock's details from his "Reminiscences."

The account of Wednesday's difficulties on the line come principally from telegrams in the Robert Kelly collection, particularly the telegram of 4:50 P.M., February 24, from O'Neill to G. W. Turner, and from Purcell's court testimony (SCT, pp. 665–71). Though the GN would later vehemently deny having too little coal on the mountain, the quoted telegram from O'Neill to Turner of 1:45 P.M., February 23, speaks for itself. The missed delivery of coal is cited in a letter from D. H. Kimball, GN general claim agent, to J. D. Armstrong, assistant general solicitor, dated March 4 (GN Legal Department Files). The fact that the rotaries would be forced to recoal at Skykomish comes from a telegram from O'Neill to Turner sent at 1:40 P.M., February 24.

The troubles experienced by the other railroads with Cascade crossings are cited in the *ST* of February 23 and 24 and the *SIH* of February 24. The performance of *The Merchant of Venice* was reported in the *ST* of February 24. Washington State's flirtation with cigarette prohibition is recounted in Cassandra Tate, "Cigarette Prohibition in Washington, 1893–1911," published on the excellent Web site www.HistoryLink.org. See also Tate's *Cigarette Wars: The Triumph of "The Little White Slaver"* (New York: Oxford University Press, 1999).

O'Neill's optimistic prediction about the opening of the line comes from the telegram of 2:50 A.M., February 24, from O'Neill to Watrous et al. The somewhat less optimistic report that followed ("If anything, it is snowing harder") is from the telegram of 8:00 A.M., February 24, also from O'Neill to Watrous et al. "O'Neill has won the fight of his life" is from the *SPI* of February 24.

The section-break excerpt from the Topping letter—"This makes 30 hours here in this spot"—is from pp. 6–7.

"The flakes became larger and heavier" is from Jesseph, p. 176, which also takes note of the food shortage at the beanery (p. 177). "They say it has snowed 13 ft" from the Covington transcript, which also describes the digging out of the roundhouse and the two horn-playing boys. Her success at telegraphing Melmoth was reported in the *SIH* of March 2. The ultimate outcome of Merritt and Jesseph's supreme court trial as reported in Jesseph, p. 177. Thelma Davis as the pet of the train comes from the *SSR* of March 3. Ned Topping's business advice to his father is from Topping, p. 8. "We visited from coach to coach" is from an interview with Rogers published in the *SPI* of March 2. Information about the Grays, the Lemmans, J. R. Vail, and Catherine O'Reilly are from Hult, *passim,* and from various newspaper accounts (including the *SSR* of March 4 and the *SDC* of March 2). Further quotes from Topping, pp. 9–10.

"Look for Nos 25 + 27" is from a telegram of 4:45 P.M., February 24.

O'Neill's participation in the efforts to free the trains at Cascade Tunnel was described in his own court testimony (SCT, p. 515ff) and in the inquest testimony of George Loveberry (CIT, p. 237). "In two minutes" is from the *ST* of March 6. The story about James J. Hill shoveling snow is from Holbrook, *Hill,* p. 3.

For the GN's cult of personality, see John Kimberly Mumford, "This Land of Opportunity," in the October 31, 1908, edition of *Harper's Weekly,* e.g., p. 21: "The longer you remain in contact with the Great Northern Railway, the more clearly you find revealed at every turn the characteristics of Hill. . . . It is hardly surprising, therefore, that the men who help him run his railroad come to think his thoughts and be in most respects echoes of his large individuality." Similarly, see John Moody and George Kibbe Turner: "The Masters of Capital in America," *McClure's* (vol. 36, no. 2, December 1910), p. 130. O'Neill's status as Hill's favorite conductor (as well as the quotation "He does not sit in his private car") comes from the *ST* of March 6.

The loss of power in the tunnel as testified in court by Walter Vogel (SCT, p. 640) and in a court affidavit by C. E. Andrews in the GN Legal Department files (Museum of History and Industry). The Thursday evening situation at Wellington as described in O'Neill's court testimony and in relevant telegrams. The two coal cars being pulled up the mountain by rotary X808 were reported in a telegram of 11:50 P.M., February 24, from O'Neill to Watrous et al. The freeing of trains at Skykomish and Scenic as reported in telegrams and in the joint affidavit of Dowling, Mackey, and Tegtmeier, which also describes the motivation for leaving the X807 on the coal-chute track. The use of coal from idle locomotives as described in a later telegram from O'Neill to H. A. Kennedy, dated March 4–6.

O'Neill's decision to go west with the double rotary on Thursday evening is from his court testimony (SCT, p. 524ff).

"24th of Feb. at night" comes from the Covington transcript.

The arrival of trains Nos. 25 and 27 at Wellington as reported in the Devery diary, an interview with Edward Sweeney by Ruby El Hult dated May 22, 1957 (Ruby El Hult Papers), and court testimony. Topping notes the snow gauge in the letter to his mother, p. 10, from which the later quotations also come. The dining room at Bailets was described in an interview with Mrs. Scott Holmes by Ruby El Hult (Ruby El Hult Papers) and in an article in the *SS* of March 8.

The layout of Wellington is described in "The Lost Communities of Stevens Pass" (*Seattle Genealogical Society Bulletin,* Spring 1999), pp. 109–12, and from plans of Wellington reprinted in Charles Wood's *Lines West* (New York: Bonanza Books, 1967), p. 117, and Charles and Dorothy Wood, p. 185. Distance to Scenic comes from the GN's Cascade Division Schedule No. 68, in effect March 1, 1910. The rocking of coaches and blowing of snow onto the slope above the trains as described by A. B. Hensel in SCT, pp. 28–29.

6: A Town at the End of the World

The opening quotation—"Too high for forest trees"—is from the *ST* of January 13, 1929 (on the eve of the town's abandonment).

Sherlock refers to Wellington as "the end of the world" in his "Reminiscences," pp. 2 and 5. "As wild a town as any" comes from an article, "Brakeman of the Great Northern," by Victor H. White (*Frontier Times*, August–September 1970), p. 10.

Railway mileage figures come from Stover, *Atlas*, p. 52. Railroad employment figures are cited in *Sayings and Writings About the Railways* (New York: Railway Age Gazette, 1913), p. 12. "An eminently locomotive people" from James Bryce's everbrilliant *The American Commonwealth*, edited by Louis M. Hacker (New York: G. P. Putnam's Sons, 1959 edition), vol. 2, p. 444. "Only one organization" from *Andrew Carnegie and the Rise of Big Business* by Harold C. Livesay (Boston: Little, Brown, 1975), p. 33. For more on the topic of how the railroads essentially invented modern business structures, see two works by Alfred D. Chandler: *The Visible Hand: The Managerial Revolution in American Business* (Cambridge: Belknap–Harvard University Press, 1977) and *The Railroad: America's First Big Business* (New York: Harcourt, Brace & World, 1965).

The discussion of the organization of a steam railroad division draws principally on *The American Railway*, p. 185ff, and Nicholas Faith's *The World the Railways Made* (New York: Carroll & Graf, 1990), pp. 210–28 (with thanks to David Sprau, retired dispatcher, for extra input). In the interest of concision, my account ignores the functions of traffic manager (in charge of soliciting freight and passengers for the railroad) and station agents and yardmasters (in charge of individual stations and rail yards). Freud's dreams of becoming an engineer are mentioned in Faith, p. 219. The cited unwritten law of railroading comes from a superb memoir by Herbert Hamblen: *The General Manager's Story* (New York: Macmillan, 1898; reprinted by Literature House, Upper Saddle River, NJ, 1970), p. 296. The rivalry between conductors and engineers is illuminated in Walter Licht's extremely useful *Working for the Railroad: The Organization of Work in the Nineteenth Century* (Princeton: Princeton University Press, 1983). Another useful source is *Railroad Conductor* by Fred A. Winkler (Spokane: Pacific Book Company, 1948). The quotation on the fireman's blackness is from B. B. Adams in *The American Railway*, p. 422. "What're brakemen for" is from Hamblen, p. 17. The average brakeman's shortage of fingers as per Licht, p. 184.

Fatality rate for rail yards in the 1870s, along with the switchman's quotation ("for the express purpose of wrapping up my mangled remains"), from Richard Reinhardt's *Workin' on the Railroad: Reminiscences from the Age of Steam* (Palo Alto: American West Publishing, 1970), p. 274–75. The 1907 injury statistic from Schwantes, p. 107. "A miserable living" comes from Hamblen, p. 52. The railroad labor surplus in most areas of the country (except the South) as per Licht, p. 64ff.

"It becomes absolutely necessary" from Hamblen, p. 131. "There was plenty of kidding" from Sherlock, pp. 9 and 5. The stories about Bob Harley, Bailets and the turkey, and the kangaroo court are from Sherlock, pp. 5–10, as is the quotation "Many times Superintendent J. H. O'Neill." Details about everyday life in Wellington (sledding, the mythical Wah-too-tie) come from the Sherlock memoir. Hill's famous comparison of a passenger train to "a male teat" is cited in H. Roger Grant's *We Took the Train* (Dekalb: Northern Illinois University Press, 1990), p. xiii.

7: First Loss

The opening quotation—"Two Men Perish in Snow Slides"—is from the *EDH* of February 25.

The 10:00 A.M. rising was recorded in the Covington diary. "It was some mountain all right" from White's court testimony (SCT, p. 97). Morning weather conditions as recorded in the Devery Operations Diary entry for 6:00 A.M. Details of the beanery slide and its location are from the inquest testimony of O'Neill and William Harrington (CIT, pp. 47 and 149).

"Some of the women became hysterical" is from Jesseph, p. 172. "Glad we moved" and "Perched on the side of a mountain" from Topping, p. 11. The condition of the mountainsides around Wellington is derived principally from Bailets's testimony (CIT, p. 341). On the fearfulness of the ladies, see also Thompson and White testimony (CIT, pp. 377, 418–19). The quotation from W. V. Avery is from his court affidavit, p. 4. Lucius Anderson's testimony is from CIT, pp. 238–39. Bailets's announcement is as reported by A. B. Hensel in his memoir published in the *SSR* of February 12, 1950. (Bailets, however, would later claim that he had seen more snow on the mountain—CIT, p. 340).

The description of digging out the buried dining hall at Cascade Tunnel Station is from the Warren Tanguy article in the *ST* of November 15, 1959.

The rising temperatures on Thursday were recorded in the Devery diary. Jill Fredston cites the ability of wind to accelerate the deposit of snow in *Snowstruck: In the Grip of Avalanches* (New York: Harcourt, 2005), p. 229. O'Neill's wiring of coroner Saunders as per the *WDW* of February 25. The two coastal-line wrecks as reported in the *SIH* of February 26. The story of the 1907 snowslide incident is related in McLaughlin, p. 6.

The bogging down and freeing of X801 as described in "Movement of Rotaries," p. 4.

The coming of the extra rotary from the Rockies was reported in the *Leavenworth Echo* of February 25. Details about the two relief trains come from the *EDH* of February 25 and two telegrams dated 9:35 A.M. (from E. L. Brown to O'Neill) and 4:30 P.M. (from O'Neill to Watrous et al.). Information about the usual duration of Cascade storms, plus the number of snowy days per season, is from the superior court testimony of O'Neill (SCT, p. 492ff) and of John Calder (SCT, p. 367).

The necessity of plundering the coal tanks of the X807 and the spare engine as cited in the Duncan affidavit. Turner's efforts to buy coal as described in a February 23 telegram from Turner to O'Neill marked 7:26 A.M.

"The first I heard of any dissatisfaction" is from CIT, p. 416.

The success of several passengers in telegraphing home as described by William Flannery (CIT, pp. 394–95) and the Covington diary. The story of Libby Latsch's smoking comes from the Topping letter, p. 9. "A good many of the passengers on this train are the smart set" and "Quite a number play cards" are from letters from Sarah Jane Covington to her husband and children, while the quotations about Frederik van Eeden are from her diary. Details about Charles Eltinge come from the *SSR* of March 3. Merritt's account of the story is from his inquest testimony (CIT, pp. 260–61), from which his three quotations come. Merritt's acquaintance with O'Neill as reported in Jesseph's memoir, p. 172. Henry White's account of sending Longcoy to summon O'Neill is from his inquest testimony (CIT, p. 421).

(NB: There is some confusion in the court testimony and other accounts about exactly when the various meetings of passengers took place. White seems to have been present at the three principal meetings, so I have given greater weight to his recollection of their order and import. Also, several newspaper reports, as well as Jesseph's memoir, would later claim—implausibly—that the *railroad* initially wanted to put the trains in the tunnel and that the *passengers* refused, for fear of being trapped. The preponderance of later testimonial evidence, however, is decisive in debunking this particular story.)

"There was not any question of slides at that time" is from Merritt's inquest testimony (CIT, p. 261). Jesseph's testimony (CIT, p. 272) concurs. "They made the argument" from White's testimony (CIT, p. 420). Similarly, "There did not seem to be any of us who had any previous experience in snowslides" is from CIT, p. 421.

"We waited for Mr. O'Neill" from White (CIT, p. 421). E. W. Boles (also identified as Bowles in some sources) mentions the rotaries throwing snow onto the train in his inquest testimony (CIT, p. 160). "Nothing doing," from the Topping letter, p. 12.

"I think the railroad men believed we would" from CIT, p. 462.

(NB: Although some crewmen were later to testify in the superior court trial that the mission of the X801 was to clear the line all the way to Leavenworth, that assertion is contradicted by several witnesses in the earlier coroner's inquest—such as J. J. Mackey [CIT, p. 74]—and by common sense. O'Neill desperately needed coal and could have no reasonable expectation that a single rotary could reach Leavenworth under current conditions. The likely explanation for the discrepancy in testimony is that by the time of the superior court trial, the GN did not wish to emphasize the shortage of coal at Wellington and so had instructed their employees to obscure the true mission of the X801.)

The Roman gladiator description of Harrington is from the *ST* of March 7. His history and his assessment of the storm are from his inquest testimony (CIT, pp. 130–40). I am also indebted to Martin Burwash for census information about the Snow King. Harrington's transfer of the extra engine from No. 25 to his own rotary train as described in superior court testimony (SCT, p. 532).

"Snow is one of the most complex materials found in nature" is from *The Avalanche Book* (Golden, CO: Fulcrum, 1986) by Betsy Armstrong and Knox Williams.

8: Closing Doors

Meath's testimony—"Had you a chance to get a meal"—from SCT, pp. 688–89.

The clearing of the second slide at Snowshed 3.3 as reported in "Movement of Rotaries" and by O'Neill in SCT, p. 527. The X808 left Scenic at 3:00 P.M. Friday according to a telegram from O'Neill to Watrous et al. dated 11:45 P.M. on February 25.

"Hello there, Bill" was recounted by Loveberry, CIT, p. 466. The fight at the tavern as per Topping, p. 13. Assistant roadmaster Thomas McIntyre confirms that most Cascade avalanches were the type that come down in draws or gulches in his inquest testimony (CIT, p. 307). Snowshed 2 was 800–900 feet long, versus 700–800 feet for train No. 25 (O'Neill, SCT, p. 560). A good summary of why the spur tracks would have been a bad place for the trains was given by F. E. Weymouth, NP Seattle Division superintendent, in his inquest testimony (CIT, p. 499ff). According to O'Neill (SCT, pp. 527–28), digging out the tracks would have required thirty to thirty-five men, each putting in ten to twenty hours of work time. The 6:00 A.M. weather conditions at

Wellington are from the Devery Operations Diary. The dimensions of the third slide at Snowshed 3.3 as per O'Neill in CIT, p. 9.

"Saturday—noon" is from Topping, p. 13.

Specifics on the interactions among the children aboard the Seattle Express are derived from the handwritten notes of a 1957 interview with Raymond Starrett conducted by Ruby El Hult (Ruby El Hult Papers). Although some latter-day Wellington accounts depict Thelma Davis's mother as dead in 1910, newspaper articles in the SSR of March 12 and the SS of March 3 indicate otherwise. The various attempts by adults to amuse the children with snowball fights, sewing circles, tap dances, and the like come principally from the Starrett interview (where he describes Lucius Anderson as "jolly") and from the inquest testimony of Henry White (CIT, pp. 430–35).

The conversations between White and Longcoy and between White and Pettit are reported in White's inquest and court testimony (CIT, pp. 421 and 437; SCT, p. 133). Longcoy's lie about O'Neill's illness is reported in CIT, p. 448. Jesseph's conversation with the mountaineers is mentioned in his memoir, p. 177, while the overheard conversation with Bailets is from Jesseph's testimony (CIT, p. 272).

In a postavalanche letter to Mrs. Covington's son Luther, Anna Gray admits that she and Ada Lemman were the two women who spent much of the time crying and requiring reassurance (letter to L. J. Covington from Mrs. Anna Gray, dated March 18, Covington/Brokaw collection). Details about Ada Lemman come from the SSR of March 4. "On Saturday the strain became too great" from the Spokane Daily Chronicle of March 2. Hensel describes seeing the departing shovelers in his superior court testimony (SCT, p. 35). "They bade us goodbye as they walked along" from CIT, p. 448. "One or two of them told me if he worked a week" from CIT, pp. 443–44. "Those men will make a pretty good trail" as quoted by White (CIT, p. 448). "The feeling prevailed" from CIT, pp. 448–49.

The 8:00 P.M. telegram is from the Robert Kelly collection.

Details about the movements of rotary X801 from Ira Clary's superior court testimony (SCT, pp. 698–700) and from the "Movement of Rotaries" document, p. 5.

The picking up of the wind on the west slope as recorded in the Devery Operations Diary entry for 6:00 P.M. "When the wind was blowing its hardest . . ." is from the Funderburk affidavit, p. 28. J. C. Wright's description of rotary operation is from his superior court testimony (SCT, p. 382). "The progress was so slow" is from the Funderburk affidavit, p. 27. O'Neill complains about the shovelers in his telegram to E. L. Brown of 4:30 P.M., February 26. The low wages paid by the GN as discussed in W. Thomas White's "A History of Railroad Workers in the Pacific Northwest, 1883–1934" (Ph.D. diss., University of Washington, 1981), p. 165. Prices paid to extra gangs also specified in the GN Corporate Office Diaries for February 8 (GN Corporate Papers, General Manager Files, Minnesota Historical Society). The encounter with the new slide at Snowshed 2.2 as described in "Movement of Rotaries," p. 4, and the E. S. Duncan affidavit, p.1. (There is some confusion in various sources over whether the shed in question was 2.1 or 2.2. I have chosen to go with the description as cited in the "Movement of Rotaries" document.) The forty-eight-hour estimate for clearing the slide at Snowshed 2.2 comes from the combined affidavit of Dowling, Mackey, and Tegtmeier, p. 3. The surrender of the double rotary as described in O'Neill's superior court testimony (SCT, p. 535).

O'Neill's admission—"That was the night that tied us up"—can be found in CIT, p. 414.

The Lemmans are described in a newspaper article in the *SSR* of March 4. "Mr. Lemman came back" from CIT, p. 250. The account of the Saturday evening meeting in the observation car comes mainly from the inquest testimony of witnesses who survived (CIT, pp. 227, 250, 426, and 461). "With that refusal" from CIT, p. 250. "If they burned up the coal" from CIT, p. 228. "I did all I could to keep down any protest" is from CIT, p. 275. "Everyone who was on the trains was in a state of quandary" is from CIT, p. 461. The Topping quotation—"If I ever make this [*indecipherable*] trip again"— comes from his letter, p. 13.

9: The Empire Builder Looks On

"He is a calculating machine" as quoted in Armbruster, p. 178.

A good overview of the transportation difficulties being caused by this storm in the entire Northwest can be found in a front-page illustration in the *Chicago Tribune* of March 2. Louis Hill's departure on Saturday night for a six-week vacation was recorded in the GN President's Files (GN Corporate Records 132.C.5.2F and 132.C.5.3B, Minnesota Historical Society) and telegram book (132.C.20.33, Nos. 189 and 194). Correspondence from Hill Sr. during Louis's absence, which normally would have been filed in the Chairman's Letterbook, was instead filed in the President's Letterbook. For the seven major railroad groups at this time (of which the Hill Roads was one), see John F. Stover, *American Railroads* (Chicago: University of Chicago Press, 1961), p. 135ff. Trackage statistics and the quotation "If the three [Hill] lines were placed end to end" from an unsigned article on Hill in *Current Literature*, January 1907, pp. 39–40. Hill's latter-day national prominence is well described in Albro Martin, *James J. Hill*, p. 525ff. For a more skeptical view of Hill's standing as an agricultural and economic guru, see Claire Strom, *Profiting from the Plains: The Great Northern Railway and Corporate Development of the West* (Seattle: University of Washington Press, 2003). Strom claims that many of the practices for which Hill proselytized in his later years were anachronistic and unsound.

"Any railroad man was popular" from Reinhardt, p. 97. Wiebe's analysis of railroad alienation is from *The Search for Order*, p. 53. The account of railroad owners as "buccaneers" is from Peter Lyon's passionate jeremiad, *To Hell in a Day Coach: An Exasperated Look at American Railroads* (Philadelphia: Lippincott, 1968), p. 17. Holbrook calls the railroad barons "men of average morals and principals but very great abilities" in *Story*, p. 10. "A vast power" comes from Frank Norris, *The Octopus* (1901; reprint: New York: Signet, 1981), p. 42.

For more background on the Granger Laws, see Stover, *Atlas*, pp. 46–47, and Holbrook, *Story*, p. 12 and pp. 231–43. For a good account of later federal attempts at regulation, see Schwantes, *Railroad Signatures*, p. 102ff, and Gordon, p. 278ff. "Hoh, yes, the Interstate Commerce Commission" is from Norris, p. 79. Hill's characterization of regulations as the work of "doctrinaires" as quoted in Malone, p. 200. "It really seems hard" as quoted in Albro Martin, *James J. Hill*, p. 494.

For this discussion of the Northern Securities case, I've drawn principally on Albro Martin, *James J. Hill*, *Theodore Rex* by Edmund Morris (New York: Random House,

2001), Richard Hofstadter's *The Age of Reform: From Bryan to F.D.R.* (1955; reprint: New York: Vintage Books, 1960), and Mowry. "The conscience of business had to be aroused" as quoted in Page Smith's *America Enters the World: A People's History of the Progressive Era and World War I* (New York: McGraw-Hill, 1985), p. 184. The *New York Times* of May 31, 1916, referred to Hill as "the Moses of the Northwestern Wilderness." The fact that Northern Securities would have been second in size to U.S. Steel is according to Morris, pp. 59–61. "God made the world" from *Life* magazine (not to be confused with Henry Luce's later, similarly named enterprise), January 24, 1902. Hill's comment about "gilded flunkies" is from Albro Martin, *James J. Hill,* p. 519.

Hill's obsession with the Northern Securities case as per Malone, p. 222. "The three railroads are still there" is cited in Morris, p. 316. Albro Martin expresses his belief in Roosevelt's disingenuousness in his biography of Hill, pp. 513–15. "To feel at last that the President" from Hofstadter, p. 237. "Uncle Sam in the fireman's seat" comes from Armbruster, p. 181. Morgan's droll comment—"I trust some lion"—is ubiquitously quoted in the literature on the era, as in Wiebe, p. 215. Taft actually called Hill to the White House to consult on his cabinet selections, according to Judith Icke Anderson, *William Howard Taft: An Intimate History* (New York: Norton, 1981), p. 209. "A platter of mush, a jellyfish" is from Albro Martin's biography, p. 599.

"Their strike is a modern repetition" comes from the *SUR* of February 12.

Among the other things Hill had on his plate at this time was his battle with the railroad interests of the recently deceased E. H. Harriman over an extension down the Deschutes Canyon in Oregon, a line that could eventually give Hill a much-needed entry point into California. John F. Stevens was even then operating in the area, discreetly procuring properties under the very cloak-and-dagger code name of "Proteus." (See Hill's letter to Stevens, dated May 30, in the Hill Personal Papers, St. Paul; see also Albro Martin, *James J. Hill,* pp. 566–67 and Hidy, pp. 95–96. Stevens's code name of "Proteus" is used in telegrams in the Hill Personal Papers.)

The looming firemen's strike as per newspaper reports, e.g., the *SPI* of March 14 and 15 (the strike was later averted).

Details of the 1909–10 switchmen's strike are from contemporary reports in *WDW, SSR, NYT,* and *SUR.* "We will fight" is from the *WDW* of November 30, 1909. "We are getting in better shape every hour" is from the *NYT* of December 5, 1909. The armed clash in Leavenworth was reported in the *WDW* of February 7, 1910. Hill's quotation about "the high cost of living" is from the *WDW* of January 29. The GN's most profitable year ever as reported in the Great Northern Railway Company's annual report for the fiscal year ending June 30, 1910, p. 13.

The GN's reputation for low wages and other ungenerous practices is corroborated in White, "History," p. 165, and Hidy, p. 144. According to William G. McAdoo, the director general of railroads during the federal takeover of the railroads after the First World War, railroad wages were "a long-standing national disgrace" (Lyon, pp. 142–43).

"Organized labor is socialistic" is quoted in W. Thomas White, "A Gilded Age Businessman in Politics: James J. Hill, the Northwest, and the American Presidency, 1884–1912" (*Pacific Historical Review,* no. 57 [November 1989]), p. 447. Hill's philosophy about wages and salaries comes from Hidy, p. 136. Hill's comment "Why should I have to pay a fireman" is cited in Phillip Dunne, ed., *Mr. Dooley Remembers: The Infor-*

mal Memoirs of Finley Peter Dunne (Boston, 1963), pp. 201–2 (as noted in Morris, *Theodore Rex,* p. 484).

The description of the 1894 strike against the Great Northern draws on accounts from Lyon, p. 108ff; Hidy, p. 109ff; Malone, p. 155ff; and Albro Martin's biography, p. 415ff. "It would be a fitting climax" as quoted in Martin, p. 416.

The press committee's accusations were aired in the *SUR* editions of March 3 and 12. Gruber and Emerson's departure as per Office Diaries (GN Corporate Records, Minnesota Historical Society) and various telegrams in the Robert Kelly collection.

10: Ways of Escape

The opening quote—"PASSENGERS ARE STILL HELD FAST"—is from the *EDH* of February 28.

Details about the Reverend James M. Thomson come from the *EDH* of March 7. "Quite a number present" is from the Covington diary. The "rough-looking fellow" is described by porter Adolph Smith in the *SPI* of March 8. "It helped those in need" from "Pull Back to the Tunnel!" by Howard E. Jackson (undated, unidentified magazine clipping in the archives of the Wenatchee Valley Museum). The reasons for O'Neill's trip to Scenic on Sunday morning are principally from his own court testimony (CIT, p. 58, and SCT, p. 546). The trek of the X801 crew back from Gaynor was described by Clary in his court testimony (SCT, pp. 698–702), from which his quotation comes.

"Everybody was making suggestions" from CIT, p. 426. The scene with Libby Latsch was related by White in CIT, p. 425. The conversation between Solomon Cohen and Antony Blomeke as related in Blomeke's court affidavit. "His chances with the kid would have been poor" as quoted in Jackson, p. 44. The negotiation with the trapper Schwartz (who in some documents is referred to as Swartz) comes from Merritt's inquest testimony (CIT, p. 276).

The transfer of coal from the Fast Mail to the Seattle Express is described in the court testimony of numerous people (CIT, p. 223; SCT, pp. 67, 155, and 628) and in the Sweeney affidavit. "I did not figure that they would open that track for three or four weeks," from CIT, p. 265. "We had a March term of court on at home," from CIT, p. 272. Merritt's account of the nicknaming banter among the passengers comes mainly from his inquest testimony (CIT, p. 267). "All the passengers on the train laughed at us" was reported in the *SDC* of March 2, while the actual begging of passengers is as per the *ST* of February 28. "We returned to the train" from Jesseph, p. 177.

The quoted Q&A—"Yes sir, we had considerable difficulty"—is from CIT, p. 59.

The fact that O'Neill slept only one night between Tuesday and Saturday comes from his own testimony (CIT, p. 51, and SCT, p. 538). "I told them I would not pay it" and other details about the walkout of gangmen are from O'Neill's inquest testimony (CIT, pp. 66–68). The story of O'Neill and the three armed men comes from the profile of the superintendent in the *ST* of March 6.

Details of weather and trail conditions on O'Neill's journey to Scenic come principally from CIT, pp. 24, 64–65 ("He [Churchill] broke trail a little ways"). Big Jerry's fall is described in CIT, pp. 102–3 and in an article quoting Merritt in the *SSR* of March 3 (from which comes the description "a giant . . . broad as a barn door").

The Merritt quotation—"That was the most thrilling experience of my life"—is quoted in the *WDW* of March 4.

The narrative of Jesseph and Merritt's hike down the mountain is based on their coroner's inquest testimony and on Jesseph's memoir in *Confluence*. Milton Horn's letter to his mother was printed in its entirety in the *WDW* of March 14. "The snow was wet and heavy" and "Silently, we stood" from Jesseph, p. 177.

Loveberry's determination to continue is cited in CIT, p. 264. (Sources conflict on whether the hikers heard about Big Jerry's fall while on the trail or only after they'd reached Scenic. Jesseph's memoir, for instance, has the group hearing about it from O'Neill at the Scenic Hot Springs Hotel. Here, however, as elsewhere, I have given priority to inquest testimony over a later memoir.) "Feeling pretty sad" from the *SSR* of March 3. Merritt's quotation—"We could look up the mountain as far as we could see"—is from CIT, p. 264. The linemen's warning about "instant death" is from the *WDW* of March 4. "Slides that fell after we had passed" is quoted in the *WDW* of March 3. "We drew our overcoats between our legs," "thumping drinks," and "Here's to happier days" from Jesseph, p. 178.

The arrival of the relief train at Scenic was recorded in Devery's diary entry for 9:30 P.M. on February 27. Big Jerry's avalanche story was told in the *SSR* of March 3. The attempt to get a message back to "Colonel Cody" (i.e., R. H. Bethel) is described throughout the inquest testimony (CIT, pp. 233, 267–68, 285); a copy of the handwritten original is in the Robert Kelly telegram collection. "After a long delay" is from Jesseph, p. 178. That the news of the slide reached them in Vancouver is cited in a letter from Jesseph's brother, Ward Jesseph, to Ruby El Hult dated August 11, 1957 (Ruby El Hult Papers).

Devery Operations Diary excerpt—"Cas. Tunnel reports worst day we have had so far"—is from the 4:30 P.M. entry for February 27.

At least one writer—Ruby El Hult—has expressed doubt about the reliability of the Sherlock memoir in which these scenes are described. Certainly Sherlock makes many claims throughout the memoir that seem dubious at best and absurdly self-serving at worst. In a letter filed at the Washington State Historical Society Library in Tacoma, Hult casts doubt on whether this scene between Sherlock and dispatcher Johnson (and the subsequent one between Sherlock and Blackburn) even took place, noting that the telegraph wires were down on Sunday. However, the Devery diary indicates that the wires to Wellington were back in service by late Sunday afternoon, and the telegram Sherlock cites, as stated in the text, does exist in the Robert Kelly collection (though its date is illegible). For reasons mentioned in the text, therefore, I have given Sherlock's account of the events themselves some credence, though I do not entirely accept his alleged prescience with regard to the imminent danger of a slide.

"We both walked down the track" is from Sherlock, p. 13. "I assume Mr. O'Neill said leave the train where it was" from Sherlock, p. 14. "A lady borrowed a phonograph" is from the Covington diary. Mrs. Covington's efforts to comfort Anna Gray and Ada Lemman are cited in the letter from Gray to Luther Covington. "It was getting warmer" from CIT, p. 255. "An enormous cap of snow" as quoted in the *WDW* of March 4. "It didn't look to me that there was any safe place there" from CIT, p. 466. "I knew it was time to act" from CIT, p. 468. The decision of the second group to hike out is confirmed in the Topping letter, p. 14. "If I should die before the night" from the Covington diary. The scene between Pettit and Laville as described in a letter from Dr. W. C. Cox to D. L. Flynn dated March 3 (GN Legal Department Files).

11: Last Chances

The opening quotation by John Rogers is from CIT, pp. 471–72.

"All day and night you could hear the reports of trees" as quoted in the *SS* of March 2. "And on Monday morning" from the *ST* of March 2. The opinion of the group of Irish mill hands is discussed in the *SPI* of March 2. In Harrington's superior court testimony (SCT, p. 720) he claims that forty-nine GN employees were now electing to sleep on the trains. "There were so many different opinions" from CIT, p. 467.

The friendship between Rogers and Pettit is mentioned in the former's inquest testimony (CIT, p. 468). "The only way to get out of there was to get out" is from CIT, p. 251. The makeup of the Rogers party as reported in the *SPI* of March 2. The story of Libby Latsch's letter comes from Jackson, p. 44. Edward Boles's story is from the inquest transcript, CIT, pp. 153–65. (NB: His surname is spelled "Bowles" in the CIT and one or two other sources, but the Coroner's Death Record for 1909–10 has his brother listed as "Albert Boles.")

"It was snowing so badly" from CIT, p. 257. The details of the Rogers party's descent come mainly from his inquest testimony (CIT, p. 469ff), from the *SPI* of March 2, and from the Avery affidavit. "I did not realize when I started" from CIT, p. 222. "We all landed in a heap" from Jackson, p. 44. "And I believe that they could have carried out" from CIT, p. 468. The account of Pettit's failed attempt to get a telegram through to the passengers at Wellington ("TELL THE PASSENGERS") comes from CIT, pp. 254 and 468. "I told him that I sympathized with him" from CIT, p. 253.

O'Neill's quoted testimony—"About noon of the 27th"—is from CIT, p. 50.

Specifics about X808's fuel and water situation come from CIT, pp. 50 and 295, and from SCT, p. 537. The problems with the rotary's injectors are discussed in the combined affidavit of Dowling, Mackey, and Tegtmeier, and in CIT, p. 50. (Some sources have Duncan, rather than Irving, Tegtmeier as the traveling engineer called down to the rotary near Corea; see notes for Chapter 12 for an explanation.) "Wellington, blowing hard, snowing" from Devery Operations Diary for 1:00 P.M., February 28. Dowling's marathon stretch on the rotary is documented in CIT, p. 294, and SCT, p. 750.

Information on the Kalispell rotary comes from extant telegrams in the Robert Kelly collection and from Devery's court testimony (SCT, p. 835ff). The coming of Gruber et al. as reported in the GN Corporate Diaries (Minnesota Historical Society) and SCT, pp. 545–46. "He is a prince" and "little less than heroic" from the *SPI* of March 1 (published before word of the slide reached Seattle). "We only get one chance to make a little money" from CIT, p. 467.

The quoted White inquest testimony—"The train was warm"—is from CIT, p. 435.

"My baby was getting so dirty" comes from the March 18 letter from Anna Gray to Luther Covington. "A man said to his little girl" is from the Covington diary. "Snow that was taken up right alongside the trail" from CIT, p. 437. The passengers' ignorance of the existence of the spring at Wellington is corroborated in CIT, p. 460. "There was a space not over a foot" from Hensel's court testimony (SCT, p. 80). The use of the mail sack to measure snowfall is mentioned in SCT, p. 75. "It was mighty deep" from SCT, p. 80. Mrs. Starrett's concern as reported in *Confluence* (Winter 1987), p. 160, as well as the *ST* of March 2 and 7. "I think we are here to stay until spring" from the Covington letter of February 27.

"We're going to get out of this," as reported in the *SSR* of March 8. Chantrell's request for a guide from CIT, p. 391. "Still in this snow" from the Topping letter, p. 15. White's discussion with Pettit as per SCT, p. 134. J. R. Vail's condition is discussed in CIT, p. 423. Pettit's implication about the train's being safer near the tunnel is cited in White's inquest testimony, CIT, p. 437. The passengers' renewed efforts to see O'Neill as recounted by White in CIT, p. 421ff. A copy of the passengers' petition is in the Robert Kelly collection.

The confrontations with Longcoy and Blackburn as depicted in Lucius Anderson's inquest testimony (CIT, pp. 244–46) and in that of R. M. Laville (missing from the transcript but quoted at length in the *ST* of March 20). "We asked him if he was in authority" and other quotations from White are from his inquest testimony (CIT, pp. 422–24). "We have only seven men on the payroll at Wellington!" from the *ST* of March 20. "We knew that 125 men were working" as quoted in an interview in the *SS* of March 8. "I heard Mr. Blackburn tell" from the *ST* of March 20. White's offer to chop wood as cited in SCT, p. 139. "Plenty of wood" from CIT, p. 426. The threat to knock down the freight house is from CIT, p. 429.

"Nearly everyone on the stalled trains was gay" from Jackson, p. 44. Dressing up Thelma Davis from the *SSR* of March 3. "A sweet little song about the sparrows" from the Anna Gray letter. Final preparations for the night as per Laville (*ST* of March 20) and White (CIT, p. 427). "When we lay in our berths" and "I don't believe anyone had a premonition" are from Jackson, p. 44. "I'll have so much to tell you" from the Topping letter, p. 16. White mentions his decision to hike out (depending on the weather) in CIT, p. 428. The final scene between Pettit and the men as per Lucius Anderson (CIT, p. 240). "The mountainside was a very beautiful sight" from SCT, p. 106. O'Neill's night of sleep in Scenic and his intent to go to Wellington the next morning come from his inquest testimony (CIT, pp. 48–51).

12: Avalanche

The opening quotation—"It was a night of heroism"—is from the *EDH* of March 2.

White's and Matthews's preparations for bed as per CIT, p. 431. Lucius Anderson's berth location on the Winnipeg from CIT, p. 240. The decision of Hensel and the other clerks to leave on Tuesday as reported in the typescript of an article written by Hensel himself for the *SSR* in the Hensel family collection. The card game in the mail car is described in a 1998 letter to Martin Burwash from Carl Hernstrom (Burwash collection). "Absolutely nothing to do" and other details of Sherlock's evening are from Sherlock, p. 16.

The rarity of electrical storms in the Cascades in winter was attested to by several witnesses in the trial (e.g., J. C. Wright, SCT, p. 379). For the physiology of wet slab avalanches, I am particularly indebted to Armstrong and Williams, Fredston, and *The Avalanche Handbook* (Seattle: The Mountaineers, 1993) by David McClung and Peter Schaerer.

Hensel's moving of his bed as per a handwritten account by Hensel himself (courtesy of Dolores Hensel Yates) and other documents in the Hensel family collection. Flannery's waking as per his court affidavit. Charles Andrews's story as related in Jackson and in the notes of an interview conducted with Ruby El Hult (Ruby El Hult Papers). Wentzel's purported eyewitness account as quoted in the *SS* of March 2.

Henry White quotations from CIT, pp. 431–32, and the *ST* and *SPI* of March 6.

Forsyth's story is retold in an article entitled "Avalanche" by Freeman Hubbard, *Argosy* (March 1959), pp. 98–99 ("Suddenly our car was lifted") and is also related in CIT, p. 216 ("It seemed more like a bad dream"). The account of the falling train hitting an obstacle as per, e.g., Starrett in "Avalanche in the Cascades" by Oliver Chapple, *American West* (January–February 1983), p. 69, and Jackson, p. 45 ("Our car popped open"). Clary's "Before I was actually awake" is from the SS of March 3. The explosion of the acetylene tank was described by several passengers (e.g., CIT, p. 432). "Everything was still" from the *SPI* of March 6.

"My God, this is an awful death to die" as quoted in the *EDH* of March 3. Clary's story of the immediate aftermath is from SCT, p. 704, and from the *ST* of March 4 ("I heard Purcell calling" and "It was raining dismally"). Hensel's story from the notes of an interview with his son-in-law, Keith Yates, in the Hensel family collection and from SCT, p. 767. The aftermath experiences of White and Harrington as per their CIT testimony (CIT, pp. 431–36 and 130–38, respectively). "Turn the steam on" was reported by Anderson himself, CIT, pp. 240–41. The rescue of Ross Phillips as per Jackson, p. 45.

The efforts of Andrews and Miles come from the notes of Ruby El Hult's interview with Andrews (Ruby El Hult Papers) and from Hubbard, p. 99. "There was a faint moaning in the gulch" was quoted in the *Tacoma Sunday Ledger–News Tribune* of March 4, 1956. "When we got down there, I saw a man laying out on the snow" from Flannery's court affidavit. (As noted earlier, some sources confuse traveling engineers Duncan and Irving Tegtmeier. That Duncan was the injured Tegtmeier, however, is supported by an *ST* article in which "D. Tegtmeier" is interviewed specifically about his injuries.) Bailets's experiences as per his inquest testimony (CIT, pp. 351–53). Preparations for the bunkhouse as hospital as recounted in Sherlock, pp. 16–18, and in Flannery's inquest testimony (CIT, p. 451).

Sherlock's account of the confrontation with a gun-toting Bailets, as related in Sherlock, p. 18, is given some credence by a similar story involving brakeman Duncan and Bailets that appeared in the *EDH* of March 3. "The stick was about two-and-a-half feet long" from Sherlock, p. 20. The surgery scene is also described in Bailets's inquest testimony (CIT, p. 353). "While carrying him" is from a letter from Sherlock to Ruby El Hult dated March 24, 1960 (Northwest Disaster Scrapbook, Ruby El Hult Papers). Flannery tells of sending an unspecified second messenger down the mountain in his court affidavit; Wentzel tells of going down the mountain in the SS of March 2, though he does not state specifically that Flannery sent him.

The detached hand was reported in the *EDH* of March 3, while the severed head was mentioned in the *SPI* of March 5. Thelma Davis's body condition as per the *SEC* of March 4 (supported by the description of her body as "badly mangled" in the 1909–10 King County Coroner's Death Record, King County Archives, Seattle). Avalanche survival statistics from McClung and Schaerer, pp. 177–78, as well as "Avalanche!!!," a Web-based handbook by Charley Shimanski (Mountain Rescue Association, www.mra.org/avalanche_2004.pdf, 1993–2004), and a lecture given by Bruce Tremper at REI in Seattle in December 2002. The two ways of dying in an avalanche are discussed in Armstrong and Williams, p. 122.

Bates's experience comes from the *EDH* of March 3. Ida Starrett's rescue story is told in Chapple, newspaper accounts, and Ruby El Hult's interviews with Charles Andrews and Ray Starrett (Ruby El Hult Papers). "I realized that I was not injured" from the *ST* of March 3.

13: "The Reddened Snow"

The Reverend Randall's sermon—"This is not an hour for reciting"—was reported in the *EDH* of March 7.

The delivery of the news of the slide to O'Neill at Scenic comes mainly from the inquest testimony of Mackey and Dowling (CIT, pp. 83–86, 295–96). (NB: Although many newspaper accounts erroneously reported Wentzel as the man who first brought news of the slide to Scenic, this is explicitly contradicted by Harrington in an article entitled "Wellington Notes" in the *ST* of March 7 and by later inquest testimony; it's likely that the original reporter confused Scenic and Skykomish.) Conductor Vogel, who was at Scenic, claimed in his testimony to have heard the overnight thunderstorm (CIT, p. 284). It was also reported in the *ST* of March 7 that some people actually heard the snowslide itself from Scenic, although this seems doubtful. "I would not have heard a cannon that night" is from SCT, p. 543.

The loss of telegraph communication to and from Scenic as reported in a telegram of Monday, February 28, 4:30 P.M. in the Robert Kelly collection. O'Neill's trip to Nippon is reported in the *SS* and the *SIH* of March 5. The telegram announcing the avalanche is from the Robert Kelly collection. (This telegram also reports the three feet of snow on the tracks west of Scenic.)

Mackey's inquest testimony is from CIT, p. 83.

The number of rescuers climbing up with Dowling from Scenic is specified in his inquest testimony (CIT, p. 295). "The bodies that are to be taken out" from the *WDW* of March 11. "I don't have any particular authority" is from Hult, p. 79. (NB: Although most of the dialogue in the Hult book is fabricated, this story and quote come directly from an interview with Sweeney that Hult conducted in the late 1950s; Ruby El Hult Papers.)

The scattering of engines and coaches in the canyon as per Dowling's testimony (CIT, pp. 183–86). The story of the 1982 slide victim who survived for five days is from Armstrong and Williams, p. 123. Speculations about the electric locomotives and why so many people from the Winnipeg escaped death come from a letter from Dorety to J. D. Armstrong, dated March 11 (GN Legal Department Files), and from Harrington's inquest testimony (CIT, p. 445).

"As if an elephant had stepped on a cigar box" is from Marion Briggs as quoted in the *SPI* of March 5. The difficulties experienced by the rescuers as outlined in the *SPI* of March 5 (the threat of a second slide), the *WDW* of March 4 (forest debris), and the *NYT* of March 6 (the leaking of snow into opened coaches). "Taking them from a river" is from the *SS* of March 3. "A car lamp, a sack of mail" from the *ST* of March 8, which also reported the baby carriage.

The rundown of injuries to survivors comes from various newspaper accounts (in particular, the *SPI* of March 4) and from Hult, pp. 214 and 217. The unidentified man who died of exposure was reported in a story by the AP dated March 1, 1960. Hensel's story as per "Survivor: A Mail Clerk's Story and the 1910 Wellington Avalanche" by Dolores Hensel Yates in the December 2004 issue of *Nostalgia*. The focus on Varden Gray as testified by Alathea Sherlock (CIT, p. 454). Sherlock's doctoring the women with hot whiskey slings is from his own "Reminiscences," p. 21. The warming of blankets, and so on, as described in Sherlock, p. 22. "I even tried to make her cry" from Hult's 1950s interview with Raymond Starrett (Ruby El Hult Papers).

The headline announcing the slide appeared in the *EDH* of March 1.

The story of Wentzel's arrival in Skykomish is from the *NYT* of March 3. "TRAVEL-ERS FACE HUNGER AND DEATH" from the *ST* of February 28. The article about the relief trains was from the *EDH* of the same day. The recruitment of homeless men from the Seattle jail was reported in the *ST* extra edition of March 2, which also noted that a supply of coffins was on the March 2 relief train from Seattle. A description of Pascoe's journey—the result of an interview with the trainman conducted in the late 1950s—is in Hult, *Northwest Disaster*, pp. 72–73. The arrival of Stockwell and the nurses as reported in Sherlock, p. 22. The dubbing of Alathea Sherlock as the "Florence Nightingale of the Cascades" is from the *SS* of March 8. The doctor's statement that all patients would recover is from the *ST* of March 3.

O'Neill's arrival at Wellington was reported in the *ST* of March 2. Dowling described the "continuous snowslide" from Windy Point to Wellington in SCT, p. 760. The description of the ten-acre slab of snow as per the *WDW* of March 3. See also Thornton Munger's "Avalanches and Forest Cover in the Northern Cascades" (U.S. Department of Agriculture, Forest Service Circular 173 [Washington: Government Printing Office, 1911]).

The Watrous telegram of Thursday, March 3, 2:38 P.M. is from the Robert Kelly collection.

The unearthing of the bodies of Bethel, McNeny, the Lemmans, and Nellie Sharp was reported in the *ST* of March 3 through 5. The return of Boles was described in the *SPI* of March 2. The arrival of various friends and relatives of victims as reported in Hult, *Northwest Disaster*, p. 70, and in the *WDW* of March 9 ("more than ordinarily pretty") and the *SSR* of March 8 ("engines and all," "There was not a sign of anything," and "a dull bruise").

The search of Luther and Frank Covington is described in a letter from Mrs. George P. Anderson to the Reverend and Mrs. A. S. Gregg dated March 6 ("My heart is well-nigh broken"), and in an unidentified newspaper clipping, both from the Covington/Brokaw family records. The seven embalmers at work were mentioned in the *SIH* of March 5. Melmoth Covington's vigil for his wife was briefly reported in the *ST* of March 2.

The lack of documentation on most of the bodies was reported in the *EDH* of March 6. The dense lineup of corpses in the depot is described in Sherlock, p. 24. "Survivors, diggers, and newspapermen have accidentally" from the *SIH* of March 5.

"Superintendent O'Neill has handled the railroad end" from the *SS* of the same date.

The discovery of the A-16 was announced in a telegram of Friday, March 4, 2:45 P.M., and was described in the *SIH* of March 4 and the *ST* of March 5. The description of Blackburn's body by W. J. Manley ("in an attitude as if he had been sleeping") as reported in the *ST* of March 5. Blackburn's gift of the Morris chair (a joint gift with Dowling and Devery) is acknowledged in the O'Neill family scrapbooks.

"Last night, when he dropped to rest on the floor" from the *SIH* of March 4.

The trouble with the foreign laborers and the arrest of "Robert Roberts" as reported in the *SDC* and the *SPI* of March 5. The account of following bloody trails in the melting snow was in the *TDL* of March 4. The blizzard on Friday night was reported in the *SIH* of March 5 and in a telegram dated March 4 at 7:30 P.M. The story of the three stranded telegraphers is from the *ST* of March 4. The unidentified body in the river was reported in the *WDW* of March 5. And the slide at Drury that killed the watchman is mentioned in a telegram of March 1, 5:00 P.M.

The incident of the snow sliding off the hotel roof is reported in the *SIH* of March 4. Bailets mentions taking his family to sleep on the outfit cars on the spur tracks in his inquest testimony (CIT, p. 343). O'Neill's nightly trips through the tunnel as per the *SPI* of March 4. The alleged quotation from Charles Andrews—"Moved by a power"—was printed in the *SPI* of March 3 and elsewhere, but Andrews denied the story in his court affidavit. The other bogus *SPI* reports are from the editions of March 4 (mountain lions and wolves; car with ten survivors) and March 5 (surviving baby; eating a cat). The French newspaper that picked up the erroneous *SPI* story was *L'Humanité* of March 5.

Underwood tells of his encounter with O'Neill in an article entitled "I Scooped the Wellington Disaster" published in *True West*, January–February 1961, p. 20. "Death everywhere" from *ST* of March 3, while "The task of digging for the dead" appeared in the *ST* of March 4. Underwood's remark that the women insisted on the train being taken out of the tunnel appeared in his *ST* report of March 3.

"I was greatly distressed" is from a letter from Charles Steele to Hill dated March 3, 1910 (James J. Hill Papers). The eighty-five deaths figure is from the March 1 entry in the general manager's office diaries (GN Corporate Records, Minnesota Historical Society). The Pueblo, Colorado, train wreck as described by Edgar A. Haine in his *Railroad Wrecks* (New York: Cornwall Books, 1993), p. 31. The issue of the thirty laborers in the smoking car as reported in *EDH* of March 7.

"The snow was packed so hard about the bodies" was said by Detective Wells and reported in the *ST* of March 7. O'Neill's estimate of one month to find all of the bodies was reported in the *SEC* of March 8. His idea of melting the snow with steam as reported in the *ST* of the same day.

"How puny is man" from the *SS* of March 7.

"The greatest blockade of a railway system" from the *ST* of March 10. The buildup of delayed freight as per the *SPI* of March 5.

The details of the east-side cleanup come primarily from two sources: John Brady's superior court testimony (SCT, pp. 804–16) and an article later written by Brady, "The Great Slide," originally published in *Railroad Magazine* in 1946 but reprinted in *Locomotives of the Empire Builder* by Charles F. Martin (Chicago: Normandie House, 1972). "One of the largest I have ever seen," from Brady's testimony, SCT, p. 808. The arrival of Northern Pacific No. 2 as per the telegram of 8:00 P.M., Thursday, March 3. "Have had considerable trouble holding men" from a telegram from E. L. Brown to O'Neill et al., 10:45 P.M., Saturday, March 5. The packing in of coal and the revival of the stalled double rotary as per Dowling (SCT, pp. 752 and 756) and the *SEC* of March 6.

Interference between the body evacuations and the plowing efforts was reported in the *ST* of March 9. Forsyth and Laville's descent as described in the *TDL* of March 3. The descent of Clary, Purcell, and Bates as per the *SS* of same date. The "pathetic procession" was described in the *SS* of March 7. "I'd rather take a chance on dying," "You can tell the people for me," and "It's not half-bad coming down that hill" as quoted in the *ST* of March 7.

O'Neill's ordering of the Alaskan sleds as per the *SPI* of March 5. "We left Wellington at noon" from the *ST* of March 6. Bill J. Moore's experience evacuating O'Reilly's body ("I seen 90 bodies") is from his handwritten margin notes in his personal copy of the Ruby El Hult book.

The discovery of the mail cars comes from Hult, *Northwest Disaster*, p. 88. The *WDW* of March 10 reported that there were still over two dozen bodies to be accounted for. The unearthing of part of the smoking car as per the *ST* of March 7. Carrie Phillips's climb to be with her husband was reported in Hult, p. 70. "Confined to the hospital" and "Let me die" are from the *SS* of March 7. "Here is a young man" and further quotes from that scene are from Sherlock, p. 24. The encounter between O'Neill and Sherlock as described in Sherlock, pp. 22–23.

"Why, get them to give me another engine" was quoted in the *ST* of March 11. Tegtmeier's early detection of Gruber's train as per the *ST* of March 10. The evacuation of the last nine of the injured as reported in the *ST* of March 11 and from transcribed notes of an interview with A. B. Hensel by Keith Yates (Robert Kelly collection). The Starretts' dread of getting back on a train as per the *SIH* of March 3.

The exact time of the rotaries' meeting was announced in a March 12 (10:49 A.M.) telegram from Gruber to Lewis Hill, cited in T. Gary Sherman's *Conquest and Catastrophe* (Bloomington, IN: Author House, 2004), p. 146. "The siege of snows is ended" was from the *ST* of March 12. Hill's congratulations are from two telegrams to Gruber dated March 8 and March 9 (Minnesota Historical Society).

The slide that hit the rotary was described in the special mail edition of the *ST* dated both March 14 and 15. That the laborer was not found for weeks was cited in the *Argus* of April 2. The majority of mail was recovered according to the *ST* of March 13. O'Neill's visits to the Longcoys and to Lewis Walker's widow are mentioned in unidentified newspaper clippings in the O'Neill family scrapbooks.

14: Inquest

The opening quotation—"That thousands of tons of snow"—is from the *SUR* of March 12.

"O'NEILL HAILED NOW AS KING OF SNOW FIGHTERS" and the subsequent quotation ("He always is cool") are from the *ST* of March 6. "What proved to be the most dangerous place possible" from the *ST* of March 3. "DOLLAR-A-DAY JAP COULD HAVE PREVENTED SLIDE" and the following quotation ("Had the slope been wooded") are from the *SS* of March 5. "[I] could not help wondering" from the Seattle *Argus* of the same date. "DID PENNY SQUEEZING COST 100 LIVES AT WELLINGTON?" and the following quotation ("The Great Northern railroad will never hire able men") are from the *SS* of the same date.

"Relatives and friends of the dead men" from the *SSR* of March 17. "It was positively known for weeks" from the *SUR* of March 12.

(NB: Despite the charges of the switchmen's union, the GN claimed to be at full operational efficiency at the time of the storm. In a letter to Armstrong dated March 11 [GN Legal Department Files], Dorety, while admitting that four cars of coal were indeed en route to Stevens Pass from Leavenworth at the time of the blockade, points out that the coal bunkers at Wellington at this time were already full. This suggests that the delay of those four cars may have been the result of a lack of urgency rather than a lack of efficiency.)

Publication of Hill's *Highways* as per Martin, p. 557. Stevens's "penny-wise, pound-wise" quip comes from his *An Engineer's Recollections* (New York: McGraw-Hill, 1935), p. 33.

Coroner Snyder's desire to have all bodies accounted for before the inquest as reported in the *SPI* of March 14. That there were still nine unidentified bodies at the morgue by the commencement of the inquest is from the *SPI* of March 14. The misidentification of Ned Topping was reported in the *SPI* of March 11 and elsewhere. The Joseph Benier anecdote ("My friends say that you have me downstairs dead") comes from the *WDW* of March 22. The difficulties with the Brockman family imposters as per the *ST* of March 20.

The disposition of the bodies was reported in the newspapers as follows: Nellie Sharp (*SPI* of March 6), George and Thelma Davis (*SSR* of March 12), the Beck family (*ST* of March 14), and the memorial service in Everett (*EDH* of March 14). Sarah Jane Covington's funeral was reported in the *Olympia Chronicle* of March 12 and in other documents in the Covington/Brokaw family records. The letter from Mrs. Gray to Luther Covington ("Dear Friend") is also from that collection.

The GN's moving behind the scenes as per a letter from Armstrong to F. V. Brown of March 9 (GN Legal Department Files), in which Armstrong states, "I am strongly of the opinion that if an inquest can be prevented it should not be held."

"Nothing in the company's affairs is of greater importance" is from a March 15 letter to Dorety from Armstrong (GN Legal Department Files). "Effort should be made to secure jury" is from a telegram pink slip from Armstrong to Brown dated March 16. The company's concern about the inquest testimony and verdict as a possible basis for future lawsuits is expressed in the March 11 letter from Dorety to Armstrong. "We are making every effort to block" from the same letter. The article citing the opinions of local lawyers appeared in the *ST* of March 4.

The original transcript of the coroner's inquest (CIT) has been missing for many years, but at least one copy recently turned up in a private collection, a second-generation copy of which is now in the Puget Sound Regional Branch of the Washington State Archives, Bellevue, WA. All of these copies are missing the testimony of R. M. Laville, but his major statements were widely reported in the newspaper accounts of the inquest.

O'Neill's arrival with the other railroaders as per the *SPI* of March 19. "Deep furrows are plowed" as per the *EDH* of March 7. The function of the railroad commission at the inquest as per the commissioner's testimony (CIT, p. 526). That this was the first train accident in Washington history to prompt an inquest is likewise mentioned in testimony (CIT, p. 526). "All kinds of rumors are in circulation" is from the *Argus* of March 12. The *Argus* of May 7 contained the story about White's being refused compensation "even for the shirt on his back."

O'Neill's attire as per an artist's rendering in the *SPI* of March 19. "I gave them orders" from CIT, p. 11. "O'NEILL ASSUMES ALL BLAME" from the *ST* of March 18. Laville's testimony ("Fear was in every heart" etc.) as reported in the *ST* of March 20. "I never met nicer gentlemen in my life" from CIT, p. 268. Perley's testimony as per CIT, p. 317. Bailets's testimony ("I asked them, I says") from CIT, p. 344. "These three tracks here contained" is from CIT, p. 369. The three questions about the spur tracks are from CIT, pp. 410–15. The claim that the railroaders backed their judgment "with their lives—and lost" comes from the *Argus* of March 12.

"So, through lack of coal and lack of help" from CIT, p. 424. Dorety's attempt to recover ("Don't you know that") from CIT, p. 438. For the record, the three non-GN officials testifying at the end of the inquest were F. E. Weymouth, superintendent of the

NP's Seattle Division; F. E. Willard, trainmaster on the Milwaukee Road, and J. E. Campbell, trainmaster on the NP's Seattle Division. "For the present, I can only say" is from a March 22 letter to Armstrong from Brown (GN Legal Department Files). The Chelan County coroner's findings are reported in the *WDW* of March 22. "If I was the manager of a railroad" is from the *Argus* of March 26.

The text of the jury's verdict is from CIT, pp. 526ff. A copy sent by Mrs. George Anderson is in the Covington/Brokaw family collection. "Hermaphrodite verdict" is the work of L. C. Gilman in a letter to Lewis W. Hill dated April 1. Brown's telegram—"WE FEEL POSITIVE NO FOUNDATION"—as cited in a March 25 letter from Armstrong to L. C. Gilman. Brown's statement to the newspapers as per the *ST* of March 25. "The verdict itself" comes from a March 25 letter from Armstrong to Brown. "If the evidence at the Coroner's Inquest" is from a March 15 letter from Armstrong to Dorety. (Letters and telegrams are from the GN Legal Department Files.)

15: Act of God

The opening headline—"WELLINGTON SLIDE LAWSUIT ON TRIAL"—is from the *WDW* of October 21, 1913.

Description of "the Cruel Castle" from HistoryLink's "Seattle's First Hill: King County Courthouse and Harborview Hospital" (www.historylink.org). Details of the Starretts' experiences after leaving Wellington, including the judgment of the GN as "most kind," are from the notes of an interview conducted by Ruby El Hult with Raymond Starrett dated February 24, 1957 (Hult Papers), and from newspaper accounts. Hensel material is from family documents and from Yates's "Survivor," p. 43. Details of the Hensel trial can be found in the *WDW* of May 7, the *SSR* of June 24, 1911, and in trial documents from the Robert Kelly collection.

Most details of the trial come from the complete transcript (SCT) in the Robert Kelly collection. Other court records, including copies of pretrial motions, are held in microfilm at the archives of the Superior Court of King County in Seattle. Two hundred witnesses as per the *WDW* of October 22, 1913. Samuel Hill's letter to James J. Hill of March 23 is from the archives of the James J. Hill Reference Library in St. Paul. Hill's response ("You can say to Governor Hay") is from his letter to Samuel Hill dated March 26 from the same collection. (This letter was later published in full in newspapers such as the *WDW* of April 2.) The railroad commission's exoneration of the GN is reported in a letter to L. C. Gilman from Armstrong dated March 31 (GN Legal Department Files).

The *WDW* of March 22 contained a report of the clearing of the last of the wreckage at Wellington. Hill's subsequent trip west as reported in the *WDW* of April 29. Commissioner Lawrence's speech ("The work will run") was quoted in the *WDW* of July 25.

The change of Wellington's name to Tye was announced in the General Manager's Circular of October 15, 1910 (GN Corporate Records).

"Those chumps would slander their parents" is from the *SUR* of March 26. Settlement terms of the strike as reported in the *SUR* of April 16 and the *WDW* of April 1 and 29. (NB: Although the switchmen working the line west of Havre got their five cents an hour, those working the line east got only a three-cent raise.)

Hill's various remarks were always widely reported in the press. "The people are living at a tremendous rate" was from the *WDW* of May 2. "The rise in the wage rate is the biggest factor" from the *SPI* of March 18. "There is a popular idea that a railroad may be compelled" from the *WDW* of June 10. For the rising tide of progressivism between 1910 and 1913, see Hofstadter, p. 248ff. "Claimed the privilege of completing" from Wiebe, p. 217. For Hill's relationships with individual presidents, I'm indebted to W. Thomas White's "A Gilded Age Businessman in Politics."

Basil Sherlock's report on the GN lawyers' collection of "every record and every bit of paper that had any writing on it" is from a letter to Ruby El Hult dated March 8, 1960 (Ruby El Hult Papers). The GN's denial of claims to all comers as per a letter of April 1 from Gilman to Louis W. Hill and other letters. The issue of ensuring the goodwill of surviving employees for the sake of the trial is explicitly mentioned in the April 1 letter from Gilman to Hill. Settlement terms for dead trainmen are cited in an undated (probably April 14) letter from Armstrong to Brown. The special compensation request from Mrs. Pettit as per a letter from L. C. Gilman to E. C. Lindley of June 7, 1910. (All from the GN Legal Department Files.)

"I believe that no employee made a single statement" is from a March 26 letter from Dorety to Armstrong (GN Legal Department Files). McFadgen's dissenting opinions discussed in a March 25 letter from Dorety to Brown. The "reasonable and prudent person" test for negligence is cited in the judge's instructions to the jury (SCT, p. 852) and is discussed in a March 29 letter from Armstrong to Dorety (GN Legal Department Files).

Judge Humphries's determination to let a jury decide the case, rather than taking presumptive action himself, is from his remarkable admission (cited later in the text— "Were I permitted, I'd like to unravel the case for you") reported in the *WDW* of October 24, 1913. The setting aside of one month for the trial as per the *ST* of October 21, 1913.

The exchange about the communication of officials on trains Nos. 2 and 27 is from SCT, p. 11. (It's worth noting that, many years later, Ross Phillips would claim that train No. 25 was also told that it would never make it over the mountains—Jackson, p. 40.) "I presume these questions are all proper" from SCT, p. 259. Williams bickers with the judge on p. 693 and makes fun of a witness's grammar on p. 773. The exchange between Williams and White ("Were you conscious when the coach went over?") is from SCT, p. 136.

(NB: A letter of September 7, 1910, from J. M. Gruber to E. C. Lindley describes an earlier, much smaller slide at Wellington that in February 1903 destroyed the sand house and killed three or four men, but this apparently happened at a point significantly west of where the trains were standing on March 1, 1910.)

For a good example of the litany of "unprecedenteds," see the testimony of J. C. Wright (SCT, p. 379). "It will be conceded by everyone" is from a March 26 letter from Dorety to Armstrong (GN Legal Department Files). "I will say, in justice to Superintendent O'Neill" is from the same letter. The birth of James O'Neill Jr. while James Sr. was at Stevens Pass as evidenced by telegrams preserved in the O'Neill family scrapbooks. The calculation of 1,350 trains per year in snowstorms as per SCT, p. 494. "I submit the motion is frivolous" is from SCT, p. 512. "Why were [the trains] put on the passing track?" is from SCT, pp. 518–19.

"Now, Mr. O'Neill, to meet such a condition" comes from SCT, pp. 605–6. "It would have buried them in" is from SCT, p. 607. Williams's frustrated wild shot ("Wouldn't it have been better") is from SCT, p. 608.

(NB: Irving Tegtmeier is identified as "Irwin" in the SCT.) "Had you tried any shoveling out by hand" from SCT, pp. 717–18. An example of Harrington's contradictory testimony can be found in SCT, p. 723, line 3, and p. 726, line 4. A denial of his inquest testimony is on SCT, p. 731. Williams's trap for Harrington ("On that trip down") from SCT, p. 741.

The lecture Judge Humphries gives to the court is on SCT, pp. 768–71. The GN's request for a directed verdict is on SCT, pp. 847–48.

The text of the supreme court's reversal is reprinted in *Washington Reports*, vol. 81. "It is plain, from the evidence in the case" is from p. 170. Other quotes are from pp. 176–77. That Topping was forced to pay back the $20,000 award plus 6 percent interest and $264 in court costs is from the court documents microfilm. "The people are rising up in arms" from a November 14, 1910, letter to E. C. Lindley from H. A. Landwehr (GN Legal Department Files).

"Corporate cunning has developed faster" as quoted in Sullivan, p. 182. Peak railroad mileage as per Stover, *Atlas*, p. 52. "By the time you're forty, be out of the railroad business" quoted in Albro Martin, *James J. Hill*, p. 571. For the discussion of wireless communications in GN operations, see Sherman, pp. 127–28. The figure of 95 percent of track under shed protection according to "Railroad Construction in Stevens Pass" by Charles F. Intlekofer (*Confluence*, Spring 1992), p. 387. "Such places would have radio" from the Sherlock memoir, p. 26. "Could not battle the clouds away" from CIT, p. 671.

Epilogue: A Memory Erased

"The mailed fist of progress" was perpetrated in the *ST* of January 11, 1929.

Details about the 1929 tunnel inauguration ceremony at Scenic come principally from contemporary newspaper accounts and from *Dedication and Opening of the New Cascade Tunnel*, which contains an account of the event and the text of the speeches given. Gilman's comment about "the weakest link in our transportation chain" is on p. 9 of the booklet. The $25 million cost of the tunnel as per General W. W. Atterbury's speech on p. 7. Other details from the *ST, SPI, EDH,* and *WDW* of January 8–13, 1929, and from McLaughlin, "How Great Northern Conquered the Cascades," pp. 10–12.

The great expense of snowshed construction and repair in the post-Wellington era is detailed in a letter of November 11, 1925, from Ralph Budd to Louis W. Hill, cited in an unpublished 2003 paper, "Great Northern Railway: The New Cascade Tunnel: Should It Have Been Built" by Jerry R. Masters and T. Michael Power (courtesy of T. Michael Power). The various slide-related mishaps of the winter of 1915–16 as reported in the *SSR* editions of December 15, 1915, and January 16, February 16, and March 17, 1916. James J. Hill's comment on his last Cascades trip ("Some of you will live to see") is cited in the dedication speech by Ralph Budd ("Dedication," p. 5).

For Hill's last days I have relied most heavily on Albro Martin's biography, pp. 608–15. "The last of the wilderness conquerors" as cited in the Holbrook biography, p. 186. "Greatness became him" from the *NYT* of May 29, 1916. "How desolately lonely the house seems" from Mary Hill's personal diary entry for June 1, 1916 (GN Corporate Records, P2210, Box 2).

Graham McNamee is identified as "the dean of American broadcasters" in the *SSR* of January 11, 1929. Ralph Budd's flu was reported in the same paper's January 13 edition. The Apple Blossom Queen's christening was dutifully recorded in the *ST* of the same date.

Hoover's celebration of American virility ("Never have we witnessed") is from *Dedication*, p. 7. John F. Stevens's oration ("And so the new tunnel is put in operation") is from p. 21 of the same source. O'Neill's experience at the ceremony as per photographs of the event, several newspaper accounts, and clippings in the O'Neill family scrapbooks, which also contain his apologetic note to his daughter ("Peggy dear, Account receiving a telegram"). Latter-day telegrams with snow-fighting reports signed by O'Neill are in the GN Corporate Records (e.g., File 132.B.18.1B, "Snow Storms and Snow Equipment"). Stories of the ring "Sunshine" and the candelabrum "George" come from an interview by the author with O'Neill's granddaughter Jeanne Patricia May. His stint as a rail tester for FDR and his love for duck hunting and steelhead fishing are from clippings in the O'Neill family scrapbooks, which also contain the note from Berenice in which she avows, "Our love was the proudest thing in my life."

Ida Starrett's later years as per a letter from Raymond Starrett to Basil J. Sherlock dated April 14, 1960 (Wenatchee Valley Museum) and from the notes of an interview with Ray Starrett by Ruby El Hult (Hult Papers). Sherlock's request for a picture and the subsequent quotations come from his letters to Raymond Starrett, one dated April 4, 1960, the other missing its first page and therefore undatable (Wenatchee Valley Museum). The effect of the slide on A. B. Hensel from the Hensel family archives and from an interview by the author with Hensel's daughter, Dolores Hensel Yates. Ira Clary's later career is detailed in George E. Leu's *A Hogshead's Random Railroad Reminiscences* (New York: Vantage, 1995). Harrington's career is from census records and a Department of Transportation report on the 1916 snowslide. Bill J. Moore's intervention on behalf of Joe Pettit Jr. is described in his letter to Ruby El Hult (Hult Papers). Varden Gray's adoption of the moniker "the Duke of Wellington" from Hult, *Northwest Disaster*, p. 210. Sherlock's quotation ("Perhaps you wish to forget it") is from the letter to Starrett dated April 4, 1960 (Wenatchee Valley Museum).

"The switchback has become tradition" is from the address by L. C. Gilman, "Dedication," p. 9. The coyotes "howling in the doorways" was cited in the *ST* of January 13, 1929.

Afterword: A Final Note on the Wellington Avalanche

The two cited reports on the avalanches of 1910 are "Avalanches in the Cascades and Northern Rocky Mountains During Winter of 1909–10" by Edward A. Beals (*Monthly Weather Review*, June 1910), pp. 951–57, and "Avalanches and Forest Cover in the Northern Cascades" by Thornton T. Munger. "Avalanches in these mountains are of common occurrence" from Beals, pp. 951–52. "Canyon slide" and "slope slide" as per Munger, p. 5.

Information about slide formation comes mainly from the following sources: Armstrong and Williams; *Secrets of the Snow: Visual Clues to Avalanche and Ski Conditions* by Edward R. LaChapelle (Seattle: University of Washington, 2001); McClung and Schaerer; and Shimanski.

"A bird or an icicle or a puff of wind" from CIT, p. 396. "Heavy wet snow on the hills" from CIT, p. 331. "As shown by conditions afterward" from SCT, p. 648.

Appendix: A Wellington Roster

The roster was assembled principally from the King County Coroner's Death Record for 1909 and 1910 (King County Archives, Seattle), cemetery records from the Evergreen Cemetery in Everett and the Mount Pleasant Cemetery in Seattle, and the official GN casualty lists published in the local press. The part of the GN Legal Department Files related to the exact number of deaths appears to be no longer extant.

BIBLIOGRAPHY

Principal Primary Sources

COURT RECORDS

Court Affidavits: A series of fourteen Wellington-related affidavits collected by Great Northern lawyers (Wenatchee Valley Museum, Wenatchee, WA).

Court Documents: Documents and motions from *Hensel vs. Great Northern Railway and James H. O'Neill,* 1910 (Superior Court, Spokane County, WA).

Court Documents: Microfilm of documents and motions from *Topping vs. Great Northern Railway* (Superior Court, King County, Seattle, WA).

Court Records: The Supreme Court appeal of *Topping vs. Great Northern Railway* (Washington State Supreme Court, Olympia, WA). The text of the court's verdict and the justices' opinions were reprinted in *Washington Reports,* vol. 81.

Coroner's Inquest Transcript: "In the matter of the inquiry into the cause of the death of John Brockman and eighty-seven, or more, others, Deceased: Testimony taken before King County Coroner J. C. Snyder, commencing March 18, 1910" (Puget Sound Regional Branch of the Washington State Archives, Bellevue, WA).

Superior Court Transcript: "Statement of Facts: *Topping vs. Great Northern Railway*" (Superior Court of the State of Washington, in and for King County: Case No. 11,949) (Robert Kelly Collection, Renton, WA).

CORPORATE ARCHIVES

Corporate Archives: Great Northern Railway Corporate Records (Minnesota Historical Society, St. Paul, MN).

Corporate Document: Excerpts from the Great Northern's Cascade Division Operations Diary (Robert Kelly Collection).

Legal Department Document: "Movement of Trains and Rotaries on the Hill from February 22d on to Slide" (Robert Kelly Collection).

Legal Department Files: An incomplete copy of the Great Northern Legal Department's Wellington file (George Fischer Collection, Museum of History and Industry, Seattle, WA).

Telegrams: A collection of Wellington-related Great Northern Railway telegrams (Robert Kelly Collection).

Letters, Memoirs, Diaries

Covington, Sarah Jane: Correspondence and diary (Washington State Historical Society, Tacoma, WA, and Covington/Brokaw family collection).

Hensel, A. B.: Memoirs, articles, and interview notes (Dolores Hensel Yates family collection).

Hill, James J.: Correspondence (James J. Hill Reference Library, St. Paul, MN).

Hult, Ruby El: Interview notes and correspondence (Ruby El Hult Papers, Washington State University Manuscripts, Archives and Special Collections, Pullman, WA).

Jesseph, Lewis C.: "We Escaped the Wellington Disaster," printed in *Confluence*, vol. 5, no. 1 (North Central Washington Museum, Wenatchee, WA, 1988).

O'Neill, James H., and Berenice O'Neill: Correspondence and scrapbooks (Jeanne Patricia May family collection).

Sherlock, Basil J.: "The Wellington Disaster—March 1, 1910: Reminiscences of Basil J. Sherlock" (unpublished ms., Washington State Historical Society, Tacoma, WA).

Topping, Edward W.: Letter to his mother (William Topping family collection).

Newspapers

Contemporaneous articles from the *Seattle Times, Seattle Post-Intelligencer, Seattle Star,* Seattle *Union Record,* Seattle *Argus, Everett Daily Herald, Wenatchee Daily World,* Spokane *Inland Herald,* Spokane *Spokesman-Review,* Spokane *Evening Chronicle, Leavenworth Echo, Tacoma Daily Ledger, St. Paul Pioneer Press, Chicago Tribune,* and *New York Times.*

Principal Secondary Sources

Abdill, George B. *This Was Railroading.* New York: Bonanza Books, 1958.

Ambrose, Stephen E. *Nothing Like It in the World.* New York: Simon & Schuster, 2000.

The American Railway: Its Construction, Development, Management, and Appliances. New York: Scribner's, 1889.

Anderson, Eva. *Rails Across the Cascades.* Wenatchee: World Publishing, 1952.

Anderson, Judith Icke. *William Howard Taft: An Intimate History.* New York: Norton, 1981.

Anonymous. "The Lost Communities of Stevens Pass." *Seattle Genealogical Society Bulletin* (Spring 1999).

Armbruster, Kurt E. *Orphan Road: The Railroad Comes to Seattle, 1853–1911.* Seattle: University of Washington Press, 1999.

Armstrong, Betsy, and Knox Williams. *The Avalanche Book.* Golden, CO: Fulcrum, 1986.

Armstrong, John. *The Railroad—What It Is, What It Does: The Introduction to Railroading.* Omaha: Simmons-Boardman, 1978.

Baker, Ray Stannard. *American Chronicle: The Autobiography of Ray Stannard Baker.* New York: Scribner's, 1945.

———. "The Great Northwest." *Century Magazine,* vol. 65, no. 5 (March 1903).

Beals, Edward A. "Avalanches in the Cascades and Northern Rocky Mountains During Winter of 1909–10." *Monthly Weather Review* (June 1910).

Becky, Fred. *Cascade Alpine Guide: Climbing and High Routes—Columbia River to Stevens Pass.* Seattle: The Mountaineers, 1973.

Belasco, Warren James. *Americans on the Road: From Autocamp to Motel, 1910–1945.* Cambridge: MIT Press, 1979.

Beniger, James. *The Control Revolution: Technological and Economic Origins of the Information Society.* Cambridge: Harvard University Press, 1986.

Blaise, Clark. *Time Lord: Sir Sandford Fleming and the Creation of Standard Time.* New York: Pantheon, 2000.

Brown, Arthur J. "The Promotion of Emigration to Washington, 1854–1909." *Pacific Northwest Quarterly* 36 (1945): pp. 3–17.

Brown, Dee. *Hear That Lonesome Whistle Blow.* New York: Holt, Rinehart and Winston, 1977.

Bryce, James. *The American Commonwealth.* Edited by Louis M. Hacker. 2 volumes. New York: G. P. Putnam's Sons, 1959 edition.

Burwash, Martin. *Cascade Division: A Pictorial Essay of the Burlington Northern and Milwaukee Road in the Washington Cascades.* Arvada, CO: Fox Publications, 1995.

———. *The Great Adventure: The Railroad Legacy of Stevens Pass.* Arvada, CO: Fox Publications, 1998.

———. "Vis Major" (unpublished Wellington novel).

Chalmers, David M. *Neither Socialism nor Monopoly: Theodore Roosevelt and the Decision to Regulate the Railroads.* The America's Alternatives Series. Philadelphia: Lippincott, 1976.

Chandler, Alfred D., ed. *The Railroad: America's First Big Business.* New York: Harcourt, Brace & World, 1965.

———. *The Visible Hand: The Managerial Revolution in American Business.* Cambridge: Belknap / Harvard University Press, 1977.

Chapple, Oliver. "Avalanche in the Cascades." *American West* (January–February 1983).

Clark, Norman H. *Mill Town: A Social History of Everett, Washington, from Its Earliest Beginnings on the Shores of Puget Sound to the Tragic and Infamous Event Known as the Everett Massacre.* Seattle: University of Washington Press, 1970.

Clark, Thomas D. *Frontier America: The Story of the Westward Movement.* 2nd ed. New York: Scribner's, 1969.

Dedication and Opening of the New Cascade Tunnel: A Monument to James J. Hill. Great Northern Railway Company, 1929.

Del Grosso, Robert C. *Railfan's Guide to Stampede and Stevens Passes.* Bonners Ferry, ID: Great Northern Pacific Publications, 1997.

DeSantis, Vincent P. *The Shaping of Modern America: 1877–1916.* Boston: Allyn and Bacon, 1973.

Duffy, Herbert S. *William Howard Taft.* New York: Minton, Balch, 1930.

Fahey, John. *The Inland Empire: The Unfolding Years, 1879–1929.* Seattle: University of Washington Press, 1986.

Faith, Nicholas. *The World the Railways Made.* New York: Carroll & Graf, 1990.

Fitzpatrick, Ellen F. *Muckraking: Three Landmark Articles.* Boston: Bedford Books–St. Martin's Press, 1994.

Flink, James J. *America Adopts the Automobile, 1895–1910*. Cambridge: MIT Press, 1970.

Fredston, Jill. *Snowstruck: In the Grip of Avalanches*. New York: Harcourt, 2005.

Garland, Hamlin. "Western Landscapes." *Atlantic Monthly* (December 1893).

Gleick, James. *Faster: The Acceleration of Just About Everything*. New York: Pantheon, 1999.

Gordon, Sarah H. *Passage to Union: How the Railroad Changed American Life, 1829–1929*. Chicago: Ivan Dee, 1996.

Grant, H. Roger, ed. *We Took the Train*. Dekalb: Northern Illinois University Press, 1990.

Haine, Edgar A. *Railroad Wrecks*. New York: Cornwall Books, 1993.

Hamberger, Eric. *Penguin Historical Atlas of North America*. New York: Viking, 1995.

Hamblen, Herbert. *The General Manager's Story*. New York: Macmillan, 1898. (Reprinted by Literature House, Upper Saddle River, NJ, 1970.)

Hartranft, W. C. "The First Cascade Tunnel." Great Northern Railway Historical Society Reference Sheet No. 175, March 1991.

———. "The Pacific Extension and Cascade Switchbacks: 1889–1892." Great Northern Railway Historical Society Reference Sheet No. 172, December 1990.

Haskell, Daniel C., ed. *On Reconnaissance for the Great Northern: Letters of C. F. B. Haskell, 1889–91*. New York: New York Public Library, 1948.

Hidy, Ralph, et al. *The Great Northern Railway: A History*. Boston: Harvard Business School Press, 1988.

Hill, James J. *Highways of Progress*. New York: Doubleday, Page, 1910.

Hofstadter, Robert. *The Age of Reform: From Bryan to F.D.R*. 1955. Reprint, New York: Vintage Books, 1960.

Holbrook, Stewart H. *James J. Hill: A Great Life in Brief*. New York: Knopf, 1955.

———. *The Story of American Railroads*. New York: Crown, 1947.

Holmquist, Stuart. "Great Northern Railway Mail Services." Great Northern Railway Historical Society Reference Sheet No. 177, June 1991.

Hult, Ruby El. *Northwest Disaster*. Portland, OR: Binford & Mort, 1960.

Intlekofer, Charles F. "Railroad Construction in Stevens Pass." *Confluence* (Spring 1992).

Jackson, Howard E. "Pull Back to the Tunnel!" Undated, unidentified magazine clipping in the archives of the Wenatchee Valley Museum.

Jeffers, H. Paul. *An Honest President: The Life and Presidencies of Grover Cleveland*. New York: Morrow, 2000.

Jenkins, Mackay. *The White Death: Tragedy and Heroism in an Avalanche Zone*. New York: Random House, 2000.

Josephson, Matthew. *The Robber Barons: The Great American Capitalists, 1861–1901*. New York: Harcourt, Brace & World, 1934, 1962.

Kalez, Jay J. *This Town of Ours . . . Spokane*. Spokane: Lawton Printing, 1973.

Kirkpatrick, O. H. *Working on the Railroad*. Philadelphia: Dorrance, 1949.

LaChapelle, Edward R. *Secrets of the Snow: Visual Clues to Avalanche and Ski Conditions*. Seattle: University of Washington, 2001.

Leu, George E. *A Hogshead's Random Railroad Reminiscences*. New York: Vantage, 1995.

Lewty, Peter J. *Across the Columbia Plain: Railroad Expansion in the Interior Northwest, 1885–1893*. Pullman: Washington State University Press, 1995.

Licht, Walter. *Working for the Railroad: The Organization of Work in the Nineteenth Century*. Princeton: Princeton University Press, 1983.

Limerick, Patricia Nelson. *The Legacy of Conquest: The Unbroken Past of the American West*. New York: Norton, 1987.

Livesay, Harold C. *Andrew Carnegie and the Rise of Big Business*. Library of American Biography. Boston: Little, Brown, 1975.

Long, Bryant Alden, and William Jefferson Dennis. *Mail by Rail: The Story of the Postal Transportation Service*. New York: Simmons-Boardman, 1951.

Lyon, Peter. *To Hell in a Day Coach: An Exasperated Look at American Railroads*. Philadelphia: Lippincott, 1968.

Mair, Walter E. "O'Neill of the Great Northern." *Railroad Stories*, May 1932.

Malone, Michael P. *James J. Hill: Empire Builder of the Northwest*. Norman: University of Oklahoma Press, 1996.

Martin, Albro. *Enterprise Denied: Origins of the Decline of American Railroads, 1897–1917*. New York: Columbia University Press, 1971.

———. *James J. Hill and the Opening of the Northwest*. New York: Oxford University Press, 1976.

Martin, Charles F. *Locomotives of the Empire Builder*. Chicago: Normandie House, 1972.

Masters, Jerry R., and T. Michael Power. "Great Northern Railway: The New Cascade Tunnel: Should It Have Been Built" (unpublished paper).

McClung, David, and Peter Schaerer. *The Avalanche Handbook*. Seattle: The Mountaineers, 1993.

McLaughlin, D. W. "How Great Northern Conquered the Cascades." Great Northern Railway Historical Society Reference Sheet No. 213, March 1994.

Meinig, D. W. *The Shaping of America*. Vol. 3, *Transcontinental America, 1850–1915*. New Haven: Yale University Press, 1998.

Middleton, Kenneth R. "Early Great Northern Sleeping Cars, Part II." Great Northern Railway Historical Society Reference Sheet No. 252, June 1997.

Middleton, William D. *When the Steam Railroads Electrified*. Rev. 2nd ed. Bloomington: Indiana University Press, 2001.

Miller, Max. *The Beginning of a Mortal*. New York: Dutton, 1933.

———. *Shinny on Your Own Side and Other Memories of Growing Up*. New York: Doubleday, 1958.

Moody, Don. *America's Worst Train Disaster: The 1910 Wellington Tragedy*. Plano, TX: Abique, 1998.

Moody, John, and George Kibbe Turner. "The Masters of Capital in America." *McClure's*, vol. 36, no. 2 (December 1910).

Morgan, Murray Cromwell. *Skid Road: An Informal Portrait of Seattle*. New York: Viking, 1960.

Morris, Edmund. *The Rise of Theodore Roosevelt*. New York: Putnam, 1979.

———. *Theodore Rex*. New York: Random House, 2001.

Mowry, George E. *The Era of Theodore Roosevelt and the Birth of Modern America, 1900–1912*. New York: Harper & Brothers, 1958.

Mumford, John Kimberly. "This Land of Opportunity: The Great 'One-Man Railroad' of the West." Parts I and II. *Harper's Weekly*, October 31 and November 14, 1908.

Munger, Thornton T. "Avalanches and Forest Cover in the Northern Cascades." U.S. Department of Agriculture, Forest Service Circular 173. Washington, DC: Government Printing Office, 1911.

Nash, Gerald D. *The American West in the Twentieth Century: A Short History of an Urban Oasis*. Englewood Cliffs, NJ: Prentice-Hall, 1973.

O'Donnell, Lawrence E. *Everett: Past and Present*. Everett: Cascade Savings Bank, 1993.

Peattie, Roderick, ed. *The Cascades: Mountains of the Pacific Northwest*. New York: Vanguard Press, 1949.

Pyle, Joseph Gilpin. *The Life of James J. Hill*. 2 vols. Garden City, N.Y.: Doubleday, Page, 1917.

Raban, Jonathan. *Bad Land: An American Romance*. New York: Pantheon, 1996.

Reinhardt, Richard, ed. *Workin' on the Railroad: Reminiscences from the Age of Steam*. Palo Alto: American West Publishing, 1970.

Rifkin, Jeremy. *Time Wars: The Primary Conflict in Human History*. New York: Holt, 1987.

Roe, JoAnn. *Stevens Pass: The Story of Railroading and Recreation in the North Cascades*. Calwell, ID: Caxton Press, 2002.

Roosevelt, Theodore. *The Autobiography of Theodore Roosevelt*. Edited by Wayne Andrews. New York: Scribners, 1958.

Roth, Jean A. "Alfred B. Hensel, Wellington Survivor." *Seattle Genealogical Society Bulletin*, vol. 48, no. 3 (Spring 1999).

Sayings and Writings About the Railways. New York: Railway Age Gazette, 1913.

Schwantes, Carlos A. *The Pacific Northwest: An Interpretive History*. Lincoln: University of Nebraska Press, 1989.

———. *Railroad Signatures Across the Pacific Northwest*. Seattle: University of Washington Press, 1993.

Sherman, T. Gary. *Conquest and Catastrophe*. Bloomington, IN: Author House, 2004.

Shimanski, Charley. "Avalanche!!!" Mountain Rescue Association, www.mra.org/avalanche_2004.pdf, 1993–2004.

Smith, Page. *America Enters the World: A People's History of the Progressive Era and World War I*. New York: McGraw-Hill, 1985.

Stevens, John F. *An Engineer's Recollections*. New York: McGraw-Hill, 1935.

Stilwell, Arthur Edward. *Confidence, or National Suicide*. New York: Bankers Publishing Company, 1910.

Stover, John F. *American Railroads*. Chicago: University of Chicago Press, 1961.

———. *Routledge Historical Atlas of American Railroads*. New York: Routledge, 1999.

Strom, Claire. *Profiting from the Plains: The Great Northern Railway and Corporate Development of the West*. Seattle: University of Washington Press, 2003.

Sullivan, Mark. *Our Times: America at the Birth of the Twentieth Century*. 1926. Abridged modern edition edited by Dan Rather. New York: Scribner, 1995.

Tate, Cassandra. *Cigarette Wars: The Triumph of "The Little White Slaver."* New York: Oxford University Press, 1999.

Taylor, George Rogers, ed. *The Turner Thesis Concerning the Role of the Frontier in American History*. Rev. ed. Problems in American Civilization. Boston: D. C. Heath, 1956.

Tucker, Louis. *Clerical Errors*. New York: Harper and Bros., 1943.

Underwood, J. J. As told to Howard E. Jackson. "I Scooped the Wellington Disaster." *True West* (January–February 1961).

U.S. Department of Labor, Bureau of Labor Statistics. *A Brief History of the American Labor Movement*. Washington, DC: U.S. Government Printing Office, 1970.

Vance, James E. *The North American Railroad: Its Origin, Evolution, and Geography*. Baltimore: Johns Hopkins University Press, 1995.

Vesper, Stuart. "Great Northern's Cascade Division Snowsheds: 1910 to 1929." Great Northern Railway Historical Society Reference Sheets Nos. 179 and 183, June and December 1991.

Wandell, Becky. *The Iron Goat Trail: A Guidebook*. 2nd ed. Seattle: The Mountaineers, 1999.

White, Victor H. "Brakeman of the Great Northern." *Frontier Times* (August–September 1970).

White, W. Thomas. "A Gilded Age Businessman in Politics: James J. Hill, the Northwest, and the American Presidency, 1884–1912." *Pacific Historical Review* 57 (November 1989): pp. 439–56.

———. "A History of Railroad Workers in the Pacific Northwest, 1883–1934." Ph.D. diss., University of Washington, 1981.

———. "Race, Ethnicity, and Gender in the Railroad Work Force: The Case of the Far Northwest, 1883–1918." *Western Historical Quarterly* 16 (July 1985): pp. 265–83.

Wiebe, Robert H. *The Search for Order: 1877–1920.* New York: Hill and Wang, 1967.

Wilson, Jeff. *The Great Northern Railway in the Pacific Northwest.* Waukesha, WI: Kalbach Books, 2001.

Wing, Warren W. *A Northwest Rail Pictorial.* Edmonds, WA: Pacific Fast Mail, 1983.

Winkler, Fred A. *Railroad Conductor.* Spokane: Pacific Book Company, 1948.

Winther, Oscar Osburn. *The Great Northwest: A History.* New York: Knopf, 1947.

Wood, Charles. *Lines West: A Pictorial History of the Great Northern Railway Operations and Motive Power from 1887 to 1967.* New York: Bonanza Books, 1967.

Wood, Charles, and Dorothy Wood. *The Great Northern Railway.* Edmonds, WA: Pacific Fast Mail, 1979.

Woodruff, R. E. *The Making of a Railroad Officer.* New York: Simmons-Boardman, 1925.

Works Projects Administration in the State of Washington. *Washington: A Guide to the Evergreen State.* Portland, OR: Binford & Mort, 1941.

Yates, Dolores Hensel. "Survivor: A Mail Clerk's Story and the 1910 Wellington Avalanche." *Nostalgia* (December 2004).

ACKNOWLEDGMENTS

One pleasant surprise for a novelist writing his first nonfiction book is the sheer sociability of the process. Instead of sitting at home in front of a blank screen, I was regularly out in the world, interacting with historians, archivists, librarians, descendants of participants in the Wellington drama, and experts of all types. Some of these people eventually became my friends, but all came to share a greater or lesser interest in the book to be written. The project of historical nonfiction, I found, generates an extraordinary spirit of community and common purpose. It also creates an enormous debt of gratitude.

The White Cascade is first and foremost a railroad story, so I owe much to the various train experts who helped lead me through the mysteries of this fascinating and complex world. For enduring my constant questions and requests for information over the course of several years, railroad historian David Sprau deserves special mention. A former telegrapher, train dispatcher, assistant chief dispatcher, and short-line superintendent, Dave has an encyclopedic knowledge of Great Northern and Northern Pacific railroad operations that proved an invaluable resource for me throughout the writing of this book.

T. Michael Power, whose thirty-four-year railroad career began with train service in Spokane and took him through management positions in the Burlington Northern Santa Fe's marketing and operations departments, was likewise a key source of guidance and information. Other experts who contributed to the book were Dr. George Fischer (who with his wife, Joan, offered me a warm welcome and a thorough GN tour of Minneapolis–St. Paul) and Father Dale Peterka (whose photography and expertise in all things GN is well known nationwide). I'm also indebted to Stu Holmquist and various other members of the Great Northern Railway Historical Society; avalanche experts Jill Fredston, codirector of the Alaska Mountain Safety Center, and Charley Shimanski, education director of the Mountain Rescue Association; Ruth Ittner, the moving force behind the Iron Goat Trail, which now traces the old GN line through Stevens Pass; and Herb Schneider, who braved the elements on a chill, snowy day in December to lead a stranger from the East along the passable sections of the trail.

I found plenty of willing assistance in libraries and archives as well. In St. Paul, Dr. W. Thomas White and Elaine McCormick of the James J. Hill Reference Library were particularly helpful. I'm also obliged to the staff of the Minnesota Historical Society, where the Great Northern's corporate records are held. Mark Behler, curator of the Wenatchee Valley Museum in Wenatchee, and Cheryl Gunselman, manuscripts librarian at the Manuscripts, Archives, and Special Collections division of the Washington State University Libraries in Pullman, were important Washington connections. Thanks also to Nicolette Bromberg, visual materials curator at the Special Collections of the University of Washington Libraries in Seattle, Elaine Miller of the Washington State Historical Society Research Center in Tacoma, Carolyn Marr of the Museum of History and Industry in Seattle, the staff of the Spokane Public Library, Steve Hubbard of the Fargo Public Library, and Leah Byzewski, director of the Grand Forks Historical Society. A special nod must go to Margaret Riddle and David Dilgard of the Northwest Room at the Everett Public Library, for assistance above and beyond the call of normal research-assistance duty. And, of course, my friend Alan Stein, staff historian of the trailblazing Web site HistoryLink.org, deserves thanks from me and everyone in the Wellington community for his on-line Wellington Scrapbook of newspaper articles (www.historylink.org/wellington/info.htm), as well as many other interesting insights into the history of the Pacific Northwest.

Those more personally connected to the story of Wellington were also extremely helpful. Jeanne Patricia ("Pat") May is the granddaughter of James H. and Berenice O'Neill; she and her husband, Ron, kindly opened their house to me on several occasions so that I could pore over Pat's collection of family photos, clippings, letters, and telegrams. (Thanks, too, to genealogist Sarah Little for finding the Mays in the first place.) I owe similar gratitude to Dolores Hensel Yates, the daughter of Wellington survivor A. B. Hensel; she and her husband, Keith, have both written about A.B.'s Wellington experience and were generous in sharing the fruits of their research with me. Among other Wellington descendants who offered their knowledge, documents, and photos were John Topping (grandson of Ned), Craig Hanson (great-grandnephew of Joe Pettit), Barney Moore (son of Bill J. Moore and a former switchman and trainmaster himself), and John Deely (great-grandson of GN traffic manager M. J. Costello). I would also like to thank Danielle Devine and Vince Decker, current residents of the O'Neill home in Everett, for inviting an unkempt loiterer into their house and sharing with him their own research about its history. A special note of thanks goes out to the amazing Ruby El Hult, who, though in her nineties, agreed to meet with me in 2004; Ruby's pioneering work in the study of the Wellington avalanche has been instrumental in keeping the story alive into a second century.

Many other friends and associates provided guidance along the way, but I'd like to make specific mention of my friends historian Michael Kazin, novelist Lisa Zeidner, law professor Bruce Morton, and all-around polymath and historical visionary Robert Wright (the last of whom has suffered through drafts of every book I have ever written). I'd also like to thank my editors at Holt, Jennifer Barth and George Hodgman, for pushing me to include all of the important things I somehow left out of my first draft and to omit all of the less important things I had left in. A special thanks goes to my agent and friend Eric Simonoff at Janklow & Nesbit, who had the insight at a lunch in Manhattan one day to ask me the question, "Have you ever thought about nonfiction?" I had, but somehow I needed Eric to propel me down this new path. I'll always be grateful to him.

And, of course, while it's vaguely insufferable when writers thank their families for putting up with them during the long, tedious process of book creation, I will risk insufferability by doing just that: To my wife, Elizabeth Cheng; my daughter, Anna; and my sweet hound, Lily, go my endless love and gratitude.

Finally, there are two people in particular without whom the writing of this book would have been all but unthinkable: Martin Burwash, railroad photographer and author of *Cascade Division, The Great Adventure,* and a still-unfinished novel about the events at Wellington, took me under his wing early in this process and has been an inexhaustible source of railroad knowledge (not to mention good-natured banter and at times almost daily e-mail companionship) ever since. No one on the planet knows more about the hour-by-hour details of what occurred at Stevens Pass in the late winter of 1910, and he has been extraordinarily forthcoming with all of it. I am happy to count Martin and his wife, Janice, librarian extraordinaire, among my friends.

But the presiding spirit over this entire project has been Robert Kelly. Widely recognized as the premier world expert on the Wellington Disaster, Bob has a passion for the subject that proves infectious to all who experience it. He has been absolutely unstinting in his generosity, providing me with encouragement, information, personal connections, books, photographs, and copies of rare documents from his own exhaustive collection of Wellingtoniana. Bob and his wife, Pam, have become my family-away-from-family in Seattle, and their companionship, conversation, and moral support have been critical to this project in more ways than I can report. My debt to Bob is, quite simply, incalculable.

INDEX

Entries in *italics* refer to illustrations.

ABOUT THE AUTHOR

GARY KRIST is the prizewinning author of three novels—*Bad Chemistry, Chaos Theory,* and *Extravagance*—and two short-story collections—*The Garden State* and *Bone by Bone.* His book reviews, short stories, articles, and travel pieces have been featured in *The New York Times, The Washington Post, Salon, National Geographic Traveler, The New Republic,* and *Esquire,* and on National Public Radio's *Selected Shorts.* His stories have also been anthologized in such collections as *Men Seeking Women, Writers' Harvest 2,* and *Best American Mystery Stories.* He has been the recipient of the Stephen Crane Award, the Sue Kaufman Prize from the American Academy of Arts and Letters, and a fellowship from the National Endowment for the Arts. He lives in Bethesda, Maryland, with his wife and their daughter.